DRAMATIC LICENCE

(50) norms
(58) ✓
(69) "a sucker from Toronto"
* (77) non-translation
(106) the desire to make
explicit
(164) Liz #yes

(7-8)(102) gov't documents
(142) Anglos

DRAMATIC LICENCE

*Translating Theatre from One Official
Language to the Other in Canada*

Louise Ladouceur

Translated by Richard Lebeau

THE UNIVERSITY OF ALBERTA PRESS

Published by
The University of Alberta Press
Ring House 2
Edmonton, Alberta, Canada   T6G 2E1
www.uap.ualberta.ca

Library and Archives Canada Cataloguing in Publication

Ladouceur, Louise, 1951–
       Dramatic licence : translating theatre from one official language to the other in Canada /
Louise Ladouceur ; translated by Richard Lebeau.

Translation of: Making the scene : la traduction du théâtre d'une langue officielle
       à l'autre au Canada.
Includes bibliographical references and index.
ISBN 978-0-88864-538-8

       1. Canadian drama—20th century—Translations—History and criticism. 2. Canadian
drama (French)—Translations into English—History and criticism. 3. Canadian drama
(French)—Québec (Province)—Translations into English—Bibliography. 4. Canadian
drama (English)—Translations into French—History and criticism. 5. Theater—Québec
(Province)—History—20th century. 6. Theater—Canada—History—20th century.
7. Translating and interpreting—Québec (Province)—History—20th century. 8. Translating
and interpreting—Canada—History—20th century. I. Title.

PS8169.T73L3213 2012   C842'.5409   C2012-902616-6

First edition, first printing, 2012.
Printed and bound in Canada by Houghton
Boston Printers, Saskatoon, Saskatchewan.
Copyediting and proofreading by
Joanne Muzak.
Indexing by Elizabeth Macfie.

The University of Alberta Press is committed
to protecting our natural environment.
As part of our efforts, this book is printed
on Enviro Paper: it contains 100% post-
consumer recycled fibres and is acid- and
chlorine-free.

The University of Alberta Press gratefully
acknowledges the support received for
its publishing program from The Canada
Council for the Arts. The University of
Alberta Press also gratefully acknowledges
the financial support of the Government
of Canada through the Canada Book Fund
(CBF) and the Government of Alberta through
the Alberta Multimedia Development Fund
(AMDF) for its publishing activities.

We acknowledge the financial support of the
Government of Canada, through the National
Translation Program for Book Publishing, for
our translation activities.

The original work, Making the Scene: la
traduction du théâtre d'une langue officiel a
l'autre, was published in French in 2005 by
Éditions Nota bene (ISBN 2-89518-196-9).

This book has been published with the help of
a grant from the Canadian Federation for the
Humanities and Social Sciences, through the
Awards to Scholarly Publications Program,
using funds provided by the Social Sciences
and Humanities Research Council of Canada.

Comparatists of Canadian subjects are themselves condemned to maintain a paradoxical duality. Blinded by proximity to their subject, swayed by politics and history, hamstrung by an inevitable, natural, linguistic and cultural affiliation to one of the two camps, they must neither unify, nor divide. They must practice subtle and unspectacular arts. They must translate while knowing that full translation is impossible. They must try to acquire the other culture while knowing full well that it will never become their true heritage. They must encourage the difficult bifocal view while knowing that it will never be understood by more than a small élite and will never represent the full reality.

—Philip Stratford,
"Canada's Two Literatures: A Search for Emblems,"
Canadian Review of Comparative Literature

CONTENTS

PREFACE

E.D. Blodgett

HOW TO EXPLAIN THE DESIRE TO TRANSLATE? One might say that it is a way to explore different cultures without ever leaving the confines of one's home. But, in contrast with reading, where one can keep a certain distance between oneself and what is foreign, translation is instead an invitation to the foreign, which in this manner becomes one's host. Of course, everything is fine if the relationship between us and our guest is personal enough, if, for example, one has been reading what is foreign long enough for the foreign to become familiar, like the relationship between two poets who enjoy their shared solitudes.

As the following study so aptly demonstrates, the translation of plays is something altogether different. For a theatre is a public space, more social and more political than the relationship between two poets who get on well together. When you translate a play, you are introducing something foreign to an audience. This is an act that requires tact and diplomacy, protocol aimed at rendering the foreign familiar.

But if the desire to translate is to make what is foreign familiar, why translate? Because those who translate are seeking the foreign. Translation is primarily a process of opening up, but is it opening towards the other or towards oneself? In principle, the goal of translation, even in cultures other than our own, is to open up to the foreign text and to get it accepted within the receptive literature. Any discussion on the subject of adequacy and equivalence is a discourse on how to do just that. As Antoine Berman and countless others have shown, there is a predilection for ethnocentric translation. Consequently, translation strives to familiarize the public with an author or a text, and the notable moments of defamiliarization, such as with the translations of Friedrich Hölderlin, are the exception.

In such circumstances, how would literary history analyze and, if necessary, judge the translations? Amongst the most efficient ways, that of the Tel Aviv School, namely that of Itamar Even-Zohar, Gideon Toury, and their disciples—José Lambert and Hendrik van Gorp, amongst others—is the one most capable of demonstrating how this openness is manifested in the translation of plays in anglophone and francophone Canada. According to them, a translation is not evaluated on the basis of its more or less narrow relationship with the source text but rather on its function within the target context. For a translation is never a mirror for reflecting the text's origin. It is a voice in a dialogue between two writers; and, far from being a faded echo of the first voice, its answer is loud and clear, to ensure it is heard in all its fullness. A translation primarily obeys a receptive system's requirements more than the constraints imposed by the text to be translated, and it is this system of requirements that gives it its context. One translates according to models deemed appropriate to the project and that respond to an audience's expectations. Translation, therefore, thoroughly belongs to the history of its receptive context. Consequently, any critical analysis must take into consideration texts rooted in this receptive context— reviews, studies, histories—to deliver its full meaning to readers.

Such a method is aptly suited to the study of theatre translation in Canada and Quebec. Because theatre is the most public of all the genres. For a play to succeed, the audience must like it for its dramatic qualities. Its success, therefore, relates to its actual ability to move its audience, without any comparison with the source text. In the history of translation, Hölderlin's German translations of the Greek tragedies, for example, are an exception; for they attempt to reproduce an exact replica of the source text. In this country, translated plays are shaped to please a targeted audience instead. To accomplish this, one disregards the other, as was the case for so long in Quebec where the naturalist model of English Canada was ignored or appropriated. Whichever it happens to be, the method favoured by each culture obeys the same rule; in other words, it attempts to protect an audience from what Berman calls "l'épreuve de l'étranger."

From Quebec's point of view, the desire to protect itself from English Canada is completely understandable; anglophone culture is ubiquitous, it's everywhere. One strives therefore to blot out the other, but that presence is discerned through what is missing, and is most apparent in what is perceived as a threat. On the other hand, despite English Canada's hegemonic position, Michel Tremblay's translators avoid the problem posed by *joual* not only, as the author makes clear, because of the difficulties of finding equivalents to this language that embodies Quebec's alterity, but also because it publicly demonstrates that language and identity go hand in hand in that province. English Canada prefers not to see this relationship that contradicts its notion of Quebec and its identity, which explains its preference for plays that depict a Quebec before the Quiet Revolution, the Quebec of Krieghoff— is this possible? By avoiding the challenge presented by the language, it is certainly possible to view the Québécois as a docile people full of old-fashioned charm. One could even conclude that it is a method, conscious or not, of condescendingly translating the other.

Although Québécois translation disregards the main tradition of the anglophone drama repertoire, that of the naturalist play, or finds ways to render it into *joual*, playwrights such as Brad Fraser and George F. Walker are, in contrast, able to freely enter into Quebec's repertoire, largely due to their deep affinities with the mentality of the target culture. But this cannot be completely explained by the fact that their plays are more violent and more surrealistic, as shown in the section of this study dedicated to the historical evolution of the two systems. Reception is never static and, consequently, the need to translate into *joual* during the 1970s and the 1980s lost its urgency; adaptations lost some of their appeal at the start of the 1990s. Identity remained no less of a concern, but it became clearer and clearer that the nation was not its only point of reference. In addition, English Canada had also begun to see that its own language had models, codes, and protocols that could vary.

The study of theatre translation thus constitutes more than a highly efficient way of looking at the other. It is also a means of gauging the evolution of a society's awareness of the other *and* of itself. Granted, the study of translation is linguistic in nature, especially when it concerns the relationship between Canada and Quebec, but, since in a certain way we are what we say we are, any study of translation is also a psychological and sociological study. It is, in spite of its stated intentions, a study of a nation or, as in Canada's case, several nations and cultures. This book clearly demonstrates that the way we use language is that of a people shaped by two languages, which themselves draw on different sources and are prismatic rather than conflictual. It also illustrates the impossibility of simply viewing translation as a problem of transfer or cultural exchange between the English and the French. These two languages exist in all their variations in a way that is evocative of a new Middle Age, a time when Latin, Vulgar Latin, Occitan, and Old French, to speak only of the situation in Quebec, have come to mingle. It is precisely here that this study proves to be most enlightening.

In her biographical note, Louise Ladouceur briefly states that early in her life she was trained in the dramatic arts and took part in numerous stage and screen productions. Her knowledge of theatre is therefore sizably greater than that of a theoretician of dramatic practices. In fact, she is not only a critic and a historian. She knows theatre from a multidimensional perspective that gives her research a particular authority. She changed course midstream to pursue the life of an intellectual and, as she has explained to me, to exchange the commotion of an actor's existence for the reflection offered by the academic life. Since life is, to use her own words, "un grand jeu," it is obvious that she is pursuing her theatre life in a complimentary vein.

When she reflects on her two careers so tightly entwined, two themes stand out: feminism and identity. The one goes nowhere without the other, and they are intimately connected. If, as she says, "acting is a way of escaping oneself" even though one has "to search for the character one takes on within oneself," acting is something profoundly ambiguous in nature. One escapes from oneself only to be rediscovered in the skin of a character constructed from within. And since one is not born a feminist, but must become one, it's an identity that must also be constructed. It is, to some degree, a role, but a role without a mask, especially when it results from a personal choice.

We can see from this that theatre, feminism, and the search for identity are all part of the same "grand jeu," the creation of oneself. So in turn, the study of translation—and especially the translation of dramatic texts—is a transposition of a personal process to one more historic and sociological in nature. In this sense, the relationship between theatre practice and her study of it remains decidedly intimate, especially in light of her life's path. Initially a theatre practitioner in Quebec, Ladouceur subsequently chose to obtain a doctorate on the other side of the country and is now teaching at the University of Alberta. She has become Canadian in the broadest sense of the word. She has a deep understanding of this country's two dominant cultures and, in a certain way, experiences the dual identity that such a life entails. She is therefore aware that one rarely has a fixed identity, that history is a constantly evolving play, and that the relationship between Canada and Quebec, between Francophone and Anglophone, is itself a game with ever changing rules. Consequently, a comparative study of cultural life in Canada demands that one abandon, as quickly as possible, any fixed idea in order to remain existentially receptive, unconditionally open to the future. From a certain point of view, the country that Ladouceur constructs is a country in constant search of itself, a country that corresponds to her idea of theatre and, above all, to her concept of acting, an activity that is invariably demanding and generous. Her country is at once the result of one's own talents and the search for oneself. It is also a country highly aware of itself, and it is on stage where this is most fully apparent. And as the role of the actor is "to reveal, to see to it that the audience sees," the role of the critic is to reveal, on one hand, to what point culture is ephemeral and, on the other hand, how it shapes the memory of a country more complex than we might have believed, and impossible to understand without keeping in mind the words of Rimbaud: "Car JE est un autre." The role sought out within oneself is the other. The shaping of identities, the translation of plays, this is the elusive country that Ladouceur constructs with her desire to know it.

ACKNOWLEDGEMENTS

Louise Ladouceur

I HOPE THAT THIS WORK WILL PROVIDE the anglophone reader, as it has previously done for the francophone reader, with certain avenues of inquiry on the relationship between Canada's official languages as it has manifested itself through theatre translation. The English translation remains very faithful to the original despite my numerous attempts at revision, and I must thank Richard Lebeau for his unfailing rigour and devotion to the task at hand. Richard and I would both like to thank Martha Laing for her much appreciated input to the translation, our copyeditor, Joanne Muzak, for her critical eye, her attention to detail, and her stamina, and Mary Lou Roy for her "oeil de lynx" and her serenity while shepherding this project to term. I am also grateful to the Canada Council for the Arts and the Canadian Federation for the Humanities and Social Sciences for their financial support for the translation. Finally, I must express my gratitude to Linda Cameron and the rest of her team at the University of Alberta Press who undertook to publish this translation and have been steadfast in their support throughout the project's numerous stages.

INTRODUCTION

IN ORDER TO ADAPT THIS WORK'S EPIGRAPH to current trends, it would be useful to give it a multicultural scope. The case could then be made for what Philip Stratford might call a "paradoxical plurality" in a study of various cultural communities that require plurifocal views. The French translation would also call for an elegant way to include and indicate the feminine in the numerous pronouns deployed in the statement. Furthermore, there can be little doubt that certain terms would have a different impact in a version destined for a French readership, given that the qualifier "Canadian"—to indicate all the subjects of the study in question—would take on a completely different value. This is a distinction that can hardly be avoided within the linguistic and political context of modern-day Canada. After all, no matter what approach is adopted when speaking of the exchange of drama repertoires between anglophone and francophone communities, it will never meet with unanimous support.

So apart from the many objections that this quotation might provoke, the very pertinence of using such an admonition to introduce a resolutely descriptive study may seem questionable. Yet it caught my attention less by what it proposes to put into practice than by what it brings to light and how it contextualizes the problem as it applies to the nature, the circumstances, and the limitations of the following study.

The methodology adopted for this study draws primarily on the functionalist hypothesis developed by Gideon Toury and Itamar Even-Zohar. Based on a descriptive analysis of translation practices as they are applied to a large corpus, the functionalist approach concentrates on the *function* assigned to translated texts within the receptive context by isolating the norms from which the translation proceeds at a given time in the evolution of a literary system. From this perspective, a translation is subject to the specific constraints of the receptive context, which affect every step of the selection and production of what is to be translated. This theoretical framework will be explored in detail.

According to Toury, the identification of constraints that act upon a translation is dependent on two sources: extratextual and textual. Sources outside the text are found in reviews, commentaries, and other metatexts devoted to the translation; those that occur within the translated text are discernible through an analytical assessment of the translations. In light of these two proposed modes of research, the present study is composed of two sections. The first section, chapters 1 through 3, provides an overview of the discourses on the translation of literary and drama repertoires in Canada, which makes it possible to identify the principles of translation already formulated. The second, chapters 4 through 6, provides a descriptive analysis of the plays of twelve authors, translated by fifteen translators, within a bipartite francophone and anglophone corpus extending from 1961 to 1999. This section aims to showcase the translative strategies applied to the works in each repertoire. We then compare the methods of translating and the functions assigned to the translation of Canadian theatre from one official language to the other in Canada.

The corpus upon which the descriptive analysis is based is derived from an inventory of the repertoires in translation for the period extending from 1950 to 1999. Covering the second half of the twentieth century, the compilation of data for this study starts at the year that marked the beginning of sustained translation activity, which gave rise to important exchanges between the drama repertoires under study. The resulting inventory constructs a statistical profile of translations and, in turn, identifies the most translated authors and the most active translators—those most representative of each repertoire. To rule out the arbitrary as far as possible in deciding on which plays to study, the choices are based strictly upon statistical criteria. In the same spirit, the method applied to the descriptive analysis of the selected plays seeks to avoid value judgements, first by employing a structure that identifies the principal microstructural and macrostructural elements of the texts and then applying this structure identically to each of the texts in the corpus.

Oriented towards the study of translated material in its most encompassing dimension, the functionalist model makes it possible to identify certain rules systematically applied to a translated repertoire at a given period in the evolution of a literature, but it ignores phenomena that do not conform to this systematization. This means that it cannot take into consideration, amongst other things, the position occupied by the translating subject within the collectivity and the subjective dimensions of the act of translating. In fact, even if it conforms to norms, a translation also defends interests more personal in nature. To compensate for the inability of the functionalist model to factor in the most individual dimension of translation, the model developed here borrows several analytical elements from Antoine Berman.

Finally, it makes little sense to explore the individuality of the translating subject without acknowledging the subjectivity of my own position as critic. The biographical note at the end of this study and the circumstantial points of reference therein were conceived with this in mind.

In this comparative study of drama repertoires translated from one official language to the other, the distribution of both official language communities in Canada is such that the Canadian francophone drama repertoire consists mostly of works from Quebec identified as Québécois; whereas the anglophone drama repertoire defines itself above all as Canadian. Yet these designations cannot accurately represent the diversity of francophone and anglophone communities within Quebec and Canada, or that of their drama repertoires.

Circumscribed such as it is, this study cannot take into account other languages and other cultures that are excluded by an official bilingualism that results from the colonial wars that shaped the New

World. Reflecting preferential treatment accorded mutually by colonial powers that perceived each other as equals, this official bilingualism underlines the lack of consideration given to the languages of the Native peoples. This oversight, however, is not the subject of this work.

Accordingly comparative in nature, this study regards translation as a mediating agent for cultural exchanges and a favoured site for the power struggle between the dramatic literatures written in Canada's two official languages. Given that translation's greatest virtue through the ages has been its ability to pass unnoticed, there is a tendency to view it as a secondary activity. Nevertheless, translation performs an important function within a literary system as it is charged with fulfilling what is perceived as a need by means of borrowing from other literary systems. In this manner, translation reveals a great deal about the state of the literatures and the relationships between them.

The research carried out here was subject to spatial and temporal considerations. While the proximity in time of certain events is bound to limit the way in which they are read, the huge distances between the Canadian and Quebec documentation centres also imposed certain restrictions, specifically in compiling the statistical component. Only plays intended for an adult audience and whose translations were produced or published during a theatre's regular season were included. The sole intention of these criteria was to establish parameters for a repertoire that was representative, operational, and readily accessible. Children's theatre is now enjoying tremendous success and has led to considerable translation activity that has certainly caught the attention of other researchers.

Finally, even though I have attempted to maintain the greatest impartiality in this study, I would never lay claim to either a complete objectivity or to an equal knowledge of the cultures in question. As Philip Stratford points out, this is an inevitable contingency of the comparative dimension, one I can only regret.

1

LITERARY TRANSLATION

IN CANADA

AN EXAMINATION OF THE CRITICAL DISCOURSES on the relationship between Canadian literatures written in English and in French reveals a significant presence of emblems and symbols encharged with representing this relationship. Expressing the positions, the presuppositions, and the aspirations of each discursive group, these symbols highlight a power struggle that, in turn, they contribute to shaping.

Originating in the discipline of Canadian comparative literature, these emblems expressed an egalitarian ideal that was highly laudable yet far removed from the actual reality. However, with the development of a critical and theoretical discourse on Canadian literary translation at the end of the 1980s, the ways of representing the dynamics of the exchange between anglophone and francophone literatures shed light upon another sort of relationship. Abandoning the analysis of similarities and differences between the two repertoires, this discourse pointed to an avowed power struggle between majority and minority literatures, a high-stakes struggle concerned with giving one's own voice and language to the words of the other.[1]

Translation is the site where literatures meet and interpenetrate, and, as such, it is shaped by the relationship they foster. More than just an instance of observing the other, the translated text proposes the substitution of its own voice and language for those of the other. This substitution cannot be carried out without modifications that profoundly affect the translated text. Inasmuch as it is impossible to reproduce the original text exactly, the linguistic means of each language being neither identical nor interchangeable, choices must be made that inevitably favour certain interpretations. These choices must also fit into a social, cultural, historical, and political context. This imbues the text with other valences than those of the original context, which also entails certain changes. Lastly, the translation is the product of an individual's subjective reading of the work and offers an interpretation informed by the translating subject's conscious and unconscious relationships with the source text and its context. At the end of the process, the translated text bears the marks of a struggle, the result of which is the representation of the other by and through the self. This makes it an avowed power struggle played out through competing identities. We will see how this relationship is expressed through the practices and the discourses that punctuate the history of literary translation in Canada.

First Literary Translations

Even though the translation of administrative, political, legal, and commercial texts had been routinely practised in Quebec since the Conquest and institution of the British regime in 1763, it took another full century for literary translation to go from being an isolated phenomenon to a practice applied, albeit very sporadically, to certain literary successes of the period.[2] It still remained a rather rare practice in Canada up until 1920, as, according to Philip Stratford, before this date only ten titles were translated into English and two into French, and all were selected from the domains of poetry and the novel.[3] This state of affairs would evolve very slowly over the next forty years, a period that, again according to Stratford, would see only thirty-nine titles translated into English and nine into French.[4] The selection, translation, and publication of these titles were often left up to individuals in Paris, London, or New York. In short, as noted by Stratford and underlined by Jean Delisle in his work *La traduction au Canada* (1987), Canada had yet to develop a tradition of literary translation. However, starting in 1960, "more translations were published than during all previous years combined and the number of books translated continued to double every five years."[5] For the period between 1960 and 1977, Stratford counted 268 titles translated into English and 190 titles translated into French, including novels, poetry, drama, letters, accounts of trips, essays, anthologies, children's books, and works on religion and folklore. How then to explain this sudden popularity of literary translation?

In the anti-establishment turmoil of the 1960s, "c'est la poésie qui canalise les plus récents efforts d'émancipation de la littérature canadienne."[6] The creative fervour and the innovations in form that engendered the revival of poetry during the 1960s led the poets themselves to create a journal devoted to the translation of Quebec and Canadian poetry. In 1969, proclaiming the conciliatory role that translation would be called upon to play, D.G. Jones founded a journal on poetry translation in Sherbrooke with the bilingual title *Ellipse*. Based on the principle of symmetry, this plane curve contains two foci, and the sums of the distances of each point in its periphery from these two fixed points are equal. The two literatures are thus joined in a single object in an equal relationship. This metaphor offers a representation of translation akin to other literary emblems based upon the ideal of equality dear to anglophone specialists in comparative literature, an ideal that is, however, far removed from the reality.

In fact, according to Stacy Churchill's statistical analysis of official-language communities, based on the 1996 census,[7] the Canadian population is composed of an anglophone majority estimated to be 67.1 per cent of the total, a bilingual group making up 16.3 per cent, and a unilingual, francophone minority of 15.2 per cent,[8] most of whom live in Quebec. In terms of territory and political power, the Anglophones enjoy a sizable majority. Except in Quebec, where the Francophones constitute a majority, English-language cultures and literatures are decidedly dominant throughout Canada.

For Jones, translation addresses a need inherent to the identity problem shared by anglophone and francophone poets alike in the colonial space that is Canada: "how to live and write when you do not appear to exist, or when your existence, first in the eyes of others, finally in your own, is an illusion."[9] Hence Jones's advice is to translate "so that we may exist, so that our particular identity may be recognized and reinforced in each other's eyes."[10] With more than sixty-four issues published between 1969 and 2000, this journal dedicated to the translation of literary works, particularly the poetry of Quebec and English Canada, is an important locus for literary interaction. According to Richard Giguère, this climate of creative exchange was such that "la traduction littéraire se développe vraiment au Canada...surtout durant la période 1965 à 1975, les événements d'octobre 1970 jouant le rôle d'un catalyseur."[11]

Literary Translation and the Canada Council

Previously a low-profile activity, literary translation really took flight in 1972 with the inception of the Canada Council's Grant Program for Literary Translation, a program designed to encourage dialogue and exchange between Canada's anglophone and francophone communities at a time when relations between the two were particularly strained. This program is exclusive inasmuch as it only funds the translation of Canadian works from one official language to the other. According to a study undertaken by Ruth Martin on the program's impact from 1972 to 1992, almost twice as many books were translated by 1977, five years into its implementation, than in the history of translation in Canada up until then.[12] It is important to note that although one might expect a francophone minority to more readily borrow from an anglophone majority, which in principle had more to offer, precisely the opposite occurred. This phenomenon found the anglophone majority more often translating works into French than the francophone minority translated into English. In fact, this phenomenon is particularly well-illustrated within the realm of theatre, given that sixty of the sixty-two theatre translations that appear in Martin's compilation were French plays translated into English.

With the canonization of *joual*, a vernacular French spoken in Quebec, as the literary language in 1968, theatre became a favoured site of identity affirmation and was called on to ensure this specifically oral language would resonate throughout the public sphere. Thanks to this new linguistic norm, Quebec French playwriting blossomed as never before. Simultaneously, an active market for theatre translation emerged as foreign plays that previously would have been sent to France were, from this point on, translated into the local vernacular on-site. However, in Quebec, the prestigious British and American repertoires were certainly preferred to what was still a rather timid Canadian repertoire that failed to elicit much interest. Accordingly, the plays that were translated into French failed to meet the requirements of the Canada Council's translation program.

If there was little interest directed towards the repertoire of English Canada, it was not simply the result of indifference or suspicion. During this period, English-Canadian theatre was borrowing heavily from the British and American repertoires that served as models and investing little in creation. It took the establishment of a network of "alternative theatres" during the 1970s to give rise to an English-Canadian repertoire from which there would be ample borrowing after 1980. No fewer than six English-Canadian plays were duly produced in translation in Quebec between 1980 and 1983, a number equal to that of the entire preceding decade.

As for the Canada Council's translation grant program, it seems to have mostly contributed to the translation of the French repertoire into English by translators who were responsible for creating bridges between the two cultures.

"A Bridge of Sorts" That Raises Suspicion

As Kathy Mezei has noted, "since the 1950s, particularly in the context of the Quiet Revolution, the 1970 October Crisis, and the rise of the Parti québécois, English-Canadian translators have proclaimed a political mission to 'bridge' the two solitudes."[13] In the nationalist fervour that accompanied the 1967 Centennial of Canadian Confederation in English Canada, the metaphor of the bridge, already present in the discourse surrounding translation, came into its own and subsequently enjoyed a long career. In anglophone texts, literary translation is thus entrusted with the mission of providing "a possible bridge over the gap between English and French Canadian writing."[14]

Employed by, amongst others, Louis Dudek and Michael Gnarowski in 1967, John Glassco in 1970, and G.V. Downes in 1973 to introduce translated poetry,[15] the symbol of the bridge was reused by Philip Stratford in 1983 in the title of his article "Literary Translation: A Bridge Between Two Solitudes." It subsequently appeared in the bilingual title of Jean Delisle's work *Au Coeur du trialogue canadien: Bureau des traductions 1934–1984 / Bridging the Language Solitudes: Translation Bureau 1934–1984* (1984). Here it is interesting to note that the metaphor is used only in the English version of the title. Whereas Anglophones are invited to a cordial meeting of linguistic solitudes, the French title highlights the role of translation as a tertiary agent vital to the process of communication, a communication rather singular in nature as it must be represented by the neologism "trialogue." In turn, Mezei borrowed the image of the bridge for an article entitled "A Bridge of Sorts: The Translation of Quebec Literature into English" (1985), in which she conceives of translation as a rare form of interaction between anglophone and francophone writers who for the most part remain isolated in mutual indifference. Sherry Simon, however, questions the representativeness of this vision of translation as an agent of fraternization: "Too closely associated with humanistic ideals of transparence and tolerance, too obviously linked to the political sphere (the final resting place of language issues in Canada), the subject of translation for a long time conjured up pious images of bridges and brotherhood, clearly out of sync with the realities of Canadian cultural politics."[16] This representation of translation as a "bridge," while dear to Anglophones, fails to kindle the same enthusiasm amongst Francophones, who perceive translation as a symbol of political domination and an agent of linguistic assimilation. In fact, within the Canadian political context, where power struggles are intimately related to linguistic duality, translation and the discourse it generates are bound to be heavily laden with political overtones. According to Larry Shouldice, not only are they unable to escape a political agenda, they serve as its tools.

In a study devoted to the Canada Council's translation grant program, Shouldice contends that the relative success of translation into English cannot be solely explained by the usual arguments that cite the dynamism of a Quebec literature of the 1960s and the 1970s, which attracted attention, even from abroad; nor can this success be explained by the fact that French Canadians can read English and that they bought fewer books than did English Canadians. Rather, he contends that "much of English Canada's interest in Quebec literature stems from a political impulse, and that this helps explain the relative proliferation of translations from Quebec. As Hubert Aquin might have expressed it, literary translation in our federal system is a form of cultural appropriation."[17] Describing the political motivations to which literary translations of that period in Canada would subscribe, Shouldice states, "It is not uncommon, I think, for English Canadians to view translation as a means of fostering national unity; and while this is no doubt true of some French Canadians as well, one senses in the latter a more pronounced impulse to intelligence gathering for strategic defence purposes: 'love thy neighbour' on the one hand, and 'know thy enemy' on the other."[18]

It should actually come as no surprise that both sides have highly divergent points of view concerning the function of literary translation and the issues surrounding it. An activity that Anglophones would like to see as convivial does in fact elicit significant suspicion on the part of Francophones, for whom translation has embodied, from the very beginning of British rule, the clear, hierarchical superiority of English vis-à-vis French. According to Ben-Zion Shek, "les documents clés de l'histoire du Canada, tels la Proclamation royale de 1763, l'Acte de Québec, l'Acte constitutionnel, le rapport Durham, l'Acte de l'Union, l'Acte de l'Amérique du Nord britannique, le Statut de Westminster, ainsi que les textes des deux référendums sur la conscription, ont été rédigés d'abord en anglais puis traduits en français....La traduction à sens unique a reproduit les rapports réels dominants-dominés de la conjoncture militaire, en premier lieu, puis et par conséquent, politique et économique."[19]

The monumental volume of translation inherent in Canadian bilingualism has therefore long embodied the clear hierarchical superiority of English vis-à-vis French, which has profoundly affected literary borrowing. In such a context, Anglophones did not hesitate when it came to translating literary texts from a French minority that posed little threat to their language and their culture. For Francophones, however,

who were obliged to translate volumes of governmental and administrative documents, the borrowing of literary texts was perceived as "à la
fois comme une menace et comme une perte d'efforts dans une entre-
prise marginale, du point de vue de la lutte pour la survie d'une langue
et d'une culture minoritaires."[20] For Francophones, this monumental amount of translation activity not only emphasizes the diglossia
between Canada's two official languages; it is prejudicial to French, a
target language constantly influenced by English as a source language.
According to Simon, the harmful effects of translation on the French
language constitute an important leitmotif in Quebec where, having
become a "topique de la défaillance, rappel de l'obligation dans laquelle
le Québec se trouve par rapport à autrui, la traduction est souvent un
sujet pénible."[21]

It was within this climate of heightened linguistic tension at the
beginning of the 1970s that Jacques Brault undertook the translation
of English-Canadian poets and published the collection *Poèmes des
quatre côtés* (1975), in which he expounds a rather unusual conception of
translation for that time in Quebec. In his opinion, by releasing it from
any responsibility to imitate, translation could acquire a certain creative autonomy that would benefit a target language, "suspendue entre
deux certitudes maintenant problématiques, langue qui reconnaît
alors sa difficulté d'être. Et sa raison d'être. Une langue qui se refuse à
pareille épreuve est d'ores et déjà condamnée."[22] By reversing the traditional argument, which holds that translation would be prejudicial to
a target language that is exposed to the influences of the source language, Brault rehabilitates an activity often deemed questionable, as
he underlines at the beginning of the work: "Les clefs de la traduction
appartiennent aux puissants. S'il n'y a pas de langue mondiale, il y a des
langues colonisatrices."[23] He then proposes to name this salutary vision
of translation, nontranslation.[24] So even when viewed as a constructive
activity, which was rare in Quebec, translation is given a prefix of negation and can only take on a positive value by negating its own action.

The inequality of Canada's two official languages influences not
only the relationship that they maintain but the way this relationship is
perceived. In 1982, E.D. Blodgett touched upon the particularly pertinent question of the ideology inherent in all literary theorizing when he
argued that literary critics must take into account the existing diglossia

in the context of Canada and Quebec: "Any literary framework that assumes equality of status between these two cultural groups mistakes the nature of the relationship."[25] From this perspective, he suggests applying the theoretical framework of polysystem literary theory developed by Itamar Even-Zohar to the comparative study of Canada's French and English literatures. He adds that the wish expressed by Jones to transcend the Canadian dilemma by means of translation is destined to fail as long as Quebec is unable to attain a more independent, and thus culturally viable, status. In his opinion, the real task does not involve wanting to unite by erasing the differences but rather by preserving the cultural pluralism and the linguistic boundaries that it dictates: "To preserve that border is, paradox as it may appear, the national Canadian task."[26] Following in the strides of André Brochu, for whom "le grand problème, toujours actuel, du peuple québécois, c'est son absence de frontières,"[27] Blodgett borrows Robert Frost's oft-quoted statement: "Good fences, I believe, do indeed make good neighbours."[28] And it is perhaps here that literary translation is most pertinent within the Canadian context inasmuch as it contributes to preserving the linguistic border while crossing it, albeit on the condition, as Blodgett notes, that it avoids assimilation by avoiding similarity: "Thus Gaston Miron would not, for example, be made to appear anglophone; nor would anglophone text be made to appear francophone and so infiltrate under the cover of language the literature of Quebec. Difference would be preserved through dialectical exchange, and so meet somewhere between the view of Jones and Shek."[29]

Yet, how can this intention be reconciled with the transparency imperative that would have a translation read as if it were an original text first conceived in the target language—inasmuch as this is the most prevalent conception of translation and hence the most widely held? Any such attempt would involve reaching a very delicate balance in what surely is an audacious yet certainly attainable undertaking, as evidenced by Brault's "familièrement étrange[s]" translations in *Poèmes des quatre côtés*.[30] It must be said that poetry readily lends itself to this type of experimentation, in contrast with other literary genres, in particular theatre, where the text is bound by a performance imperative.

At the beginning of the 1980s, with the blossoming of feminist writing and the dynamism of the exchanges initiated between Canadian anglophone and francophone women writers, a dialogue was established through translation. No longer an undertaking carried out as a reaction to the imbalance between the dominant and dominated cultures, translation responded to a desire to cross the limits placed on sense by a phallocentric language. Where once the act of translation prided itself on reproducing an equivalent message with the utmost discretion, there was a new insistence on the visibility of the female translating subject. Accordingly, for texts full of cultural references, neologisms, and word play impossible to reproduce, feminist translation advocates a re-creation in the target language and reveals its efforts to inscribe the feminine in the symbolic order of the language. In this, the act of translating serves feminist criticism remarkably well, as it brings to light the mechanisms of the production of meaning.

For example, in Barbara Godard's translation of Nicole Brossard's book *Amantes*, entitled *Lovhers*, a concrete subversion of the supposed neutrality of the English term serves to emphasize the "genders of language" by distorting the linguistic code.[31] This emphasis on translation as discursive production and manipulation contributed to the theoretic renewal of translation studies in the 1980s.

Without putting forward an emblem intended to represent the two literatures, certain metaphors may thus serve as models for a feminist practice of literary translation. Godard creates a neologism that conjures up notions of transformation and of performance in a process of "transformance."[32] By insisting on the visibility of the female translator in the endeavour to recreate the text, this method of translation breaks new ground by attaching importance to the role of the translating subject. In this case, presented as a work of text transformation, translation avoids the clichés that see it as a faithful reproduction of the original text. Subsequently, signalling the emergence of new images resulting from the exchanges between feminist writers in Quebec and Canada made possible through translation, Mezei focusses attention on an erotic image borrowed from Brossard's *French Kiss*, which refers to "sa langue dans la bouche de l'autre": "The use of an English expression containing the adjective 'French' to describe a sexual act in a French text is a multi-layered parody in which stereotyped perceptions of sexuality (English puritanism versus French hot-bloodedness) reflect cultural positions. (English wariness of the French difference;

French alienation and subordination under the English). This inversion of French/English also mirrors the sexual inversion of the traditional heterosexual binary male/female romance in Brossard's tale of lesbian love."[33] The meeting of tongues/languages appears in a critical text in English dealing with a work of fiction in French that sports an English title containing the word "French." This *mise en abyme*[34] demonstrates not only the intricately entwined position of each literature, but also the playful and specular aspects of the exchange itself.

The same year, Simon published a study in which she identified two cultural goals as they apply to literary translation within the Canadian context. Inspired by the work of Annie Brisset on theatre translation in Quebec before 1988, Simon attributes to Franco-Québécois theatre translation a "visée *identitaire*"[35] destined to affirm a Quebec identity by obscuring the foreign origins of the borrowed text in order to contribute to the construction of a local drama repertoire. She compares this approach to the "visée *ethnographique*" of the English-Canadian translations of novels that, in contrast, emphasize the cultural alterity of Quebec works, thereby demonstrating a "surconscience de la différence."[36] It must be said that we are dealing here with two literary genres that each present constraints specific to the act of translating. Given that a theatre text is destined to be staged, translating a play calls upon strategies related to performance requirements that are very different from those needed to translate a novel, as will become apparent in chapter 2.

2

FROM ONE STAGE TO THE OTHER

AS WE HAVE BEEN ABLE TO OBSERVE, reflection on literary translation within a Canadian context has primarily favoured two genres: the novel and poetry. Theatre translation in Canada is in fact a relatively recent phenomenon, and it was only during the 1980s that it became the object of systematic study. With the exception of the rare play translated especially for its historic value,[1] not until the birth of the modern francophone and anglophone theatre repertoires did an active market in Canadian theatre translation develop.

First Theatre Translations

Through the auspices of translation, burlesque had already widely availed itself of the American repertoire for performances in "canayen" that were all the rage on Quebec stages from 1920 until the beginning of the 1950s. The vernacular was thus front and centre during the golden age of burlesque, and it was in this language that Gratien Gélinas undertook to write the play that, according to Jean-Cléo Godin and

Laurent Mailhot, heralded "la véritable naissance d'un théâtre populaire québécois."[2] Originally staged at the Monument-National in 1948, *Tit-Coq* was translated into English by Kenneth Johnstone and Gélinas and produced in English on the same stage in 1950 and then at the Royal Alexandra in Toronto in 1951. This marked the inauguration of an active market for the translation of Canadian theatre. Even though translations into English appeared at the beginning of the 1950s, it was not until the end of the 1960s that exchanges in the other direction began.

As early as 1966, Montreal's Instant Theatre was already alternating presentations in English and in French of Aviva Ravel's short play *Shoulder Pads*, translated by Luce Guilbault under the title *Les épaulettes*. This practice of alternating English and French performances was specific to Montreal's bilingual theatre milieu, which catered to francophone and anglophone audiences. In this same vein, Gélinas had already produced English translations of his own plays at Montreal's Comédie-Canadienne, and, on this same stage, he once again undertook to translate and produce an English-Canadian work that had enjoyed considerable success at the Vancouver Playhouse in 1967. The play in question was George Ryga's *The Ecstasy of Rita Joe*, which, according to Christopher Innes, "marked the birth of modern Canadian drama."[3] As the driving force behind the first productions of Canadian plays translated from one official language into the other, Gélinas actually set in motion the practice of Canadian theatre translation.

In addition to the evident time gap between the first translations into English and those into French, the statistics gathered in the course of this study reveal a decided asymmetry in the number of plays translated.[4] Without taking into consideration children's theatre, summer theatre, or amateur theatre, a total of 146 works by francophone playwrights and sixty-nine works by their anglophone counterparts were produced or published in translation in the other official language from 1951 to 2000. Though they reflect an inequality in the relationship between the two languages, these asymmetries can also be explained by the way in which the francophone and anglophone drama repertoires have developed.

A Theatre Meant to Be Québécois

During Quebec's relentless campaigns promoting the use of "bon français," the stages of burlesque theatres resonated with "la langue du
peuple." These shows were often translated from the American original and would contain "cinquante pour cent de joual pour cinquante
pour cent de sl(ang) [sic]" before the English was completely eliminated
towards the end of the 1920s.[5] Burlesque enjoyed its golden age between
1930 and 1950, and its popularity "repose beaucoup sur l'utilisation
de la langue vernaculaire."[6] This vernacular is also the one used by
the characters in Petitjean and Rollin's *Aurore, l'enfant martyre*, the
melodrama that "fit pleurer tout le Québec de 1920 à 1950."[7] The characters in Gélinas's *Fridolin* (1941–1946) and *Tit-Coq* also spoke with a
Québécois-accented French, as did those in Marcel Dubé's *Zone*, which
was presented in 1953 at the Dominion Drama Festival in Victoria.

Following in the footsteps of those rare companies already in existence, one of which was the famous Compagnons de Saint-Laurent
directed by Father Émile Legault from 1937 to 1952, several theatre companies were created: the Théâtre du Rideau Vert in 1949, the Théâtre
du Nouveau Monde in 1951, and the Théâtre de Quat'Sous in 1955.
However, the majority of the repertoire presented on these stages was
inspired by bedroom comedy or drawn from classical foreign theatre,
French or translated into French. Several years later, three government
bodies in charge of funding cultural activities were established: the
Canada Council for the Arts and the Montreal Regional Arts Council in
1957, and the Quebec Ministry of Cultural Affairs in 1961. At the same
time, the vogue for small theatres contributed to the discovery of the
European avant-garde, while in 1954 the Conservatoire d'art dramatique was founded, followed by the National Theatre School in 1962.
This period also saw the construction of Montreal's Place des Arts and
the Grand Théâtre in Quebec City, both among the regional theatres
built to celebrate the Centennial of Canadian Confederation. Lastly,
in 1965, the Centre d'essai des auteurs dramatiques was established to
promote Quebec plays and playwrights. So, by the middle of the 1960s,
the institutional apparatus of Quebec theatre was in place and ready to
promote its own values. Even though it was already present on Quebec
stages, the vernacular language was previously unable to benefit from

the institutional support of a theatre system that had yet to acquire the necessary apparatus to assure its legitimacy.

It was in 1968 at the Théâtre du Rideau Vert, with the support of the Centre d'essai des auteurs dramatiques, that Michel Tremblay's *Les belles-sœurs* would stir up a great deal of controversy before establishing *joual* as the language for the stage in Quebec. With the normalization of *joual*, the drama repertoire would undergo a period of rapid development, as massive borrowing from the French repertoire would cease in favour of elaborating a specifically Québécois repertoire. Charged with the responsibility of publicly embodying the essentially oral specificity of *joual*, theatre became a privileged site of identity affirmation. As a result, theatre translation would also have to submit to this new linguistic norm, and foreign plays, which previously had to pass through France, would from then on be translated into the local vernacular in Quebec. In 1970, Tremblay confirmed the status of *joual* as the language of theatre translation with the remarkable success of *L'effet des rayons gamma sur les vieux-garçons*, an adaptation of Paul Zindel's play created in New York the same year.

A poor and lame sociolect of French origin, isolated by the break with France and alienated by the crushing presence of English in North America, *joual* lays claim to its accents, proclaims its difference, and repudiates the French model once seen as the only one capable of expressing an authentic francophone culture. The triumph of *joual* challenges a twofold colonial tradition and leads to a radical about-face, as a language embodying the difficulty to express oneself becomes an identity-affirming tool. It is particularly in this respect that the canonization of *joual* on the Quebec stage at the end of the 1960s established a new set of expectations. As Annie Brisset notes, this "modifie...le rapport des forces linguistiques sur le plan institutionnel et sur le plan symbolique, en permettant que le langage vernaculaire prenne la place du langage référentiaire."[8] Brisset borrows this terminology from categories defined by Henri Gobard, according to whom any given cultural sphere comprises four types of language.

1. Un *langage vernaculaire*, local, parlé spontanément, moins fait pour communiquer que pour *communier* et qui seul peut être considéré comme langue maternelle (ou langue natale).

II. Un *langage véhiculaire*, national ou régional, appris par nécessité, destiné aux *communications* à l'échelle des villes.

III. Un *langage référentiaire*, lié aux traditions culturelles, orales ou écrites, assurant la continuité des valeurs par une référence systématique aux oeuvres du passé pérennisées...

IV. Un *langage mythique*, qui fonctionne comme ultime recours, magie verbale dont on comprend l'incompréhensibilité comme preuve irréfutable du sacré.[9]

The categorical shift that results in a vernacular language infused with a high quotient of Quebec territoriality becoming a national language of cultural affirmation brings about what Itamar Even-Zohar refers to as a "conversion" within Quebec's literary polysystem.[10] Such a conversion occurs when a popular language, heretofore confined to the non-canonized periphery, comes to occupy a central position and subsequently imposes itself as the dominant norm. From this moment on, if it wished to be authentic and to be considered as such, Québécois drama written or translated in Quebec would have to employ the vernacular language of Quebec.

Dominant during the 1970s, the predilection for *joual* nonetheless faded during the 1980s, a period where Quebec playwriting diversified as much in the themes it dealt with as in the stylistic forms it explored. Freed from its mission to affirm identity, Quebec theatre experimented with new topics and new resources. Whether feminist, gay, experimental, or visual, theatre presented an exuberant manner of speaking that called upon several levels of language. This speech reflected the linguistic freedom enjoyed in Quebec after the adoption of severe measures aimed at protecting the French language in the province. As Jean-Luc Denis noted in 1990, "auparavant confiné à un niveau populaire, archaïsant et fortement anglicisé, le français parlé au Québec parcourt aujourd'hui tout le registre des niveaux de langue et coïncide souvent, à ses niveaux supérieurs, avec le français standard."[11]

Even though it has since been set aside by playwrights, *joual* remained the favoured language of theatre translation and of adaptation, a translation strategy that would reach its zenith in the middle of the 1980s. Adaptation or "tradaptation," a term borrowed from Michel Garneau,[12] represents 80 per cent of the Quebec translations presented by the theatre companies Jean-Duceppe, Rideau Vert, and Nouveau Monde during the 1985–1986 season.[13] This translative strategy involves more than simply utilizing the vernacular as a target language as it entails transposing the action into a Quebec setting and totally appropriating the initial play to the target context; the names of places and characters, along with their titles and functions, as well as sociocultural references are modified as a result. Here, the translation process becomes solipsistic and rejects any intertextual connections, referring only to itself and creating the illusion that the play is an original. This explains why there is a passage in the program for a production of *Chacun son tour*, a Quebec adaptation of Ray Clooney's *One for the Pot* produced by the Compagnie Jean-Duceppe in January 1991, that reads: "Ce soir, vous ne vous rendrez pas compte que vous entendrez une traduction. Vous allez avoir l'illusion que la pièce a été écrite ici à Montréal. Une bonne traduction, c'est ça." By the end of the 1980s, this translative strategy had been seriously re-evaluated by the translators themselves and subsequently fell into disuse. Denis aptly describes the position it has since occupied: "pour donner accès à l'oeuvre d'un auteur étranger, doit-on traduire ou adapter? On doit traduire. L'adaptation n'est pas en soi quelque chose d'illégitime; c'est lorsqu'elle est érigée en système qu'elle fait problème....Elle doit être reléguée le plus vite possible au territoire qu'elle n'aurait jamais dû quitter: celui du phénomène épisodique."[14]

The remarkable dynamism that characterized playwriting and theatre translation in Quebec beginning in 1968 resulted, according to Brisset, in theatre becoming "le genre favori de la traduction littéraire."[15] In her study of translations, imitations, and parodies presented in Quebec between 1968 and 1988, Brisset contends that during a period of nationalist fervour, translations are not designed to reveal the borrowed work, but to "cautionner son propre discours, celui de l'émancipation nationale."[16] This ethnocentric approach requires any signs of alterity to be removed so that the translated text is able to reflect the reality of the Quebec society and thus contribute to the development of a repertoire claiming to be specifically Québécois. In *Sociocritique de la traduction: théâtre et altérité au Québec (1968–1988)*,

Brisset's study of translations, imitations, and parodies presented in Quebec, she contends, that this practice is common for emerging literatures at various periods and in various places.[17] Historically, translation is in fact closely related to the emergence and evolution of numerous literary systems. As Edmond Cary argues, "la traduction a, en règle générale, précédé la création littéraire autonome, elle a été la grande accoucheuse des littératures"[18] inasmuch as "c'est par des traductions et des adaptations que les littératures modernes ont commencé."[19]

Brisset's work demonstrates that before 1990 borrowing from the prestigious American and British repertoires was prevalent, while the Canadian repertoire, as yet unsure of itself, was for the most part ignored.

Borrowing from the Anglophone Repertoire

To mark the occasion of the Centennial of Canadian Confederation in 1967, many Canadian plays were created throughout the country. Amongst these plays, George Ryga's *The Ecstasy of Rita Joe*, presented at the Vancouver Playhouse, met with such success that Gratien Gélinas decided to adapt and produce it in Quebec. Entitled *Rita Joe*, the play was produced at the Comédie-Canadienne in November 1969 in a version stripped of its initial geographical and sociocultural references in such a manner that it could fit within a Quebec reality.

The translations of seven Canadian plays were produced in Quebec during the 1970s, four of which were published, and another French translation was published in Nova Scotia.[20] One of the plays translated for Quebec audiences, John Herbert's *Fortune and Men's Eyes*, enjoyed great success in New York, London, and Los Angeles prior to being made into a movie that was filmed in Quebec City just before it was presented on stage in Montreal. Another play was a huge hit in translation while the original had passed largely unnoticed—*Charbonneau et le Chef*, translated and adapted by Paul Hébert and Pierre Morency from John McDonough's *Charbonneau and Le Chef*. It told the story of the confrontation between Duplessis and Monsignor Charbonneau during the Asbestos strike in 1949. *Charbonneau et le Chef* was presented at Quebec City's Théâtre du Trident in March 1971 and in May 1972, and then restaged in Montreal by the Compagnie Jean-Duceppe in November 1973 and in February 1986. It was published by Éditions Leméac in 1974 in the collection Traduction et adaptation.

The 1980s were certainly more propitious when it came to productions, yet publications remained rare; only three of the twenty-six plays enumerated in the statistical component of this study were published. Amongst these productions, three translated plays—two produced in Vanier, Ontario and one in Edmonton, Alberta—are particularly noteworthy. Kent Stetson's *Comme un vent chaud de Chine*, published in a bilingual edition in 1989 by Montreal's NuAge Editions, was nominated for a Governor General's Award. The original play was first produced in Halifax at the Neptune Theatre in 1988, while the translation was presented the same year in Hull at the Théâtre de l'Île.

From 1990 to 1993, borrowing increased. More than thirteen French translations of English plays were produced in Canada, including two in Saskatoon. Judith Thompson led things off with *Je suis à toi*, Robert Vézina's French translation of *I Am Yours*, produced in 1990 at La Licorne by the Théâtre de la Manufacture. Another of Thompson's plays and one of Brad Fraser's were presented the following year at Théâtre de Quat'Sous, and, the same year, Robert Nunn published an article entitled "Canada Incognita: Has Quebec Theatre Discovered English Canadian Plays?" in which he described the phenomenon of the apparent popularity of English-Canadian plays in Quebec. Boréal published two plays by Fraser, in 1991 and 1993 respectively. Faced with such an abundance, the theatre critic at the *Montreal Gazette*, Pat Donnelly, concluded, "contemporary English-Canadian playwrights are finally being recognized in Quebec."[21] The *Globe and Mail* theatre critic, Ray Conlogue, explains Quebec's previous indifference to the English-Canadian drama repertoire thus: "English Canada's love affair with a plodding American-style naturalism which bored Quebec to tears."[22] Robert Wallace points out that it is also necessary to realize that the Canadian political climate was such that many Quebec theatre directors did not look to English Canada when seeking interesting plays to borrow: "Many of these people see no reason to introduce Canadian Theatre to Quebec audiences; not considering themselves part of Canadian culture, they feel no obligation to privilege Canadian plays."[23]

However, as Pierre Bernard, the artistic director of the Théâtre de Quat'Sous, which produced Thompson's play and two of Fraser's plays, is quick to add, "the quality of the writing is now stronger than it was before."[24] According to Bernard, this evolution in playwriting is manifest in a rejection of conventional structures and in a subversion that in his opinion constitutes the raison d'être of the artistic discourse: "Les artistes sont la [sic] pour le desordre [sic]."[25]

Of the thirteen English-Canadian plays produced in translation between 1990 and 1993, only a few were critically acclaimed for their audacious novelty. Amongst these, a play by Thompson and two by Fraser attracted considerable attention on Quebec stages, where their spectacular and even shocking qualities, which sometimes verged on the scandalous, were extolled. Vézina's translations *Je suis à toi* and *Lion dans les rues* brought Thompson's plays to the stage in 1990 at La Licorne and in 1991 at the Théâtre de Quat'Sous, respectively. The "rock and roll"[26] aspect of the staging was singled out for praise in *Je suis à toi*, which also featured "formidables numéros d'acteurs."[27] The laudable staging and acting, however, were undermined by incoherent translation choices; for example, class conflict is a central theme in the play and, inappropriately, all the characters speak in a highly-accentuated *joual*. However, the second production was a great success. Quebec critics were surprised to discover a vigorous style of writing that was a clear departure from the conventional naturalism for which they had previously criticized English-Canadian theatre. Thompson was consequently described as the "auteure la plus provocante au Canada anglais,"[28] with a play that attains "un véritable état hypomaniaque que la mise en scène de Claude Poissant et le jeu de tous les comédiens rendent bien."[29] The play's staging did indeed flirt with the frenetic, as anglophone critic Donnelly noted in her astonishment at the success of a production that is "about as much fun as a hellfire sermon [with] performances pitched to a passionate screech."[30]

Several months earlier, in March 1991, the Théâtre de Quat'Sous had first produced another of Fraser's plays, *Des restes humains non identifiés et la véritable nature de l'amour*, translated and directed by André Brassard. The production met with considerable success despite the controversy it engendered. After all, coarse language, murder, nudity, mental cruelty, and sadomasochistic games were all on the menu. As Benoit Melançon pointed out, the play "ne fait l'économie d'aucune violence, physique ou verbale."[31] Fresh from this previous, scandal-tinged success, Fraser was once again found on stage at Théâtre de Quat'Sous in 1993 in Maryse Warda's translation L'homme laid. This time, the production provoked widespread indignation: "L'homme laid est la pièce la plus violente, la plus vulgaire, la plus horrible que j'ai vue."[32] The play was described as a "carnaval sanguinolent...spectaculaire plus que tragique, grossière plus qu'étrange."[33] And many took umbrage at a "surenchère de sexe, de violence et d'horreur digne des films les plus sensationnalistes."[34] Nevertheless, Fraser would return to Quat'Sous in 1995 with Poor Super Man, but would be criticized for a routine sensationalism that had become "le plus scabreux de la dramaturgie actuelle."[35]

The two other English-Canadian plays produced in translation between 1990 and 1993 met with a lukewarm reception from the theatre-going public. They were criticized for a lack of originality in both theme and treatment, and for poor and awkward writing. The choice of appropriating the play into a target context through the use of a highly-accentuated vernacular came under fire as well.[36] The critical discourse that accompanied these productions highlighted what seemed to have become a new norm of acceptability regarding English-Canadian theatre translated in Quebec. The specular imperative that had previously rendered it necessary to obscure the English-Canadian origin of translated plays had given way to a "spectacular" aesthetic that sought to accentuate the dramatic potential of the plays in order to justify this sudden interest in a theatre repertoire that had once been considered boring due to its dull naturalism. At a time when Quebec theatre was becoming known on the international stage for productions acclaimed for their scenographic or choreographic prowess, such as those produced by Carbone 14 and Robert Lepage, the spectacular value of the recently translated Canadian plays was used to justify borrowing them. Thus, the specular imperative gave way to an imperious spectacularity. From then on, the disturbing, even shocking qualities of the English-Canadian product served to legitimize it in the French context.

Twenty-two other Canadian plays were produced in French translation between 1994 and 2000, eight of which were published. Moreover, there were more publishers interested in publishing these translations, including Humanitas, Les Herbes Rouges, Dramaturges Éditeurs, and VLB Éditeur. Within this group of published plays, four were written by George Walker, which makes him the English-Canadian playwright with the most plays produced or published in French translation in Canada. A little more than a decade after the 1986 production of *Le théâtre du film noir* at the Théâtre d'la Corvée in Ontario, and the 1989 production of *Amours passibles d'amendes* at Montreal's Théâtre Denise-Pelletier, the year 1998 saw the beginning of a veritable Walker marathon at the Théâtre de Quat'Sous, where four of Walker's plays were staged within thirteen months: *L'enfant-problème* in October 1998, *Pour adultes seulement* and *Le génie du crime* in April 1999, and *La fin de la civilisation* in October 1999, all translated by Maryse Warda.

Amongst the plays translated since 1969, several had received prizes or awards and had therefore been recognized by the source literary establishment before being borrowed. We can also chart the cities in which the plays originated: Toronto, Calgary, Montreal, Fredericton, Blyth (Ontario), Vancouver, Edmonton, Winnipeg, and Ottawa.

As detailed in Appendix 1, sixty-nine English-Canadian plays were produced or published in translation in Canada between 1966 and 2000. The authors most often translated are George F. Walker, with six plays produced in translation, and Norm Foster, with four; while Brad Fraser had three translations produced, followed by David Freeman, Sharon Pollock, Bernard Slade, and Judith Thompson, each of whom had two of their plays translated and produced. The most active translators were Maryse Warda, with five translations, René Dionne, and Louison Danis, with four translations apiece, while Guy Beausoleil, Josée Labossière, Michel Garneau, Francine Pominville, and Robert Vézina were responsible for three each. This information reveals which playwrights were most often translated as well as which translators were most active within each drama repertoire. This, in turn, guided the selection of the most representative plays within each repertoire and thereby determined the corpus that undergoes a detailed descriptive analysis later in the book.

The Canadian Alternative

With the celebration of the Centennial of Canadian Confederation in 1967, the English-Canadian drama repertoire went through a period of unprecedented rapid expansion. Animated by a nationalist flame rekindled for the occasion, the federal and provincial governments undertook the construction of prestigious cultural structures, such as Ottawa's National Arts Centre. Some of these buildings would house repertory companies that were part of the network of regional theatres, institutional theatres that have received financial support from the Canada Council for the Arts since 1957. These theatres included the Manitoba Theatre Centre, founded in Winnipeg in 1958 as well as the Vancouver Playhouse and Halifax's Neptune Theatre, both founded in 1963. They were followed by Edmonton's Citadel Theatre in 1965; Montreal's Saidye Bronfman Centre and Saint John's Arts and Culture Centre in 1967; Theatre Calgary and Theatre New Brunswick in 1968; and Toronto's St. Lawrence Centre in 1970.

Even though the blossoming of theatre during the 1960s cannot be entirely credited to the recent establishment of the Canada Council for the Arts, it is clear that this new source of funding dedicated to the development of the arts had a profound affect on the changing Canadian theatre scene. Since 1935, radio had already given many playwrights, actors, and directors their first opportunities, and the arrival of television in the early 1950s provided new challenges. The inaugural edition of the Dominion Drama Festival took place in Ottawa in 1933, and, this same year, the Banff School of Fine Arts opened its doors. In 1945, the University of Saskatchewan created the first chair of drama, and, in 1947, the University of Alberta and Queen's University inaugurated their departments of theatre studies. When the Stratford Festival was launched in 1953, some professional companies had already been established, including the John Holden Players of Bala, Ontario in 1934, Vancouver's Everyman Theatre Company in 1946, Toronto's New Play Society, also in 1946, and, finally, Toronto's Jupiter Theatre in 1951. Toronto's Crest Theatre was founded in 1954; this young, vibrant professional company did not shut its doors until 1966.[37]

Thus, the foundations were in place for the establishment of institutional structures that would be consolidated with the creation of the

Canada Council for the Arts in 1957. Henceforth a network of regional professional theatres as well as various theatre festivals would receive financial support from the Canada Council, provincial governments, and concerned municipal agencies. Canada's first bilingual theatre school, the National Theatre School of Canada, was founded in 1962. The Shaw Festival was launched that same year, and the Charlottetown Festival was established two years later in 1964. Nevertheless, the majority of the plays produced on the stages of these new Canadian institutions were borrowed from the American or British repertoires, which still dictated the norm on Canadian stages.

Then, in 1967, the word went out: for the Centennial of Canadian Confederation, Canadian content was to take centre stage. The regional theatres sought plays by Canadian authors, and the Dominion Drama Festival considered only Canadian works for that year's competition. Ironically, Michel Tremblay's *Les belles-sœurs*, the play that would forever change Quebec theatre the following year, was rejected by the Dominion Drama Festival's jury in 1967. It was nonetheless an exceptional year that gave rise to several remarkable productions, including that of George Ryga's celebrated play, *The Ecstasy of Rita Joe*, which describes the tragic fate awaiting Native people in a hostile urban centre. This blistering social critique set the tone for Canadian drama of the late 1960s and the 1970s in keeping with the time's spirit of social dissent and raising social awareness. As Jerry Wasserman has noted, "modern Canadian drama was born out of an amalgam of the new consciousness of the age—social, political, and aesthetic—with the new Canadian self-consciousness."[38]

However, the institutional theatres' enthusiasm for Canadian content was short-lived. Once the centennial celebrations subsided, audacity declined, and the American and British norms once more dominated Canadian stages. Faced with this development, some artists rebelled, and a dissenting movement was born. The Gaspé Manifesto appeared in 1971 and called for granting agencies to encourage the formation of a Canadian repertoire by awarding grants only to theatres whose programs contained at least 50 per cent Canadian content as of 1973. This objective would never be realized; but the call to action was out, and an alternative movement, dubbed "alternative" or "alternate" theatre, emerged with the mission of promoting Canadian theatre through the exploration of Canadian history, culture, and social institutions. With funding assistance from two federal work programs—the Local Initiatives Program and Opportunities for Youth—alternate theatre companies multiplied across the country: Vancouver's New Play Centre (1970) and Tamahnous Theatre (1971); Calgary's Alberta Theatre Projects (1972); Edmonton's Theatre 3 (1970) and Theatre Network (1975); Saskatoon's 25th Street Theatre (1971); Halifax's Pier One (1971); Newfoundland's Mummers Troupe (1972) and Codco (1973); and several in Toronto, including Theatre Passe Muraille (1968), Factory Theatre Lab (1970), Tarragon Theatre (1971), and Toronto Free Theatre (1972).[39]

The few alternative companies still active at the end of the 1970s, however, acquired the status of institutional theatres. They were intensively involved in collective creations, not unlike the young companies in Quebec at this time, to discuss subjects drawn from local realities with which the public could directly identify. They also encouraged playwriting through a formula particularly favourable to the elaboration of a specifically Canadian repertoire: the docudrama. Very popular with the alternative theatres, this dramatic genre was intended to dramatize and, eventually, mythify segments of Canadian history. Some of these productions, such as *1837: The Farmers' Revolt*, presented at Theatre Passe Muraille in 1975, were remarkably successful.

During the 1970s, certain agencies were established to encourage the publication of plays, including the Playwrights Co-op, now known as Playwrights Canada. Hundreds of plays were published, and Canadian playwrights began to develop a name for themselves.

As was the case in Quebec, Canadian playwrights of the 1980s abandoned their nationalistically-oriented efforts to explore other avenues and other themes. Festivals multiplied and international exchanges were encouraged. However, through translation, the francophone repertoire would continue to prove valuable in the efforts to create a national repertoire.

Borrowing from the Francophone Repertoire

During the 1950s and the 1960s, successful francophone plays were already produced in English translation for the Canadian public. No fewer than ten plays, by Gratien Gélinas, Jacques Languirand, Marcel Dubé, and Robert Gurik, among others, were duly produced in English in Montreal, Toronto, London, and Edmonton before 1969. Four of these plays were published before 1970 by Clarke, Irwin, and Company, and two others were published by the Playwrights Co-op in 1973, which is particularly impressive considering that the English-Canadian repertoire had just begun to appear in translation in Quebec.

During the 1970s, and particularly with the creation of the Canada Council's Grant Program for Literary Translation, the borrowing continued at an astonishing pace. Forty francophone plays were produced in English translation, thirty of which were published by companies such as Talonbooks, Simon & Pierre, and Coach House Press. Amongst these plays, there were twelve by Michel Tremblay and five by Jean Barbeau. John Van Burek translated three plays by Barbeau and ten of Tremblay's, three in collaboration with Bill Glassco. However, these numerous productions were not all welcomed with the same enthusiasm.

Already, at the end of the Quiet Revolution, plays that presented a changing Quebec had little to reassure an anglophone audience. The first translation of a new theatrical genre written in *joual*, Jean-Claude Germain's *Notes from Quebec* produced at Theatre Passe Muraille in 1970, met with little success. As Jane Koustas noted, the play was described as absurd, soporific, and amateur; it "was judged to have lost 'some pertinence in translation.'"[40]

According to Koustas, "the negative reaction elicited by a play's québécitude as well as by the use of 'joual' was even more evident in Jean Barbeau's Toronto experience."[41] Barbeau was criticized for speaking specifically to a Quebec audience, thereby delivering a social critique irrelevant to the target context. Koustas attributes this attitude to the fact that certain critics "failed to acknowledge or explain the importance of the political background, namely the October Crisis."[42] Aware of the problems involved in transposing *joual* into the English language, Urjo Kareda, then drama critic for the *Toronto Star*, raised the question of the translatability of plays written in *joual*.[43]

Even so, several months later, another play originally written in *joual* enjoyed great success with the anglophone audience. If the 1971 production of Tremblay's *Forever Yours, Marie-Lou* at the Tarragon

Theatre was a box-office success, despite the reservations of certain critics, it is because it had a comforting effect on a Toronto public anxious to understand what was shaking up Quebec playwriting. "As we appreciated the skill with which Tremblay led us over old, rocky ground, we had to suppress an urge to pop up and say 'I knew that! Teacher, I knew that. Everybody knows that!'"[44] With characters from the 1960s dear to Tremblay's heart, Torontonians could, in effect, reconnect with a familiar image—that of a Quebec before the Quiet Revolution—without having to take into account a revolutionary aspect of Tremblay's writing, which the translation process would by definition erase—the use of *joual*. It was therefore quite a different portrayal of Tremblay's voice, and the movement springing from it, that was conveyed to a unilingual anglophone audience, unable to perceive what was at stake both linguistically and culturally in this new type of theatre. Moreover, according to Koustas, the reviews Tremblay received in Toronto "indicate that he triumphed as a Canadian, not Quebec, playwright due primarily to the universality, not *québécitude* of his plays."[45]

After many attempts, some more convincing than others, the question of how to translate *joual* into English, particularly at the beginning of the 1970s, had yet to be answered. What linguistic equivalent would have enabled an English-Canadian audience to understand the socio-cultural connotations inherent in the use and the canonization of *joual* on Quebec stages at that time? In this regard, the extraordinary success of the Scottish translations of Tremblay's plays is rather instructive. If *The Guid Sisters*, Bill Findlay's 1989 Scottish translation, became the most often produced play in Scotland, it is because sociolinguistic communities in Scotland and Quebec have a great deal in common: "Both cultures have been, if not oppressed, then circumscribed....Both cultures have grappled with 'English' contempt; their churches have lionized self-denial and guilt; nostalgia for the rural past runs deep; even the populations have roughly the same size."[46] Furthermore, both languages exhibit strong similarities; much like the relationship that the Franco-Québécois language has with French, Scottish originates from Old English and follows a curve that travels from the vernacular, with its rural accents, towards a more formal urban language, in which a Standard English serves as the language of communication. And finally, in each of these societies, the vernacular, despite inherent stigmatization, performs a symbolic function. "Quebec and Scotland are still plagued by the same unresolved ambivalence: the vernacular is loudly touted as a pillar of nationhood and quietly reviled for its proletarian associations."[47] Although *joual* no longer carries the symbolic value it once did, this does not alter the fact that its arrival on Quebec stages at the end of the 1960s was a highly significant cultural event that remains largely misunderstood by an anglophone public.

According to Koustas, the quaint vision of a Quebec predating the Quiet Revolution was favoured in the English translations of the Quebec drama repertoire presented in Toronto from 1951 up until the middle of the 1980s. These translated plays fell victim to what Pierre Hébert refers to as "le syndrome de Krieghoff," defined as being the "perpétuation du mythe selon lequel le Canadien français est jovial, animé certes mais aussi grossier, anarchique, irrespectueux des conventions, insubordonné."[48] This vision of what was perceived as typically Québécois in the borrowed plays depleted them of their nationalist content and the inherent political implications in favour of a more familiar and non-threatening representation of Quebec.

The arrival of the 1980s saw little decrease in activity; there were forty-three francophone plays translated into English, twenty-eight of which were published. The playwrights most often translated were Tremblay, still at the head of the list with English versions of four of his plays, along with Jovette Marchessault, René-Daniel Dubois, Marco Micone, and Antonine Maillet, with two plays each. Notably, like many other Quebec plays, those of Marchessault and Dubois were henceforth translated into English in Montreal; indeed, by 1985, Montreal was the theatre translation capital of Canada.

With the establishment of support structures for translation in 1985, the mission of the Centre d'essai des auteurs dramatiques (CEAD) was to promote the circulation of Québécois theatre in English translation. This program initially concentrated on an exchange between Montreal and New York before turning its attention to the English-Canadian drama repertoire. In 1985, the CEAD and Playwright's Workshop Montreal founded an exchange program for theatre translations called Transmissions. It consisted of workshops on theatre translation wherein the translator worked closely with the playwright and those responsible for the public reading of the translated play. From 1985 to 1999, these workshops were co-ordinated by the CEAD's Linda Gaboriau, who was in charge of promoting the Québécois drama repertoire in English translation. Still in 1985, the CEAD and the Factory Theatre undertook a series of exchanges within the Interact program, one of the exchange programs offered by the CEAD. In 1987, the Passages project was inaugurated by the CEAD and the Prairie Theatre Exchange; and, in 1992, Banff Playwrights' Colony and the Alberta Theatre Projects took the opportunity to participate in these exchanges. The CEAD subsequently collaborated with Toronto's Tarragon Theatre and with Vancouver theatres Pink Ink and Ruby Slippers to present public readings of plays in translation. Since 1985, no fewer than forty-three francophone plays have been translated into English and been the object of public readings in Montreal, Toronto, Winnipeg, Banff, Calgary, and Vancouver, a testament to the dynamic nature of these organizations and these programs, which have greatly contributed to theatre exchanges through translation in Canada.

The foundation of these programs marks the emergence of an extremely interesting phenomenon concerning the market for theatre translation in Quebec: not only is Montreal the site of numerous Franco-Québécois translations of English works, but it has also become a prolific exporter of Quebec plays in English translation. Furthermore, the Centre d'essai des auteurs dramatiques, renamed the Centre des auteurs dramatiques in 1990, even devotes a publication to the English translations of Quebec plays it promotes. Published and regularly updated since 1990, *Quebec Plays in Translation: A Catalogue of Quebec Playwrights and Plays in English Translation* boasted some 168 plays for adults and children by 1994, written by fifty-four authors since 1951. The most active of the Quebec translators is Linda Gaboriau, followed by John Van Burek, Maureen Labonté, and Shelley Tepperman. With the exception of Van Burek, the most active anglophone translators live and work in Montreal. Thus, from the middle of the 1980s on, the choice of works entrusted to represent the francophone repertoire and their translation were responsibilities undertaken within Quebec itself. In contrast with the usual mediation governing the migration of a work in translation from one culture to another, in order to fulfill a need in the target context, the selection of the works to be translated and the strategies to use is made according to the norms of the source context through the intervention of an institution eager to promote the franco-phone repertoire to an anglophone public in Canada and abroad. By analyzing the plays included in the corpus one can see how, beginning in 1985, this new practice affected the image of the francophone drama repertoire and how it was received in English Canada.

From 1990 to 2000, fifty-three francophone plays were translated into English, thirty-three of which were published. This translated repertoire was mainly published by Talonbooks, Coach House Press, Playwrights Canada, and the University of Toronto Press, although some of these translations were also published by smaller presses, such as Guernica, Scirocco, Éditions Trois, and NuAge. This decade was dominated by Michel Marc Bouchard who had seven of his plays produced in translation, five of which were published. François Archambault, Daniel Danis, and Jean Marc Dalpé each had three plays produced in translation. Michel Garneau had the translation of one of his plays produced and published, while two others were staged as public readings. Normand Chaurette and Michel Tremblay each had two plays produced and published in translation during this period. As for the translators, Gaboriau translated six of Bouchard's plays and three works by Daniel Danis. Tepperman and Labonté were the other most active translators of this decade.

Between 1951 and 2000, there were 146 plays produced or published in English translation in Canada. With eighteen of his plays in translation, Michel Tremblay is the most-often translated francophone playwright, followed by Michel Marc Bouchard, who has eight plays in translation. Jean Barbeau and Robert Gurik have each seen six of their plays translated. As for Jovette Marchessault, she has five, while Gratien Gélinas has four. François Archambault, Normand Chaurette, Daniel Danis, Jean Marc Dalpé, Marcel Dubé, René-Daniel Dubois, Michel Garneau, Marie Laberge, and Robert Marinier have each had three plays translated. Turning to the translators, the scene is dominated by Linda Gaboriau, who has twenty-three translations to her credit, and John Van Burek, who is responsible for twelve translations, seven of which were done with Bill Glassco. Two other translators, Allan Van Meer and Shelley Tepperman, have penned six apiece. Finally, Henry Beissel, Marc F. Gélinas, Kenneth Johnstone, Maureen Labonté, and Philip W. London are each responsible for three translations.

Works Included in the Corpus

To select the works that would form a segment of the corpus and thus undergo a descriptive analysis, synchronic selections were performed along a diachronic axis at the point representing the greatest congruity in francophone and anglophone translation activity. Each of the six segments thus obtained includes both francophone and anglophone plays in translation, selected from the work of the authors and translators whose names appeared most frequently in the statistical study that accompanies this work. (Refer to the appendices for a list of the translations produced or published in each decade from 1950 to 2000.) Texts whose translations had been produced once or several times and had been published were given priority.

While Gratien Gélinas's *Tit-Coq*, in an English version by Kenneth Johnstone produced in 1951 in Toronto, ushered in the era of theatrical exchange through translation outside of Quebec, it was another eighteen years before the first French translation of an Anglo-Canadian play appeared—Gélinas's Québécois adaptation of George Ryga's *The Ecstasy of Rita Joe*. Given this temporal imbalance of exchange, it is necessary to ensure that the first segment of texts is large enough to take into account translation's beginnings on both French and English sides, but without covering periods that are too far apart. Because the 1969 adaptation of George Ryga's play by Gélinas was never published, and given that it is difficult to ascertain which is the final version amongst the numerous manuscripts conserved in the archives of the Bibliothèque et Archives nationale du Québec, another English-Canadian work—John Herbert's celebrated play *Fortune and Men's Eyes*, translated in 1970 by René Dionne and published that same year as *Aux yeux des hommes*—was selected for this first segment. This choice is all the more appropriate because Dionne is one of the most active francophone translators. As for the francophone side, the translation of Gélinas's second play, *Bousille and the Just*, published in 1961 and produced in Toronto in 1962, falls midway between the first English translations of French plays and the production of Herbert's play. It fills out this first segment of descriptive analysis, which therefore runs from 1961 to 1970.

The choices for the second segment, which covers the early 1970s, are more obvious. After all, John McDonough's *Charbonneau et le Chef* was enormously successful in Quebec, where the play was published in 1974 following numerous productions in 1971, 1972, and 1973. It was in 1973 as well that Toronto enthusiastically welcomed Michel Tremblay's celebrated play *Les Belles Soeurs* in a translation by Bill Glassco and John Van Burek. *Les Belles Soeurs* was the flagship play of the most-translated francophone playwright in Canada, and the English version was penned by a duo that included Van Burek, one of the most active anglophone translators. In addition, the two plays that make up this second segment were published in 1974.

The beginning of the 1980s found both sides ardently involved in translating. Eight English-language plays and seventeen works originating in French were produced in translation between 1980 and 1984. David Freeman was one of this period's new authors; Louison Danis, at the time one of the most active translators, translated two of Freeman's plays, one in 1981 and another in 1984. These translations are available in manuscript form in the library at the National Theatre School of Canada, but are sometimes difficult to decipher. Of the two, *Le bélier*, produced at the Théâtre d'Aujourd'hui in 1984, contains the fewest deletions, which makes it more readable and reliable. This text, therefore, undergoes a descriptive analysis later in the book. Representing the francophone repertoire is Jovette Marchessault's *The Edge of Earth is Too Near, Violette Leduc*, in an English translation by Susanne de Lotbinière-Harwood, produced in Toronto in 1986 but not published. This choice was motivated by a concern for variety because Linda Gaboriau translated all of Marchessault's other plays during this period; one of Gaboriau's translations is included in the next segment. Yvonne Klein also translated two of Marchessault's plays, one of which, *Night Cows*, was presented in Toronto in 1980. *Night Cows*, however, was composed of short monologues that are less representative of her other plays, which feature many characters inspired by the lives of women artists—a model that would become the hallmark of Marchessault's plays.

The end of the 1980s saw the rapid rise to prominence of anglophone playwright Norm Foster, who had five plays produced in translation between 1989 and 1996. His play *The Melville Boys* turned him into "one of Canada's most produced playwrights."[49] The French version of this play was presented in 1989 at Hull's Théâtre de l'Île, an important site of English-Canadian theatre production; the theatre staged seven Canadian plays in translation between 1988 and 1999. *Les frères Mainville* was the work of Paul Latreille, who had previously translated another Anglo-Canadian play in 1984; Foster's *Les frères Mainville* will also be included in the descriptive analysis. Joining this play is Normand Chaurette's *Provincetown Playhouse, July 1919*, which was produced in a translation by William Boulet in 1986 and published in an anthology the same year. The play had a significant impact on Quebec theatre and brought Chaurette to the attention of an anglophone audience.

The beginning of the 1980s signalled English-Canadian theatre's arrival in force on Quebec's francophone stages. Brad Fraser was evidently popular, as three of his plays were produced in translation between 1991 and 1995, including one translated by Maryse Warda. At the same time, on the francophone side, Michel Marc Bouchard enjoyed considerable success in English Canada as three of his plays were produced for the first time in English translations by Linda Gaboriau. For the next segment, two plays by each author will be jointly examined to discern the various strategies at work in their translation and those favoured by the most active translators in the Canadian repertoire. Fraser's *Des restes humains non identifiés et de la véritable nature de l'amour*, translated and directed by André Brassard for the Théâtre de Quat'Sous in 1991 and published by Boréal in 1993, and *L'homme laid*, translated by Warda, also produced by the Théâtre de Quat'Sous and published by Boréal in 1993, will be examined. And as for Bouchard, the plays *Lilies or The Revival of a Romantic Drama*, translated by Linda Gaboriau, published by Coach House in 1990 and produced by Theatre Passe Muraille in 1991, and *The Orphan Muses*, also translated by Gaboriau, published by Scirocco in 1993 and produced at Touchstone Theatre in 1996, have been selected for analysis.

The last segment includes a play by George F. Walker, the English-Canadian playwright most often translated into French in Canada, who really became known on the francophone scene with the success of *L'enfant-problème*. This is the first play of the Motel de passage series presented at the Théâtre de Quat'Sous in 1998 and 1999 in French translations by Warda that were published by VLB Éditeur in 2001. On the francophone side, the selected work is by Jean Marc Dalpé, a Franco-Ontarian author whose popularity has continued to rise since 1988 and whose writing depicts a linguistic reality peculiar to francophone minorities outside of Quebec. The play in question is *Lucky Lady* and it was translated by Robert Dickson, a native-Ontarian francophile, and produced by the Great Canadian Theatre Company in 1997.

The following section lists the plays that constitute the corpus for the purposes of this study. The list is arranged chronologically, which allows the reader to clearly recognize the distinct segments of the study. This list also identifies the plays' translators and catalogues the production and publication details.

Corpus

First segment: 1962, 1971

Gratien Gélinas, *Bousille and the Just* (*Bousille et les justes*). Translation: Kenneth Johnstone and Joffre Miville-Deschêne. Production: Comédie-Canadienne, Montreal, 1961; Royal Alexandra, Toronto, 1962. Publication: Clarke, Irwin and Company, 1961.

John Herbert, *Aux yeux des hommes* (*Fortune and Men's Eyes*). Translation and adaptation: René Dionne. Production: Théâtre de Quat'Sous, Montreal, 1971. Publication: Leméac, 1971.

Second segment: 1972, 1974

John McDonough, *Charbonneau et le Chef* (*Charbonneau and Le Chef*). Translation and adaptation: Paul Hébert and Pierre Morency. Production: Théâtre du trident, Quebec City, 1971, 1972; Compagnie Jean-Duceppe, Montreal, 1973, 1986. Publication: Leméac, 1974.

Michel Tremblay, *Les Belles Soeurs* (*Les belles-sœurs*). Translation: Bill Glassco and John Van Burek. Production: St. Lawrence Centre, Toronto, 1973. Publication: Talonbooks, 1974, 1992.

Third segment: 1984, 1986

David Freeman, *Le bélier* (*Battering Ram*). Adaptation: Louison Danis. Production: Théâtre d'Aujourd'hui, Montreal, 1984.

Jovette Marchessault, *The Edge of Earth is Too Near, Violette Leduc* (*La terre est trop courte, Violette Leduc*). Translation: Susanne de Lotbinière-Harwood. Production: Nightwood Theatre, Toronto, 1986.

Fourth segment: 1986, 1989

Normand Chaurette, *Provincetown Playhouse, July 1919 (Provincetown Playhouse, juillet 1919, j'avais 19 ans)*. Translation: William Boulet. Production: Buddies in Bad Times Theatre, Toronto, 1986. Publication: Coach House Press, 1986.

Norm Foster, *Les frères Mainville (The Melville Brothers)*. Translation: Paul Latreille. Production: Théâtre de l'Île, Hull, 1989.

Fifth segment: 1990, 1991

Brad Fraser, *Des restes humains non identifiés et de la véritable nature de l'amour (Unidentified Human Remains and the True Nature of Love)*. Translation: André Brassard. Production: Théâtre de Quat'Sous, Montreal, 1991. Publication: Boréal, 1993; *L'homme laid (The Ugly Man)*. Translation: Maryse Warda. Production: Théâtre de Quat'Sous, Montreal, 1993. Publication: Boréal, 1993.

Michel Marc Bouchard, *Lilies or The Revival of a Romantic Drama (Les feluettes ou la répétition d'un drame romantique)*. Translation: Linda Gaboriau. Production: Theatre Passe Muraille, Toronto, 1991; Touchstone Theatre, Vancouver 1994. Publication: Coach House Press, 1990; *The Orphan Muses (Les muses orphelines)*. Translation: Linda Gaboriau. Production: Western Canada Theatre Company, Kamloops and Belfry Theatre, Victoria, 1995; Touchstone Theatre, Vancouver, 1996. Publication: Scirocco Drama, 1993.

Sixth segment: 1997, 1998

George F. Walker. *L'enfant-problème (Problem Child)*. Translation: Maryse Warda. Production: Théâtre de Quat'Sous, Montreal, 1998. Publication: VLB Éditeur, 2001.

Jean Marc Dalpé, *Lucky Lady (Lucky Lady)*. Translation: Robert Dickson. Production: Great Canadian Theatre Company, Ottawa, 1997.

Chapter 3 discusses the methodological framework and theoretical reference points that will be employed in the descriptive analysis of the plays in the corpus.

3

TRANSLATING FOR THE STAGE

THE TRANSLATION OF A THEATRE TEXT involves a difficulty not to be found in any other type of translation. This difficulty resides in the very nature of the dramatic work, the translation of which involves not only a textual transfer from the source language to the target language, but also the transfer of numerous linguistic and paralinguistic factors that are intrinsic to its performative function and that shape the text in various ways. As Susan Bassnett-McGuire puts it, "A theatre text exists in a dialectical relationship with the performance of that text. The two texts—written and performed—are coexistent and inseparable, and it is in this relationship that the paradox for the translator lies."[1]

Orality and Immediacy

The dramatic work is subject to unique communicative and receptive modalities. Through its performance, it is conveyed orally to an audience that receives and judges it immediately. Originating in written form, a theatre text is destined to be performed in a language that will seem spontaneous to the intended audience and with which it will readily be able to identify. Except for experimental performances that explore other functions of a text, it is of paramount importance that dialogue be natural and authentic. These characteristics of theatre works require the translator to take into consideration the oral language of the intended audience and ways of speaking that are likely to deliver the desired effect. This process may result in the use of language resources other than those of the language spoken locally; but, whatever type of language is chosen, the audience must easily be able to identify with it.

In contrast with other literary texts that are perceived by way of individual processes and rhythms repeated over years and sometimes centuries, the dramatic text is delivered to an audience during a single performance that must convey everything right away. "Cette lutte que représente une traduction théâtrale, c'est une bataille dont le résultat se joue en une seule fois: la pièce passe ou ne passe pas la rampe, les auditeurs jugent sans appel."[2] The immediacy of theatrical communication requires that the message delivered must be immediately understandable. As Paul Lefebvre has noted, "si le traducteur de roman ou de poème est toujours libre d'ajouter une note explicative au bas de la page, cette pratique est impossible au théâtre."[3] So the performative function of the theatre text imposes specific linguistic constraints upon its translation, insofar as it acts upon the way this information is delivered to an audience, as much on the signifiers verbally transmitted as on what is signified throughout the performance.

Inasmuch as it must transmit everything "dans les limites du temps et dans l'espace circonscrit de la representation,"[4] a dramatic work is particularly dependent on where and when it is performed. Intended for a given community at a given moment in its history, it is bound to be rooted in a specific social, cultural, and political context. Therefore, the dramatic work obeys a logic that closely links it with the context in which it is produced and received.

Interactions with Other Sign Systems

Given that theatre is a multi-dimensional art composed of linguistic, visual, and auditory elements, it is impossible to isolate linguistic signs from the other sign systems that contribute to the makeup of the performance. Subject as it is to the needs of the performance, the theatre text is part of a complex network of semiotic codes with which it maintains close links that influence the verbal message expressed on stage. Tadeusz Kowzan defines five categories of signs that contribute to the theatre act: the spoken text, physical expression, the external appearance of the actor, the performance space, and the unspoken sounds.[5] The superimposition of these varied semiotic systems belonging to a performance implies that "le texte de théâtre est le seul texte littéraire qui ne puisse absolument pas se lire dans la suite diachronique d'une lecture, et qui ne se livre que dans une épaisseur de signes synchroniques, c'est-à-dire étagés dans l'espace, spatialisés."[6]

Accordingly, the manner in which the text is delivered, the intonation, the rhythm, and the actor's accent can infuse the words with connotations that modify its impact. The actor's body language and gestures can also affect the text. A shrug of the shoulders can be eloquent enough to render the accompanying dialogue superfluous. It can also act to affirm, contradict, or ridicule its meaning. The outward appearance of the actors, the sets they move through onstage, and what their attire and environment reveal about their social condition can also have an impact on the discourse. Thereby identified with a function, a community, and a background, it is most likely that a given character must adopt the linguistic behaviours linked to these associations.

The lighting and the sound design are two other sign systems, one visual and the other auditory, that must be integrated with the linguistic, physical, and visual aspects of the performance. The sound design can affect what unfolds onstage when, for example, it's a question of matching lyrics to music, as is the case for songs, or when one part of a text is conceived and recorded to fit with a specific, fixed-length moment within the performance. Lighting can intensify a specific moment, highlight an aspect of the message, and, to some extent, create an extra-linguistic situation that underlies the text, thereby imbuing it with additional references.

Finally, the type of stage upon which the play is produced and the time allotted to the production provide a rigid spatiotemporal framework within which each semiotic system must signify according to the protocol established by the director's vision. The aim of this complex orchestration is to transmit everything within the time and space allotted to the performance while constantly maintaining the audience's interest. If, for example, the pace of a scene needs to be adjusted, or if the space is incongruous with the message expressed, revisions can be made to the text in a search for greater conciseness, precision, or unity in the dialogue.

The Collective Art of Theatre

The decision on the role of the different semiotic systems that are juxtaposed with the linguistic sign is usually handed over to specialists who collaborate on putting the show together under the guidance of a director, who in turn is subject to the demands of a producer. Then the text is given to actors, who transmit it to an audience. Due to the production and performance requirements, theatre is by definition a collective art where choices concerning the performance and, as a result, the text do not solely belong to the translator. Jan Ferencik maintains that, because it must pass through several intermediaries, the stage performance of a dramatic work "se caractérise par la subjectivité"[7] inasmuch as each intermediary creates a subjective reading of the work. This means that "le traducteur de l'oeuvre dramatique doit donc, avant de commencer la traduction, connaître la réalisation fonctionnelle, éventuellement la conception pour laquelle il la prépare."[8]

While ensuring that the author's text and intent are respected, the translator will attempt to "rapprocher le plus possible la traduction de la conception de la mise en scène par le choix approprié des moyens et des formes d'expression."[9] For example, where the choices made by a director orient a play in a manner that favours the gestural code at the expense of the linguistic code, the text could be substantially modified.

The actors, in turn, could superimpose their understanding of their character onto that of the director and propose a different interpretation, which could necessitate a reworking of the text. Or they might ask that the text be adapted to fit more closely with their style of acting or to enable them to more readily master the dialogue. Finally, the performance will depend on the overall policy of a production company that wants to ensure that the show conforms to certain aesthetic or discursive criteria.

Adapting to Enhance Understanding[10]

The specific constraints that the nature and the function of a theatre text impose upon a translation are such that "le traducteur d'une oeuvre théâtrale...recourra presque toujours aux procédés les moins textuellement fidèles...parce qu'il doit traduire non seulement des énoncés, mais des contextes et des situations, de façon qu'on puisse immédiatement les comprendre au point d'en rire ou d'en pleurer."[11] Indeed, in the case of theatre, the "contraintes péritextuelles sont à ce point fortes qu'elles amènent des 'adaptations' ou 'versions'"[12] in order to meet one of the enunciative conditions imposed by the target context: "L'arrière-plan socio-culturel varie d'une langue à l'autre. Il faut donc s'attendre à des modifications (superstructurelles, macrostructurelles ou microstructurelles) dans une traduction à vecteurs socio-culturels. Ces modifications seront dictées cependant par un principe 'de nécessité,' c'est-à-dire le souci de faire comprendre un texte par un destinataire donné."[13] Accordingly, as René Dionne explains in the program for *La cuisine*, the Québécois adaptation of Arnold Wesker's *The Kitchen* presented at the Théâtre du Nouveau Monde in 1985, it is sometimes necessary to modify the context of the action in order to "transmettre le message d'un auteur dans une autre langue en le rendant le plus accessible possible au public...[et] favoriser l'identification du public aux personnages qui évoluent devant lui."

Along the same lines, adaptation facilitates a recreation of the relationship between the performance and the audience of the original play.

Le traducteur théâtral ne travaille pas que sur le texte; il a en plus une fonction extralittéraire. Non seulement il doit être fidèle aux structures du texte, mais il doit aussi tenir compte des relations qui unissent la pièce au public....Remplaçant un contexte étranger par un contexte connu du spectateur, l'adaptateur permet de signifier par des moyens connotatifs ce qui, dans une traduction littérale, aurait été l'objet de la part du spectateur d'une démarche dénotative. Le grand avantage de l'adaptation est de faire appel à un réseau de connotations connu du spectateur; ce dernier est alors en mesure de comprendre plus facilement le déroulement du spectacle et de communiquer avec les intentions de l'auteur.[14]

In order to render a text more understandable for the target audience by recreating the performance/audience relationship sought by the author, a translator will adapt the sociocultural context of the original work and substitute another one deemed to be equivalent.

Needless to say, this transposition of the context leads to numerous spatial and temporal readjustments in keeping with the adaptation. Undertaking a modification of the era and of the locales where the action unfolds in order to adapt it to another social and cultural reality involves taking into consideration, among other things, the geography, the religious and political climate, the institutions and traditions, the history and all customs connected with this new context. In addition to changing the names of places and characters, it is necessary to alter the surroundings in which characters interact, the functions they perform, the links that connect them, the sociolects and dialects that they use— in short, everything that defines them socially and culturally.

Adapting to Better Translate Emotion

If the sociocultural equivalents proposed by the adaptation can render the message more readily understandable for the recipient, it is because, beyond words, the adaptation serves to translate an emotional quality. According to the participants in a roundtable discussion on theatre adaptation held during the Salon du livre de l'Outaouais in 1985, "traduire, c'est s'attacher à trouver des équivalences lexicales, c'est vouer un grand respect à la formulation originale, tandis qu'adapter consiste plutôt à rechercher, au-delà des mots, une correspondance des émotions et des sentiments, à avoir le souci de la fluidité et du naturel des dialogues....Ce qu'il faut faire passer, ce qu'il faut traduire (au sens propre et au figuré), ce sont avant tout les émotions, la force dramatique d'une oeuvre, en un mot, sa théâtralité. Le vocabulaire, la syntaxe, les effets prosodiques ne sont que des moyens pour y parvenir."[15] This emphasis on the necessity of translating emotions in a way that produces an effect similar to that of the original message is similar to the concept of dynamic equivalence developed by Eugène Nida some twenty years earlier,[16] which states that priority should be given to translating the meaning of an utterance rather than its form in order to elicit in the targeted recipient a result equivalent to the one felt by the source-text recipient. In doing so, the translator enjoys "une liberté de récréation qui s'apparente beaucoup à celle du créateur original."[17]

Subject to the imperatives of orality and immediacy unique to performance, the translation of a dramatic text must also take into consideration the various interpretations put forward by the theatre artists and the multiple sign systems that contribute to the theatrical act. Amongst other things, it must deliver a message with cognitive and emotional value equivalent to that of the source text. Only then can it fulfill the performative function it has been assigned to ensure that the play successfully communicates with optimum effectiveness.

Methodological and Theoretical Framework[18]

Inspired by Itamar Even-Zohar's work on the literary polysystem, the functionalist hypothesis as described by Gideon Toury in *In Search of a Theory of Translation* (1980) and *Descriptive Translation Studies and Beyond* (1995) provides a theoretical and methodological framework for the analysis of the corpus. It will be complemented with elements borrowed from the critical methodology outlined by Antoine Berman in *Pour une critiqué des traductions: John Donne* (1995), translated by Françoise Massardier-Kenney under the title *Toward a Translation Criticism: John Donne* (2009).

Based on the descriptive analysis of translative strategies applied to target texts, the functionalist approach seeks to observe the function of the translated literature in its adopted context and the position it has been assigned within the receptive polysystem. The "function" of a text is defined by Toury as "the 'value' assigned to an item belonging in a certain system by virtue of the network of relations it enters into."[19] This notion of system is borrowed from the polysystem theory put forward by Even-Zohar, which draws its inspiration from the communication model elaborated by Roman Jakobson and the concept of the literary system developed by Boris Eichenbaum and Jurij Tynjanov.

The Literary Polysystem

Even-Zohar takes up Jakobson's model of communication to apply it not only to an isolated act or text but to a group of phenomena that make up a literary system,[20] which is viewed as being "an aggregate of activities, which in terms of systemic relations behaves as a whole, although each separate activity among these (or any part thereof) may at the same time participate in some other whole, yet be governed there by different rules and correlated with different factors."[21] This aggregate of activities related to literary matters obeys certain laws that are inherent in the system and govern literary production. These activities, diverse in nature, are grouped into six functions derived from those identified by Jakobson and presented within the following systemic model put forward by Even-Zohar.[22]

Model of the Literary System

Each of these components represents the literary system's different sectors of activity, which are interdependent. The producer represents groups or social communities of people organized and engaged in literary production. These groups also make up part of the institution inasmuch as they actively contribute, together with government agencies, the education system, criticism, and the media, to the development of institutional norms employed to maintain and pursue the sociocultural activity that is literature. The consumer is a social entity that represents the public in general. The market is the group of elements related to the buying and selling of literary products, their promotion and their consumption. The repertoire refers to the set of codes and laws that governs literary production and what use is made of the resulting products. Based on a knowledge and an acceptance of these laws, the notion of a repertoire resembles the concept of *habitus* developed by Pierre Bourdieu that Even-Zohar defines as "a repertoire of models acquired and adopted (as well as adapted) by individuals and groups in a given milieu, and under the constraints of the prevailing system relations dominating this milieu."[23] Finally, the product corresponds to any group of signs or behaviours resulting from an activity within the system. Although texts are the most obvious literary products, they can also provide support for other products.

Having thus defined the nature of a literary system, Even-Zohar underlines that this system is not homogenous. In fact, each literary genre constitutes a system in and of itself, possessing its own laws yet all the while dependent on the other systems with which it interacts. The same applies to literature in translation, which also obeys a set of laws, some of which are uniquely its own. In addition, the historical dimension of the system, which is in constant evolution inasmuch as it must continuously renew itself, means that several options simultaneously coexist at varying degrees of intensity depending on whether they belong to tradition or make up the avant-garde.

Within this polysystemic model, each system has a hierarchical structure wherein the dominant norm at its centre serves as a model for elements in the peripheral layers. In keeping with an evolutionary imperative, the centre of the system must utilize the most recent model until its novelty fades and another model is subsequently singled out. This is how the literary institution establishes a norm and maintains it, until it is pushed to the periphery by a new element that in turn occupies the centre of the system and constitutes the new norm. Such a conversion took place within the Québécois polysystem in 1968 with the canonization of *joual* as the language of the stage. Previously confined to the peripheral and non-canonized layers of the polysystem, this vernacular language thus came to occupy a central position and established itself as the dominant norm. Twenty years later, however, it had been supplanted by a more diversified Québécois language. In brief, the literary polysystem appears as "a heterogeneous open structure…a system of various systems which intersect with each other and partly overlap, using concurrently different options, yet functioning as one structured whole, whose members are interdependent."[24]

Literary Translation within the Polysystem

Toury applies the polysystem model developed by Even-Zohar to the study of translation and considers literature in translation as one of the constituent systems of the receptive literary polysystem. Albeit subject to certain general laws within the receptive literary polysystem, literature in translation also has its own dynamic and performs a specific function within this polysystem. To determine the function performed by the translation, it is important to thoroughly understand the phenomenon of literary translation.

From the functionalist perspective, literary translation is firstly a linguistic product belonging to the system of the target language itself, which means that it depends on the resources available within this target language. Secondly, it is a textual product shaped by the receptive literary system, the "secondary modelling system" that serves as a model for it.[25] This concept is borrowed from the structuralist semiotician Iouri Lotman, for whom "l'art est un système modélisant secondaire" in that it constitutes one of the "structures de communication qui se superposent au niveau linguistique naturel" as, for example, is the case for myths or religion.[26] "Ainsi l'art peut être décrit comme un langage secondaire et l'oeuvre d'art, comme un texte dans ce langage."[27] In the case of theatre, the text is subject to a series of dialogical, scenographic, and performance codes that form a secondary semiotic structure specific to the drama repertoire within a given literary system. Therefore, the study of the translation must take into account not only the linguistic constraints imposed upon the translated text, but also the literary polysystem that shapes it and of which it is a product.

Expanded by Annie Brisset, the functionalist model went beyond the literary polysystem to include the sociocultural context that encompasses it. From this perspective, the translation of a literary text, like the literary system that receives it, cannot escape the social discourse, which is "formé de tous les énoncés qui surgissent dans une société"[28] insofar as they are caught up in "configurations idéologiques."[29] Thus, subject to the prevalent discourse in the target society, a literary translation is not only shaped by literary and linguistic constraints but by discursive codes as well.

However, even when expanded, this theoretical framework does not take into consideration an element essential to the study of the translation process: the action of the translating subject informed by conscious and unconscious forces related to individuality and to the social field to which the subject belongs. Although indicative of the values, ideas, tensions, and tendencies shared by a given community and that influence translation, the study of linguistic, literary, and discursive norms cannot explain all the evident shifts observed within translated texts. As Antoine Berman points out, a translation is necessarily personal as, ultimately, it "proceeds from an individuality, even one subjected to 'norms.'"[30] Further on in this chapter, the critical reflections of Berman and Bourdieu will be used in an attempt to define the translator's more personal contribution to the function of literature in translation.

The Functional Equivalence

Developed at first within a prescriptive linguistic framework, equivalence represents an "identité de signification" put forward by the translation to account for the initial signification.[31] Rejecting this ideal conception as unrepresentative of reality, the functionalist approach understands equivalence as an empirical and observable phenomenon in which an utterance in the source language is represented by an utterance in the target language within the target context. Even though the two texts are similar in terms of relevant characteristics, the hierarchy of these characteristics may differ in the target and source texts, each respectively subject to distinct systemic constraints.

Shaped by this polarity, the equivalence of a literary translation is determined by the position that it occupies between the adequacy pole, which represents faithfulness to the source text and its norms, and the acceptability pole, which governs the insertion of the translation and its reception within the receptive linguistic and literary systems.[32] Exactly where the translation is positioned between adequacy towards the source text and acceptability within the target context is determined by the norms that govern it. These norms are meant to ensure that it is a worthwhile literary work within the target language and that it occupies an appropriate position within the targeted literary polysystem, while it continues to represent a text written in another language that itself already occupies a position in another literary polysystem. These two principles are often incompatible.

Even-Zohar maintains that the position occupied by the translation within the receptive polysystem depends on the state of the receptive system and on the need fulfilled by the translation within this system. It follows that young literatures and weak literary systems, or those in a state of crisis, will resort to translation to fill in what they feel is missing. In such circumstances, the translated text will lean towards adequacy to the original text and will establish itself as a model and occupy a central position within the receptive context. By contrast, when the translation is inserted into a stable system that enjoys a long tradition or that is rapidly developing, it will tend to reproduce the existing dominant model and seek to attain maximum acceptability within the receptive polysystem. As Even-Zohar points out, "not only is the socio-literary status of translation dependent upon its position within the system, but the very practice of translation is also strongly subordinated to that position."[33] Therefore, depending on the state of the receptive polysystem, the translation will favour adequacy to the source text or acceptability within the target system.

This theoretical framework enabled E.D. Blodgett to attribute Quebec's indifference towards English Canada's writing to their second-ary position within the target system: "the writing of English Canada had, until recently, only rarely possessed, to use Even-Zohar's terms, a 'primary activity' representing 'the principle of innovation,' as opposed to a secondary activity whose role is to maintain 'the established code.'"[34] According to Blodgett, this model also has the benefit of allowing for the study of translation carried out "under intra-national conditions,"[35] in contrast with models developed to study literature in an international context. After all, the constraints imposed upon literary systems within a bilingual state "are not the same as those that exist between sovereign nations,"[36] and international models are incapable of factoring in the diglossia that governs the relationship between literature written in English and in French in Canada. Not only is the dynamic of the relationship between the different national literatures affected by power struggles of every sort, as evidenced by the present linguistic hegemony of English throughout the world and the difficult enfranchisement of postcolonial literatures, but this dynamic is most often constructed from a position of national autonomy.

Pursuing his reflection on the polysystem and its application to the study of literary translation within the context of Canadian and Quebec literatures, Blodgett cites the critical paradigm developed by Toury: "the translation becomes the field that both relates the literatures of Canada and problematizes their relationship. It also makes it impossible to speak, as most critics do, of these literatures as if there were only one....Another consequence is that it permits literary activity to be defined with respect to the systems within which it operates and with which it interferes."[37]

The Norms

In any given society, how translation is carried out is subject to constraints that, to varying degrees, shape the behaviour of individuals who belong to this society and share its values and ideas. These explicit or implicit rules, learned through the process of socialization, constitute what is referred to in sociological terms as norms. Inter-subjective in nature, norms form a continuum extending from an absolute extreme, represented by prescribed laws, to a subjective extreme, manifested idiosyncratically. To be recognized as such, a norm must appear with a certain regularity, despite being fundamentally unstable and exhibiting a sociocultural specificity, inasmuch as each norm does not apply to the same degree to all sectors of cultural activity. They in turn form a set of norms peculiar to each linguistic, literary, and sociocultural community, and affect every step of the translation process and all levels of the translation's production.

Although they differ in nature and vary in intensity, translation norms all originate from an initial norm. This "norm of norms" determines the type of equivalence sought, and consequently where the translation is positioned between the search for adequacy—adherence to the source text and its norms—and the search for acceptability—adherence to the norms within the linguistic, literary, and discursive systems of the receptive context. In practice, the overall approach that an individual adopts for the translation of a specific text will take the form of a compromise, at once a meeting and a confrontation between the two opposing systems.

The translational norms are divided into two groups issuing respectively from two central questions posed by the functionalist hypothesis: what works are chosen to be translated, and how are they translated? Or more precisely, how does the receptive polysystem govern the choice of what text to translate, and how it is to be translated? Presiding over the selection of texts to translate, the preliminary norms deal with the translation strategy adopted, the systematic factors pertaining to the choice of works, authors, translators, and types of texts favoured or rejected for translation, as well as the use of intermediate versions in the translation process. Various factors, commercial, aesthetic, or sociocultural in nature, may be at play in these choices.

At a different level, operational norms chiefly direct the decisions made during the act of translation itself. They are of two types. Matricial norms are derived from the primary modelling system and are related to "the very existence of target-language material intended as a substitute for the corresponding source language material...its location in the text...as well as the textual segmentation."[38] Textual, linguistic, or discursive norms belong to the secondary modelling system and "govern the selection of material to formulate the target text in or replace the original textual and linguistic material with."[39] This choice is linguistic when it relates to lexical, grammatical, syntaxical, or stylistic norms peculiar to a given literature; it is textual when it conforms to what is considered appropriate for a translation of a literary work according to the location, the period, the type of translation or the technique employed; it is discursive when it is the result of ideological configurations peculiar to the receptive sociocultural context.

As for the level of intensity of the norms, Toury draws upon a model by Jay Jackson to develop a tripartite representation of distribution. The norms are primary when they represent a more-or-less mandatory phenomenon and offer the translator minimum latitude; they are secondary when they express tendencies generally acceptable to the group under study; finally, they become idiosyncratic when they result from an individual choice and offer the translator maximum latitude. However, the norms must not be mistaken for "*universals of translational behaviour,*"[40] such as the tendency to clarify, which is to say rendering something explicit in the translated text that is implicit in the original, or rendering the text more idiomatic by accentuating the use of structures peculiar to the target language at the expense of the elements of meaning contained in the source text.

Lastly, the unstable nature of norms is such that they can be contradictory, causing them to thus compete with one another and to act simultaneously. Their value will be dominant when they are in fashion and occupy the centre of the system; it will be peripheral when they act as remnants of past norms related to a tradition or rudiments of new norms constituting the avant-garde. This allocation underlines the dynamic aspect of normative systems and allows them to be studied from a diachronic perspective. Here is an outline of the norms applied to the translation of a literary work.

Type

INITIAL NORM: position of the translation between adequacy to
    the source text and acceptability within the receptive context
TRANSLATIONAL NORMS: preliminary and operational (matricial
    [language] and literary [linguistic, textual, discursive])

Intensity

PRIMARY and SECONDARY: more or less collective
IDIOSYNCRASY: more individual

Value

CENTRAL: dominant, proposes a model

PERIPHERAL: reproduces the dominant model

Translational norms are identified by way of two sources: textual, i.e., the translated texts themselves and their analytical inventory; and extratextual, i.e., semi-theoretical or critical formulations, such as prescriptive theories of translation, statements made by translators, editors or publishers, criticism, comments, analyses as well as metatexts and introductions relating to the translation. The first group of sources enable the reconstruction of the active norms in the texts under study, while the second contain norms that are already formulated. However, according to Toury, as the goal of the formulation is often, intentional or not, to promote rather than to reveal a way of translating, it is not unusual to note a gap between the norms drawn from extratextual sources and those obtained by analyzing the translated texts.

This disparity between the discourse on the translation and the actual strategies that shape it exposes an aspect of the translation process that as yet remains obscure: the translating subject and his or her conscious or unconscious relation to the text and to more personal issues it may raise. Because they are not statistically measurable and do not conform to systematic linguistic or literary norms and social codes, these aspects of the translation operation elude the functionalist model. Revealing ideas and values shared by a given community, the model offers a homogenous vision of this community in that it presents what therein constitutes the norm. Consequently, it can hardly take into account the translating subject's position within the community and the subjective dimensions of translating.

In this vein, one wonders how the countless choices made during a translation are affected by the translator's race, ethnicity, gender, social class, personal history, sexual orientation, aesthetic preferences, and political, moral, or religious convictions—in short, all that informs a subject and his or her position within the community. We could also consider the influence of other subjectivities involved at different stages of the translation process, be it the acting, the direction, the production, or the publication.

With this in mind, the French version of Judith Thompson's *I Am Yours*, translated by Robert Vézina in 1990 under the title *Je suis à toi*, is quite revealing. The play deals with an unwanted pregnancy, but the translation has erased any indication of the young pregnant woman's fears about possible pathological behaviour that, according to her mother, could be triggered by the pregnancy. This significant omission seems to suggest that the translator has a conflict with the representation of maternity in the original play. Moreover, this conflict with the relationship to motherhood as it is portrayed in the original runs throughout the whole translation.[41] In this text, where parents from different social classes confront each other over custody of a soon-to-be-born child, all differences in the levels of language have been erased, thereby eliminating the class antagonism between the parents, which effectively displaces the conflict solely into the territory of the couple and the power struggle between the sexes. This displacement discredits the mother to the father's advantage; now that he is freed from the stigma of belonging to an inferior social class, he becomes the innocent victim of the battle of the sexes. This linguistic strategy reinforces the message already conveyed by the title ("toi" is a diminutive of Toilane, the father's name) and is consistent with a thematic isotopy that results in the promotion of the rights of the father. Furthermore, various translative choices are discernible throughout the French text that exhibit, consciously or not, a resistance to the representation of maternity and motherhood put forward in the original text. In this sense, it is conceivable that certain themes can be particularly prone to unconscious investment during the translation, certainly not the least of which would be representations of motherhood.

On a broader level, it is necessary to take into account the material conditions in which the translation is done, the allegiances from which it results, the working relationships, and the interests at stake. Here "interests" is understood to be what Bourdieu defines as "un investissement spécifique dans les enjeux, qui est à la fois la condition et le produit de l'appartenance à un champ,"[42] which causes one to fight in order to maintain or improve one's position as an agent belonging to a given social field where all activity is conceived as a fight for legitimacy. As noted by Jean-Marc Gouanvic, who studies translation from a Bourdieusian perspective, it is also necessary to ask: "dans quelle

dynamique sociale [le traducteur] s'inscrit-il dans le champ, autrement dit comment négocie-t-il sa position par rapport aux autres agents
avec lesquels il est en concurrence pour la légitimité?"[43] From this perspective, it is conceivable that translation is dependent on the specific
interests of the translator within the field where she or he works and the
group to which she or he belongs, and that it is affected by the conge-
nial relations and the competition amongst the agents that contribute
to its production.

Accordingly, one can see, for example, that a translation undertaken
for an experimental feminist theatre company would be conceived in
light of values and objectives suitable to such an artistic and ideological orientation. This orientation would inform the reading given to
the text and suggest certain correlations at the expense of other potential equivalences, which could otherwise be activated in a translation
intended for another stage and concerned with promoting another discourse. The translator would take into account the specific orientation
of the company in question, as it aims to occupy a more or less radical, more or less exclusive, or more or less subversive position within
the artistic and ideological fields to which it lays claim, on a regional,
national, or international level.

Whether in the realm of the strictly private or within the context of
the field wherein an agent is striving for legitimacy, we find ourselves in
the presence of a multi-dimensional translating subject whose choices,
be they collective or individual, act upon the text to be translated in a
variety of ways. Luise von Flotow contends: "Though subjective aspects
of translation such as the translator's biographical, psychological, ideological, and professional background—her positionality—are rarely
reflected upon, they certainly have an impact on the final text."[44] This
is also the opinion of Berman, whose critical method sheds light on the
subjective aspects of translation.

Outline of a "Productive Criticism"

Derived from a post-Heideggerian hermeneutics developed by Paul
Ricoeur and Hans Robert Jauss, and the concept of literary criticism put
forward by Walter Benjamin, Berman developed a method of critical

analysis for translation that he describes as "productive criticism"; it is meant to be an illumination, manifestation, and perpetuation of the aforementioned theorists' work. He details the fundamental traits of productive criticism in a posthumous work entitled *Pour une critique des traductions: John Donne*. Aimed at "bringing out the truth of a translation,"[45] Berman's productive crticicism calls for a rigorous analysis of the translation and the original, and a consideration not only of the historico-cultural context of the work in translation, but also of the subjectivity that informs it. Moreover, Berman pays particular attention to the responsibility of the translator, given that translation is always individual and always carried out by an author-translator who "has every right as soon as he is open"[46]—which is to say that a translator has every right to translate as he or she wishes as long as he or she plays fair. This ethical consideration, with which one cannot help but sympathize, is nonetheless perplexing. If the translator's "*ethics* lies in the respect, or rather *in a certain respect for the original*,"[47] what about unconscious or subconscious factors that participate in the act of translation without her or his knowledge? Without aspiring to provide an answer to this question within the framework of this study, I nevertheless propose to explore certain critical notions put forward by Berman in order to shed light on the study of the translating subject, including her or his translating position and translation project in relation to a given translation horizon.

The Translation Horizon

To define the translation horizon, Berman draws upon the notion of the horizon of expectations, developed by Hans Robert Jauss in his aesthetic of literary reception. According to Jauss, the perception of a work is subject to a set of rules based on the reader's previous experiences, determining what he refers to as this work's "horizon of expectations."[48] Applied by Berman to an hermeneutic of translation, the notion of an horizon of expectations includes "the set of linguistic, literary, cultural, and historical parameters that 'determine' the ways of feeling, acting, and thinking of the translator."[49] The notion of horizon has a dual nature: "On one hand, referring to the place from which the action of the translator has meaning and can unfold, it points to the open space of this action. On the other hand, it refers to what closes, what encloses, the translator in a circle of limited possibilities."[50] Within the methodological framework devised for this study, the translation horizon corresponds to the linguistic, textual, and discursive norms active within the receptive context and orienting a priori the translative choices made by the translating subject.

The Position of the Translating Subject

Caught in this horizon, the translating subject reaches a compromise between her conception of translation or her "*translation drive*"[51] and the manner in which she has internalized the prevailing discourse on translation as represented by the norms. According to Berman, this urge that propels the translation and that "is at the base of every *destiny* of translation"[52] remains to be defined inasmuch as there had yet to be a theory on the translating subject. For him, the translating position "is the self-positioning of the translator vis-à-vis translation, a self-positioning that, once chosen (for it is, in fact, a choice) *binds* the translator, in the sense given by the philosopher Alain when he said that character is an oath."[53] All translators develop a translating position of their own, through which they exercise their subjectivity. The translator's position can be pieced together from the translations themselves, which implicitly express it, and from any remarks that the translator has made on the translations or any other related subject matter. However, according to Berman, "these representations do not always express the truth of the translation position, especially when they appear in strongly coded texts like prefaces or conventional speaking situations like interviews. Here the translator tends to give voice to the doxa and to impersonal topoi about translation."[54] This mistrust regarding how representative translators' remarks actually are of their translating position brings to mind Toury's warning concerning the actual value of norms drawn from extratextual sources. This shared reservation underlines the elusive aspect of the translating subject whose remarks are more likely to conceal rather than reveal an action. Is it that translators can no longer escape the anonymity that has been their lot? The invisibility of the work carried out by the translation, long considered a measure of its quality, is moreover vigorously called into question by recent translation criticism, notably within the framework of feminist analysis, wherein there is an insistence on the visibility of the feminine translating subject. Be that as it may, the confrontation of extratextual and textual norms within the current analysis will highlight the disparities between the translator's position and the discourse it engenders.

Finally, according to Berman, the translating position is also connected to translators' "*language position,*" which is to say, "their relation to foreign languages and to the mother-tongue" and their "*scriptural position* (their relation to writing and to literary works)."[55] Berman adds, "A theory of the translating subject will be possible only when we are able to consider together the translator's translating position, language position, and scriptural position."[56]

The Translation Project

The project, or the aim of the translation, depends on the translating position adopted by the translator and the specific demands of the work to be translated. On one hand, the project dictates the mode of transcultural passage, namely the forms favoured by the translator to reveal the foreign work to the receptive culture—chosen excerpts or the whole work, partial or complete translation, adaptation, retranslation, bilingual or unilingual publication, etc.—what Berman refers to as "la translation" or "literary transfer."[57] On the other hand, the aim of the translation lies in the very manner in which the translation is carried out. The position and project are therefore inseparable and introduce the critic to "an absolute circle not a vicious one."[58] Berman explains:

> [the critic] must read the translation on the basis of its project, but the truth of this project is, in the end, accessible only based on the translation itself and on the type of literary transfer that it achieves. For everything that a translator can say and write about his project becomes a reality only in the translation. And yet the translation is never more than the realization of the project: it goes *where* and *up to the limits* of where the project leads it. It tells us the

truth of the project only by revealing to us *how* it was carried out (and not whether in the end it has been carried out) and what the *consequences* of the project in relation to the original were.[59]

In other words, the project and the results are inseparable. The object of translation criticism can only be the project itself, inasmuch as the chosen mode of translation is the very manifestation of this project. The success or failure of the translation is only attributable to the project, which determined that certain means were chosen rather than others. For Berman, these choices can only be personal and subjective. It is possible that a project's lack of coherence is the cause of contradictions in the translation, but this should be strictly viewed as a result of the project. It is also not unusual for the doxa to interfere in certain translative choices that "momentarily violate the project because they follow different laws."[60] However, what can create real discordance between the project and its realization is "the defectiveness inherent in the act of translation,"[61] which cannot be attributed to the project, but rather to the subjectivity of the translator. "It is the *finitude* of the translator that explains the discordances in relation to the project. But it can only be a matter of limited discordances, although they may be numerous."[62]

Thus, according to Berman, the translation project is defined by how translators negotiate their translating position—their conception of the translation vis-à-vis the prevailing doxa—in relation to the specific constraints of a work. In other words, the translation project represents the compromise translators make between their translating position and the demands of the work to be translated. The subjectivity of translating subjects can appear overtly in remarks or comments on the translating position, but it pays to be cautious because they can be mistaken about themselves. This subjectivity can also be concealed within the disparities between the declared translating position and how it is represented in the translated text, as well as in the discordances observed in the translation project.

This brief critical incursion into the realm of the translating subject foreshadows the difficulty inherent in the understanding of this enigmatic but unavoidable element of the translation process. For the purpose of this study, we shall consider the translating subject in terms of the subject's collective dimension through primary and secondary norms, and in the subject's more individual dimensions within the category of idiosyncratic behaviours resulting from the position of the translator.

Model of a Descriptive Analysis

Among the researchers who have contributed to the elaboration of the functionalist model to be used in the study of translation, José Lambert and Hendrik van Gorp put forward a frame of reference, which is to say a third element necessary in the comparison of original and translated texts. Equally applicable to all the pairs of texts studied, this model makes it possible to identify strategies specific to each translation, their order of priority, and the nature of the norms from which they originate. The results obtained can then be compared with the systemic context in which they take part.

Based on a principle of correspondence between mechanisms working at different levels of the textual structure, this model advocates a telescopic study of translation strategies proceeding from a general presentation of the text, wherein an overall strategy is discernible, to its macrostructure, and, finally, to its microstructural strategies. The advantage of such a model is that it allows for the classification of observable phenomena according to specific parameters and facilitates their inventory. Essentially systemic, this approach examines the translation solely in terms of its relation with the system that encompasses it, meaning the greatest number of written or translated texts involved in the formation of a literature. Moreover, it permits the individual or collective character of a norm to be evaluated according to the frequency of the phenomena attributable to it.

Derived from a model developed by Lambert and van Gorp to describe a translation,[63] and amended in light of the distinctive features of the dramatic work, the proposed descriptive analysis comprises the following four steps.

1. *The compilation of preliminary data* informs us of the overall translative strategy exhibited in the presentation of the text and

through the type of transcultural passage it has undergone. The metatexts can also provide indications of the subject's translating position, the processes favoured by the translation project, the preliminary norms specific to the text under study, and, finally, the initial norm, which means the preference shown for adequacy to the source text or for acceptability within the receptive context.

2. *The macrostructural analysis* investigates the translation of the text itself in terms of its structure in the broadest sense. Here, once again, the strategies favoured by the translation project can be identified. The examination of these macrostructural elements can unearth certain preliminary or operational norms, and indicate the type of strategies at work at the microstructural level.

3. *The microstructural analysis* deals with the translative strategies at work at the level of the text's smallest integral unit. In uncovering the translative strategies actually applied to the text, the analysis of the textual microstructure makes it possible to compare the phenomena observed at each level of analysis and identify operational norms influencing the translation. Furthermore, it can provide elements that reveal the position of the translating subject, the manner in which the translation project is being carried out and the degree of coherence of this project. Finally, these textual results are compared with the systemic context in which the text finds itself.

4. *The comparison with the systemic context* serves to compare the norms observed in the text under study with those of other translations belonging to the same literary system. These textual norms can then be compared to the extratextual norms specific to the systemic context in which the translated texts now belong. In thereby situating the texts in their translation horizon, it is possible to measure the nature, the intensity, and the value of a norm or a translative strategy. Collating the results thus acquired enables the identification of the initial norm governing the texts under study, their position within the receptive polysystem, and the resulting function assigned to them.

As for the translating subject, the comparison with other works by the same translator along with that individual's reflections on subjects concerning translation can reveal certain subjective factors within the repertoire under study.

The following compilation outlines the model that will serve as a referential framework for the descriptive analysis of the corpus.[64]

1. Preliminary data

a. *Presentation of the text*
- title of the translation
- translator
- original title of the play
- author
- indications of genre
- date, place, production

b. *Metatext*
- preliminary pages
- preface, postface, glossary
- notes, included or separate

c. *Indications of translative strategy*
- complete, partial, amplified
- adaptation, imitation, etc.

2. Macrostructural analysis

a. *Surrounding texts*
- prologue, epilogue

b. *Text divisions*
- acts, scenes
- titles

c. *Staging information*
- characters
- setting
- period
- set and accessories
- costumes
- description of the action
- stage directions

3. Microstructural analysis

a. *Levels of language*	• literary, formal, informal, colloquial, vernacular, slang • dialects
b. *Grammatical models*	• elisions, repetitions, unusual stylistic inversions, omissions, etc. • strategies
c. *Vocabulary*	• spelling discrepancies • lexico-semantic discrepancies
d. *Semantic discrepancies*	• additions, suppressions, substitutions • other modifications

4. Comparison with the systemic context

a. *Comparison of the results obtained for each text and examination of intertextual relations*

b. *Comparison with the extratextual norms belonging to the system under study and to the polysystem that encompasses it*

c. *Identification of subjective factors and idiosyncratic behaviour within the translations*

By using this model, the descriptive analysis will attempt to identify the norms that are of particular interest to this study. Though the preliminary norms related to the choice of works, authors, translators, and the politics that precede the translation itself will be discussed, our attention will be mainly focussed upon the linguistic operational norms, both textual and discursive, governing the choices made in replacing the original text. The regularity with which these norms appear will attest to their intensity and provide information on the initial norm that governed the translation. Ultimately, the function thereby assigned to the translated text within the receptive context will be revealed.

4

DESCRIPTIVE ANALYSIS

The French Repertoire
Translated into English

THIS CHAPTER IS DEVOTED TO the English versions of the Franco-Canadian plays selected in chapter 2. In keeping with the proposed model, this analysis will first present the translated work and the circumstances surrounding the transcultural passage. It will then examine the preliminary data, the metatext, and the macrostructure. Lastly, the microstrucural analysis will serve to reveal the strategies operating at the smallest integral unit of the translation. This examination will make it possible to identify the norms that govern the translation of each text and the type of equivalence upon which they are based. However, it is only after all the texts belonging to the same repertoire and representing various moments in the evolution of this repertoire have been analyzed that one can evaluate the importance of the observed norms and the function attributed to the translated texts within the target context.

Gélinas, *Bousille*, and Quaint Appeal

In 1958, Gratien Gélinas founded the Comédie-Canadienne, a Montreal theatre company dedicated to producing Canadian works. The following year he staged his second play, *Bousille et les justes*, which met with the greatest success in the theatre company's history, with more than 300 performances in French and in English. Gélinas's first play *Tit-Coq* had been a huge hit at the Monument-National in 1948. He was already famous for Fridolin, the mischievous character he brought to life in 1938, whose funny, touching remarks were firmly anchored in Quebec's popular reality and were the subject matter of annual revues up until 1956. Moreover, according to Jean-Cléo Godin and Laurent Mailhot, "Fridolin et *Tit-Coq*...apparaissent comme les contributions les plus significatives du dramaturge. Elles représentent un moment privilégié: la véritable naissance d'un théâtre populaire québécois."[1] Internationally acclaimed, *Bousille et les justes* enjoyed lasting success, and, by 1976, following 567 official performances, broke the national record for performances set by *Tit-Coq*.[2] The original play was published in 1960 by Éditions de l'Institut littéraire du Québec, then again in 1967 by Montreal's Éditions de l'Homme, and, finally, by Quinze Éditeur in 1981. *Bousille and the Just*, the translation by Kenneth Johnstone and Joffre Miville-Deschêne, was published in 1961 by Toronto's Clarke, Irwin and Company.

Created at the very beginning of the Quiet Revolution, *Bousille et les justes* attests to the spirit of dissent that at the time was beginning to take hold throughout Quebec. Written in the form of a tragicomical satire, the play is a blistering criticism of religious and moral hypocrisy existing under the guise of respectability. The plot can be summarized thus: following the arrest of their youngest child on the charge of involuntary manslaughter, the Grenons are willing to do whatever it takes to protect their reputation. Bousille, a simple-minded individual employed by the family, is the sole witness to the crime. Profoundly religious and incapable of understanding what is at stake in the trial, Bousille is terrified at the idea of perjuring himself, even involuntarily. Despite the religious bartering undertaken by the mother, for whom heaven's blessings are received in exchange for promises of pilgrimages and novenas, it is obvious that the murderer will be found guilty as a result of Bousille's testimony. It is at this point that the oldest brother, backed by his brother-in-law, indulges first in blackmail and then in intimidation and physical violence to convince Bousille to commit perjury. At the very moment when the family is celebrating the outcome of the trial, we learn that Bousille has killed himself and that an inquiry will be held. Here the character's name takes on a specific meaning in the sense that Bousille's integrity managed to "bousiller," or ruin, the family's dishonest designs.

This play is indicative of Gélinas's particular style. The metaphors are colourful and numerous; the tone is imbued with a disconcerting sincerity that renders the dialogue extremely effective, despite the clumsiness of certain quaint descriptions. Though it sometimes verges on caricature, the humour is scathing, and the satire pitiless. The language is informal, which is to say neither colloquial nor formal, with rare examples of the vernacular such as "guidoune" (floozie), "cenne" (penny), "quêteux" (beggar), and "comprenure" (comprehension). The spelling generally respects the standard French model, except for certain markers of orality, such as "mam'zelle" for mademoiselle, or "v'là" for voilà. This psychological drama is naturalist in style and respects the classical tradition of the unity of time and space.

As noted in the introductory pages of the 1960 publication, the play is divided into four acts that all take place in the hotel room rented by the family, which has come to Montreal from Saint-Tite for the trial. The characters are listed in the order that they appear on stage: "le garçon, Phil Vezeau, Henri Grenon, Aurore Vezeau, Blaise Belzile dit Bousille, la mère, Noëlla Grenon, l'avocat, le frère Nolasque, Colette Marcoux." This list is followed by a description of the set, in which the action is said to take place in Montreal, and the reader is advised to consult the glossary that explains the nine "mots et expressions propres au Canada français [qui] sont imprimés en italiques dans le texte."[3] There is no mention of the era in which the action unfolds, but one assumes the play is set in the early 1950s. Numerous stage directions mostly serve to indicate movements or emphasize intent.

The English version appeared the year after the original publication, with but a single introductory page stating that the translation was first produced at the Comédie-Canadienne in February 1961, with a cast that included several actors from the original production. It also indicates that the play takes place in the present-day and that it is divided into two acts of two scenes each. So, there were structural modifications, apparent in the written text yet imperceptible at the performance level. As for the characters, one notices that the first names have been retained, yet the family names have been replaced by other French names; Vezeau, Grenon, and Marcoux become Vézina, Gravel, and Richard respectively, and le frère Nolasque is rechristened Brother Théophile. Within the text itself, other characters also have their first or last names changed; Jean-Paul is replaced by Pierre, le frère Théophane by Brother Stanislas, Madame Laberge by Mrs. Larose, and Maître Lacroix by Mr. Fontaine. The same thing occurs with place names when Saint-Lambert becomes Pont-Viau and Saint-Hubert Street replaces la rue Saint-André. Only Saint-Tite is retained. It seems rather likely that such onomastic and toponymic modifications were intended to appropriate the Franco-Québécois reality for something more familiar to the anglophone audience. Not only must the name be obviously French, it must correspond to something already entrenched in the anglophone imagination.

In the English version, there is no indication of the author's style or the use of certain local expressions that appear in the original. The English title is accompanied by the author's name as well as that of one of the translators, but there is no mention of the translative strategy employed, the original title, or the version of the original upon which it was based. Generally, the English version adopts a more neutral and less colourful tone than the original. In the words of Renate Usmiani, "the English dialogue as a whole seems somewhat anemic compared to the French....Gélinas's dialogue captures the spirit of his characters from Saint-Tite so realistically that a full transposition into another cultural background is simply not possible."[4]

Indeed, many local expressions and some rather awkward figures of speech have either been removed or replaced by less quaint equivalents, such as "I am just as upset"[5] for "ça me chiffonne la tranquillité, à moi aussi."[6] Certain religious details considered superfluous or insignificant for an anglophone audience have been deleted or removed in favour of a more acceptable equivalent. Thus, "Je mettrais ma main au feu qu'elle n'a pas fait ses Pâques depuis au moins deux ans"[7] becomes "I'd swear she hasn't received holy communion for at least two years."[8] Here, it is preferable to refer to a religious custom that is more widely known to an audience that is not necessarily conversant with all the rites of the Catholic Church. The same approach is taken with "le saint Vincent de Paul" to whom Henri is compared and who becomes "a philanthropist" in the translated version.[9]

The translation also modifies the dialogue by deleting certain remarks or explanations considered unnecessary, as in the following example:

> L'AVOCAT. Jusqu'ici, je comptais justifier le geste malheureux de l'accusé par le raisonnement suivant, que je vous exposais ce matin: au moment de l'accident, Aimé se trouvait—ou croyait se trouver— en état de légitime défense devant un homme qui avait déjà levé la main sur lui quelques secondes plus tôt.[10]

Here is what appears in the English version:

> LAWYER. As I told you this morning, I intended to plead legitimate self-defence.[11]

One has to wonder, though, why the English version would omit dialogue where Bousille empathizes with his dog Fido, a pet that is not very smart but has a heart of gold, when this analogy describes his own character with remarkable efficiency and rare eloquence. Here is the missing excerpt in which Bousille talks about his dog:

> BOUSILLE. Il n'est pas beau, il n'est pas très intelligent non plus...

> NOËLLA. ...mais il a un coeur d'or.

> BOUSILLE. Là tu dis vrai! L'autre soir, Aurore avait fait des saucisses pour le repas. Comme il avait faim, lui aussi, je lui ai donné la moitié de la mienne. Cinq minutes plus tard, crois-le ou non, il vient me déposer un os sur les genoux! Comme geste de reconnaissance, pas un chien de race n'aurait pu trouver mieux.[12]

The translation only includes the ensuing exchange:

NOËLLA. He's a good dog, all right.

BOUSILLE. It seems to me the family doesn't appreciate him enough.

NOËLLA. I am afraid not.[13]

This dialogue about the dog clearly illustrates Bousille's character and alludes to the position he holds within the family. Why was it cut? This question is all the more relevant because the dog makes another symbolic appearance later in the play; right before the dreadful interview in which Henri resorts to physical violence to persuade Bousille to perjure himself, there is a reference to the affection that Fido feels for Bousille. Phil then leaps at the chance to compare Bousille to his dog and tries to mollify him by exploiting this comparison. It is tempting to see this deletion as the result of an aesthetic judgement or a subjective choice that intervenes in the translation project and is aimed at attenuating the analogy between Bousille and his dog Fido.

On a different note, the translation occasionally amplifies jokes or comments designed to underline the sense of belonging to the Québécois context, as in the following excerpt.

PHIL. (*Baissant la voix pour qu'Henri n'entende pas.*) Pas d'erreur, le bluff, ça le connaît.

BOUSILLE. Je voudrais bien être aussi à l'aise que lui quand le moment viendra pour moi de vider mon sac devant le juge.[14]

In the English version, two lines have been added to this exchange and they contain an analogy to hockey, a very popular sport in Quebec.

PHIL. (*Lowering his voice so that Henri cannot hear him.*) No doubt about it, the kid's a good bluffer!

BOUSILLE. He seemed upset but not too much.

PHIL. Yeah! Just like a hockey player in the penalty box.

BOUSILLE. I'd sure like to be that relaxed when the time comes for me to face the judge.[15]

Another stereotypical cultural substitution sees to it that the client who has been overcharged at the Gravels' garage is no longer "un gars de La Tuque qu'on ne reverra jamais," but "a sucker from Toronto."[16] It is not hard to see here the effect of an "idéologème"[17] that calls for a Francophone's favourite target to be an Anglophone. This substitution endows the fraudulent scheme with obvious sociopolitical connotations.

Following the author's revisions to the last act, in which Bousille commits suicide rather than dying of a heart attack, the play enjoyed considerable critical success and became one of Quebec theatre's most widely acclaimed works. It is interesting to compare the reactions of the anglophone critics in Montreal and Toronto. On the one hand, the *Montreal Star*'s Sydney Johnson considers that "because the dramatic theme is universal rather than French-Canadian the language makes no difference to the effectiveness of the melodrama."[18] On the other hand, Jane Koustas cites Herbert Whittaker, who, in a *Globe and Mail* article dated January 16, 1962, describes the play as "a melodrama that takes a cold look at hypocrisy as it flourishes in [Gélinas's] native Quebec."[19] This is a view shared by the *Toronto Star*'s Nathan Cohen, who wrote, "the things that make the play worthwhile can only be effective in their native tongue."[20] Here one notes a clear divergence of opinion between the Montreal critic, for whom the theme of the play is universal, and the Toronto critics, who see in this melodrama a reality typical to Quebec. This latter point of view undoubtedly owes a great deal to the fact that the English version of the play was cast with francophone actors, whose accents underlined the play's origin, in a translation that Cohen found "stilted and somewhat antiquated."[21]

Koustas also points out that the critical reception in Toronto was split between admiration for this "memorable creation" from the hand of "the most honoured man in Canadian theatre"[22] and a rather unflattering opinion of the play, "an awkwardly constructed, ineptly staged and performed melodrama."[23] According to Koustas, this ambivalence is derived from the attitude of English-Canadian critics, thus described by Paul Leonard: "They tend to collapse the distinction between author and text while widening the chasm between the production and the playwright's script. Even those critics who move beyond the simplicity of authorial intention can still doggedly insist that the performance event is best regarded as primarily an expression of a transcendent meaning—the script."[24]

This initial analysis reveals certain norms applied to the translation of Gélinas's text. At the preliminary level, providing any information on the original play and its subsequent productions was deemed irrelevant. Similarly, there is nothing on the approach taken towards the translation or on the particularities of the original work that it might have come up against, especially in relation to the style of writing. In fact, there is no mention of Gélinas's extremely colourful language or the dialectal expressions that he uses, even though the latter are mentioned by the author in a note contained in the original publication.

The macrostructural analysis does however indicate that an onomastic modification has taken place; French names that are more familiar to the anglophone audience and considered more representative or more authentic for the recipient replace the original French names. The microstructural analysis reveals that the same strategy has been applied to place names in the play. The authenticity of the Québécois dialogue has also been emphasized by the addition of a remark pertaining to hockey, the quintessential Québécois sport. Certain religious references have also been adapted to the target context. Finally, the substitution calling for the victim of a fraudulent scheme to be "a sucker from Toronto" rather than a Francophone from La Tuque exploits a cultural presupposition that maintains a certain anglophone suspicion towards Francophones. In doing so, it obeys a discursive norm in effect within the target context.

With the exception of these few strategies aimed at furthering the acceptance of the translated product within the target context, the translation closely follows Gélinas's text and attests to a search for equivalence that most often tends towards adequacy with the original. Though well-suited to Gélinas's quaintness, this search for adequacy would however be severely tested by the new theatre coming out of Quebec, ushered in by the work of Robert Gurik, Jean Barbeau, and Jean-Claude Germain before being institutionalized with the presentation of Michel Tremblay's Les belles-sœurs in 1968.

Tremblay's *Les Belles-Soeurs*: More Québécois Than the Original[25]

In April 1973, Toronto's St. Lawrence Centre was the site of the English-Canadian premiere of Michel Tremblay's *Les Belles Soeurs* in a production directed by André Brassard. John Van Burek and Bill Glassco's translation was published in Vancouver the following year by Talonbooks. The original play, created in 1968 at Montreal's Théâtre du Rideau Vert, was published that same year by Holt, Rinehart and Winston, in cooperation with Centre d'essai des auteurs dramatiques, in a series entitled Théâtre Vivant. It was republished in 1972 by Éditions Leméac in a slightly revised version with an introduction by Alain Pontaut. In 1992, Talonbooks brought out a revised translation by Van Burek and Glassco that was also included in the 1993 anthology *Modern Canadian Plays*, edited by Jerry Wasserman. This revised version adheres more closely to the form of the original dialogue, as indicated, incidentally, by the spelling of the new title, *Les Belles-Soeurs*, which, with the addition of a hyphen, now conforms to the original. The excerpts cited in this study render us aware of these changes, as they are taken from the two versions of the original (1968 and 1972) as well as the two versions of the translation (1974 and 1992). The dates that accompany these excerpts correspond to these publications. Also of note is that the three Tremblay plays translated in the 1970s by the tandem of Van Burek and Glassco, *Les Belles Soeurs* (1974), *Hosanna* (1974), and *Bonjour, Là, Bonjour* (1975), were corrected and published in revised editions in the late 1980s and early 1990s. Comparing these different translations will serve to support the study of the English versions of *Les belles-sœurs*.[26]

Reflecting a neo-realist aesthetic in which the naturalness of the dialogue is intercut with independent monologues and tirades delivered in chorus in a style occasionally bordering on the burlesque, *Les belles-sœurs* introduces fifteen women from a Montreal working-class neighbourhood who have gotten together to glue the one million saving stamps that Germaine Lauzon has just won.[27] Consumed by the envy, prejudices, and frustrations that are their lot, the women tear each other apart with a sometimes comic cruelty while stealing Germaine's precious merchandise. They end up coming to blows, and Germaine, crushed, barely recovers from the affront in a shower of saving stamps accompanied by the Canadian national anthem. The language used is a *joual* heartily seasoned with barbarisms, solepcisms, and Anglicisms such as "c'tait ben l'fun," "un party de collage de timbres," "le boss m'a même dit qu'y pourrait embarquer dans les grosses payes ben vite, pis devenir p'tit boss." The spelling of these dialectal expressions carries the markers of the spoken language, something attested to by the numerous "pis" (puis), "pus" (plus), "chu" (je suis), or "entéka" (en tout cas), the pronouns "y" (il/s, lui), and "a" (elle/s), the demonstrative adjective "à" (ce), the repetition or the addition of "tu" in the interrogative form as in "A vas-tu y parler?" and the suppression of "ne," the initial part of the negation.

The English production of *Les Belles Soeurs* met with resounding success. The *Globe and Mail*'s Herbert Whittaker described it as a "milestone play...a historic document of some significance"[28] whose triumph "can be seen to have saved the season for the St. Lawrence."[29] According to Urjo Kareda of the *Toronto Star*, this redemption is all the more gratifying as it is the work of a Canadian playwright: "For the first time all season that stage has found and exhaled the breath of life. And that breath—also for the first time all season—is Canadian."[30] Commenting on the 1975 revival of *Forever Yours, Marie-Lou*, Kareda also wrote, "Tremblay himself would say that he's a Quebec playwright, not Canadian at all, but never mind."[31]

Amidst the triumphant reception extended to the play by Toronto audiences, Stephen Mezei nevertheless detected a certain reservation. In *Performing Arts in Canada*, he suggests that the play "scored because Tremblay's characters belong to a class that doesn't exist in Toronto and the women on stage represented something alien with an exotic flavour."[32] Whittaker also mentions this remoteness from the subject matter of the play and describes the St. Lawrence Centre's audience "splitting its reaction between a laughter at the ignorance and prejudice the play deals with [and] a kind of muted edge of condescension."[33] In the same vein, Myron Galloway of the *Montreal Star* thinks that "the big applause and the standing ovation...considering the [poor] quality of the production and the fact that the play in no way came across... sounded suspiciously patronizing."[34] As Whittaker explains, a long tradition of refinement "established through the playing of English imports" is affected by the saltiness of the language.[35] Toronto audiences had experienced a foretaste of this language the previous year when the Tarragon Theatre, with Bill Glassco as artistic director, presented *Forever Yours, Marie-Lou* in a production directed by Glassco from a translation on which he collaborated with John Van Burek. The *Globe and Mail* critic had then deplored the sense of déjà-vu in *Forever Yours, Marie-Lou* because for "an Ontario audience in the mainstream of North American psychological drama for the past quarter century, the surprise is that Quebec's novelty today was ours earlier."[36] Michel Tremblay's talent was nonetheless recognized; according to *Saturday Night's* Marianne Ackerman, Tremblay, "more than any other artist...has provided English Canada with a window on Quebec."[37] Moreover, this production of *Forever Yours, Marie-Lou* earned him the 1973 Chalmers Award for the best Canadian play of the Toronto season.

The translation attracted a certain amount of attention from newspaper critics, who reported that a first version by René Dionne was rejected three weeks before the play's premiere. Glassco and Van Burek came to the rescue, producing a translation that Kareda considered "splendid and brilliant" and that succeeded in capturing, according to David McCaughna of the *Toronto Citizen*, "the flavour and earthiness of the language."[38] However, Kareda added that "the play's strong political implications would be largely lost in English," while the Montreal critic Galloway described the English version as a "massacre."[39] There was no mention, however, of the effect of the strategy Glassco and Van Burek initiated with this play, which would somehow become the trademark of the translations of Tremblay's plays: the calque of the title.

With a title borrowed from the original and lacking any meaning in English, *Les Belles Soeurs* affirms from the outset that there is no cultural equivalent for the play within the receptive context; it attests to an untranslatable reality with which an anglophone public is unable to identify. Here, resorting to a strategy that obscures more of the meaning of the original title than it reveals has the effect of emphasizing the Québécois product's irreducible alterity. This, according to Vivien Bosley, contributed to the play's reception by the anglophone public: "It is my contention that, instead of identifying with what is happening on stage, we become observers of an ethnological situation which strikes us as interesting and amusing and quaint."[40]

In the same spirit, these anglophone *belles soeurs* would be provided with a strong Québécois accent, as would later be the case in another of Tremblay's plays, *Hosanna*. According to Koustas, the character of Hosanna, a flamboyant transvestite played by Richard Monette in the original Toronto production of the play, displayed a Québécois accent unlike that of his partner Cuirette. This diglossia introduces a conflict into their relationship that would take on connotations of a cultural nature: "English (dominant/male) versus French (passive/female)."[41] Furthermore, this first translation of *Hosanna* by the duo of Van Burek and Glassco, produced at the Tarragon Theatre in 1974 and published the same year by Talonbooks, was generously seasoned with French expressions delivered exclusively by Hosanna. For example, at the beginning of the first act, the character reacts to Cuirette's unpleasant remarks.

> **HOSANNA.** Just the overall effect...Regardes [sic]...
>
> *She smokes voluptuously.*
>
> **CUIRETTE.** Well, baby, the effect you have on me...
>
> **HOSANNA.** Oh, go take a shit, you!
>
> **CUIRETTE.** That's how you take care of everything, eh? Tell people to go take a shit.
>
> **HOSANNA.** Precisely. It's less complicated. That way you know where they are and they don't bother you...Me, I'm just not up to it tonight. "Les poses voluptueuses et provocantes" will have to wait.[42]

This excerpt reveals two types of Gallicisms:[43] one in which a term or an excerpt from the original text is borrowed exactly as it is, and the other wherein a literal translation is produced for a vernacular expression for which there are many idiomatic equivalents in the target language. The 1974 version of the play is replete with words borrowed from the French such as "stupide," "oui, allô," "ah oui," "ben oui," "hein," "aie," "ouais," "ayoye," "dégoûtant," "chriss," "câlice," and "sacrement." Amongst the few corrections that were made to the revised edition of the play published in 1991, the most notable change concerns the disappearance of the Franco-Québécois calques. Here is the same excerpt taken from the revised translation in which the corrections made to the initial version have been underlined.

HOSANNA. Just the overall effect...Regarde...

She smokes voluptuously.

CUIRETTE. Well, baby, the effect you have on me...

HOSANNA. Oh, go take a shit _____!

CUIRETTE. That's <u>your answer to</u> everything, eh? Tell people to go take a shit.

HOSANNA. Precisely. It's less complicated. That way you know where they are and they don't bother you...<u>Oh no</u>, tonight I'm <u>just</u> not up to it. <u>The voluptuous, provocative poses</u> will have to wait.[44]

Later we will see how these revisions, made after a seventeen-year interval, reflect a new attitude towards mediating the Québécois product through translation.

The insistence placed on the alterity of the Québécois theatrical product in the early 1970s subscribes to a norm already systematically applied to novels borrowed from Quebec, as underlined by Sherry Simon for whom "la visée ethnographique joue à plein dans la traduction du Québec par le Canada anglais."[45] Simon contends that this attitude has prevailed since Sir Charles G.D. Roberts's declaration in his influential 1890 translation of Philippe Aubert de Gaspé's *Les Anciens Canadiens*: "We of English speech turn naturally to French-Canadian literature for knowledge of the French-Canadian people."[46] The anglophone translator's ethnographic task of revealing the Québécois to English Canadians by way of their literature was thus stated more than a century ago.

The strategy involved with the calque of the title was applied to eight other Tremblay plays translated into English: *Hosanna* (1974) and *Bonjour, Là, Bonjour* (1975) by Van Burek and Glassco; *Surprise!*

Surprise! (1975), *La Duchesse de Langeais* (1976), *Trois Petits Tours* (1977) and *Damnée Manon, Sacrée Sandra* (1981) by Van Burek; and finally *En Pièces Détachées* (1975) by Allan Van Meer, after he changed the title three times—*Like Death Warmed Over* (1973), *Montreal Smoked Meat* (1974), and *Broken Pieces* (1974). More recently, Van Burek and Glassco once again resorted to a calque in the translation of *La Maison Suspendue* (1991).

Notably, except for Tremblay's plays, borrowing the original title rarely occurs in the English translations of the Québécois repertoire, and the popularity of such borrowing appears to correspond to a well-defined period of Quebec history preceding the Quiet Revolution. After Gratien Gélinas's *Tit-Coq*, a title borrowed from the eponymous character of the play whose name was retained in Kenneth Johnstone and Gélinas's English version presented in Toronto in 1951, Anne Hébert's *Le Temps Sauvage* was translated by Elizabeth Mascall and produced under the same title at Toronto's Firehall Theatre in 1972, only a few months before *Les Belles Soeurs*. Sheila Fischman subsequently retained the original title of Roland Lepage's *Le Temps d'une Vie* when the English version was staged at the Tarragon Theatre in 1978, before opting for the English equivalent *In a Lifetime*.[47] Interestingly, what the plays by Hébert and Lepage have in common is that they both reveal the mentality of an era, that of a society under the influence of religious and moral dogma prevalent in rural Quebec for the first half of the twentieth century. It is a reality belonging to a past that is still redolent of the "romans de la terre," such an authentic French reality that the English translation must retain the original French title. Thus, given that Tremblay's plays most closely resemble the image of a pre-modern Quebec, it is little surprise that borrowing the French title is a popular strategy in the English translations of the play.

The aforementioned list shows that the borrowing was first applied to Tremblay's plays that feature the sisters-in-law and their families, la Duchesse, Hosanna, Manon, Sandra, Carmen, Berthe, and Gloria Star, characters who are grappling with an alienating reality that imprisons them in the ghettos of Plateau Mont-Royal and Boulevard Saint-Laurent. With *The Impromptu of Outremont*, translated by Van Burek in 1980, and *Remember Me*, translated by John Stowe in 1984, we travel to a different geographic location and mental space. Having managed to leave the stifling universe of rue Fabre and the false promise of the "Main," the characters in these plays inhabit an upscale Montreal neighbourhood.

In *Albertine, in Five Times*, translated by Van Burek and Glassco in 1986, Albertine recalls five periods in her life and attempts to come to terms with them. Although the play alludes to the Plateau Mont-Royal, where Albertine and her family resided, the author has placed Albertine outside the time and space of the events she recounts in the play. It is a reflection on a character's life, the assessment of an existence that unfolds before her and that she observes with a critical eye. A similar situation occurs in the play *The Real World?*, translated in 1988 by Van Burek and Glassco, in which the author explores the question of developing plot and theatre characters from models based on "real" life.

Then, in 1990, Tremblay envisions a reunion for recurring characters, the members of Jean-Marc's family, who have come to Duhamel to spend their summer holidays in the house that has been their ancestral home since 1910. Translated that same year by Van Burek and Glassco under the title *La Maison Suspendue*, the play takes us back in time as it brings together several well-known characters from Tremblay's first plays and the novels that make up Chroniques du Plateau Mont-Royal. The original title was retained for this family gathering that takes place in a village in the Laurentians at a time preceding the exodus to the city. The following play, *Marcel Pursued by the Hounds*, translated in 1996 by Van Burek and Glassco, brings Albertine's children to the stage in a period close to the one evoked in Tremblay's initial plays.

In attempting to find what the plays bearing a borrowed title have in common, we can see that, with the exception of *Forever Yours, Marie-Lou* and *Marcel Pursued by the Hounds*, the translators seem to have systematically resorted to the French title when the play deals with characters who inhabit a historical Quebec yet untouched by the social and political upheavals that followed the Quiet Revolution. The representation of an alterity evoking a traditional Quebec is thus expressed in a strategy that emphasizes the authentically French value of the title and, consequently, the play's subject matter.

As for the preliminary and macrostructural data, the English versions of *Les belles-sœurs*, published in 1974, 1992, and 1993, include the name of the author and the two translators along with the title *Les Belles Soeurs*. The site of the original production, as well as the original cast and director, André Brassard, are also indicated. The same information is subsequently provided for the original English production. The 1974 and 1992 publications lack an introduction and make no reference to Jean-Claude Germain's preface or Brassard's commentary that accompanied the play's original publication in 1968. Nor is there any reference to Alain Pontaut's introduction to the 1972 publication. Yet these metatexts explained how "la pièce de Tremblay est d'ores et déjà un point tournant dans l'histoire du théâtre québécois"[48] and analyzed "la place considérable tenue par *Les belles-sœurs* dans la dramaturgie québécoise."[49] In the 1993 anthology *Modern Canadian Plays*, the play was preceded by an introduction in which Jerry Wasserman presents the author and his work. However, not one of the three editions supplied any information on the original production, what was at stake with the original text, and what approach was adopted in its translation.

How can the silence surrounding these translations be anything but surprising given the striking novelty of Tremblay's writing and the difficulties, in both linguistic and sociocultural terms, involved in transposing it to an Anglo-Canadian context? This question is all the more significant because 1974 saw the first English publication of a play by an author who had just revolutionized Quebec theatre by establishing *joual* as the language of the stage. Thus, not mentioning how the translation acts as an intermediary for the original text gives the impression of a faithful reproduction that results from a total compatibility of the two cultures. It is still too often a translation's fate to be consumed like a naturally-occurring product, without a history or a brand name.

On the macrostructural level, the proper names were retained in their entirety in the three Tremblay plays translated by Glassco and Van Burek, i.e., *Les Belles Soeurs*, *Hosanna*, and *Bonjour, Là, Bonjour*. In the two versions of *Les Belles Soeurs*, "Madame" is used in front of the characters' names. So, Germaine addresses her neighbour in English as "Mme. [sic] Brouillette."[50] This search for adequacy with respect to the original text is also found in the place names, the majority of which remain French, although some toponymical references deemed unessential have been altered. Such is the case for "le théâtre Amherst,"[51] which the 1974 translation turns into the generalization of "a two-bit show," and the 1992 translation later replaces with "the local movie house."[52] Later, while Marie Ange explains that "chus t'allée voir une vieille vue d'Eddie Constantine,"[53] the English version erases the cultural reference to Constantine, an actor who would be unknown to an anglophone audience, in favour of a cultural reference that is an overlapping combination of the audience's knowledge of French cinema and its own cultural establishments, which results in the following hybridization: "I went to the Rex the other day to see Belmondo in something."[54] This formulation is surprising, though, as it is doubtful that an Anglophone would have been aware of Belmondo at the time the play takes place. Nevertheless, the semantic shift here does attest to the translators' interest in adapting the dialogue to suit the target audience, without removing it from the original context. Similar strategies have been adopted in the initial English translation of *Hosanna* where the Bijou theatre becomes "the La Scala Theatre" and where "la pharmacie Beaubien" relinquishes its name by becoming "the pharmacy."[55] However, these equivalents were revised in the 1991 edition, which provides us with an exact reproduction of the toponymic references found in the original.

The translation seems to be most strongly influenced by the receptive cultural context in the choice of the level of language employed to represent Tremblay's *joual*. Even though certain elements of the original language are difficult to transpose into English, particularly the frequent use of Anglicisms in the urban-Montreal *joual*, the fact remains that English certainly possesses numerous linguistic resources of a vernacular nature, as illustrated in John Herbert's play *Fortune and Men's Eyes*, which will be examined in chapter 5, or in more recent works by playwrights such as Judith Thompson or Brad Fraser. One wonders why Tremblay's translators elected to retain a certain propriety of expression, albeit one offset by a heightened use of swear words or *sacres*,[56] as can be seen in the following excerpt from the very beginning of the play where Germaine addresses her daughter Linda.

> **GERMAINE.** C'est ça, méprise-moé! Bon, c'est correct, sors, fais à ta tête! Tu fais toujours à ta tête, c'est pas ben ben mêlant! Maudite vie! J'peux même pas avoir une p'tite joie, y faut toujours que quelqu'un vienne toute gâter! Vas-y aux vues, Linda, vas-y, sors à'soir, fais à ta tête! Maudit verrat de bâtard que chus donc tannée![57]

Here is the same excerpt taken from each of the English versions:

GERMAINE. That's right. You've always said so. I'm dumb. Okay Linda, go ahead. Do what you like. That's all you ever do anyway. It's nothing new. Christ, I can't have a bit of pleasure for myself. Someone's always got to spoil it for me. It's okay, Linda, if that's what you want. Go ahead. Go to your goddamn show![58]

GERMAINE. Sure, that's right. Put me down. Fine, you go out, do just as you like. That's all you ever do anyway. Nothing new. I never have any pleasure. Someone's always got to spoil it for me. Go ahead Linda, you go out tonight, go to your goddamned show. Jesus Christ Almighty, I'm so fed up.[59]

First, we can see that, in the original, the obvious markers of *joual* such as "moé," "ben ben mêlant," "toute gâter," "vues," "à'soir," "chus," and "tannée," inform us immediately of the sociocultural context in question, that of the impoverished, poorly educated residents of a Franco-Québécois urban neighbourhood. Tremblay lays claim to this vernacular, establishing it as the language of the stage, thus creating a rupture within the Franco-Québécois drama repertoire previously subject to the norm of "bon français." How is this information delivered in the English translation of the same excerpt?

Apart from the swearing and the elisions specific to orality, the language in the English translations is representative of everyday usage. Although the original place names and the names of the characters indicate that the play was written in French and takes place in Montreal, nothing in the English versions indicates the sociolect and the class depicted in the original. Without this information, the translated versions lack the subversive effect inherent in the recourse to *joual* as a dramatic idiom within the Québécois context.

Furthermore, while the rewriting of the text in the first translation strives to reproduce a large part of the semantic content of the original excerpt, it readily dispenses with the form. The second version eliminates certain distortions and more closely follows the original text. However, the swearing remains just as excessive.

Various idiomatic expressions of the sociolect employed in the original are themselves untranslatable and must be adapted according to the linguistic means of the target language. The expression "c'est pas ben ben mêlant" mostly fulfills a phatic function, which is to say that it conveys no information and serves only to sustain the communication. It is quite another story for the oath "maudit verrat de bâtard" that expresses an intense anger without however borrowing the liturgical terminology, as do the *sacres*. It's not that Tremblay's "belles-sœurs" never resort to *sacres*, but they do so reservedly as it is an act that remains taboo. It is only after Germaine has been pushed to her limit by her daughter Linda's stubbornness that she uses *sacres*, and she points out the exceptional nature of the occurrence.

> **GERMAINE.** Linda tu fais exprès pour me faire damner! Tu veux me faire sacrer devant le monde! Hein, c'est ça, tu veux me faire sacrer devant le monde? Ben crisse, tu vas avoir réussi.[60]

Here, the use of "crisse" represents the ultimate *sacre* in the language of the "belles-sœurs," and, with the exception of Pierrette who works in a club and has renounced their world, they only use it twice in the whole play. Within this context, it is unlikely that they would have rashly employed "goddamn," which appears often in the English translation, and even less likely "Christ" and "Jesus Christ Almighty" from the excerpt cited above. Be that as it may, it seems that the translators systematically relied upon *sacres* as the equivalents of all types of cursing and of idiomatic expressions such as "c'est pas mêlant" or "j'ai mon voyage."

If it is difficult to reproduce Québécois swear words in English, it is nevertheless possible to resort to English expressions devoid of religious references, such as "damn," "dammit," "shit," "hell," "good gracious," "my goodness," etc. Incidentally, the first word in the text, "Misère," is a swear word that has been replaced in the English versions by "Sweet Jesus," thus from the outset creating an isotopy of profanity that abounds throughout the play. This repetition of a single element of meaning, which A.J. Greimas defines as an isotopy,[61] creates a subtext that informs our reading of the play. To illustrate the difference in number and intensity of the swear words in each version, I compared their occurrence in the dialogue preceding the recitation of the rosary. The two Québécois versions (1968 and 1972) each contain three: "Ma grand-foi du bon Dieu," "Mon Dieu," and again "Mon Dieu."[62] Within the same dialogue, the first English version contains the following fourteen: "Sweet Jesus," "Jesus," "Christ," "goddamn show," "Mother of God," "Jesus," "Jesus," "goddamn thing," "goddamn thing," "my God," "the God's truth," "Goddamn sex," "Dear God," and "Goddamn it."[63] The second English version contains thirteen: "God," "Jesus," "goddamned show," "Jesus Christ Almighty," "Mother of God," "Jesus," "goddamned stamps," "goddamn thing," "My God," "God's truth," "Goddamn sex," "Dear God," and "Goddamn it."[64] Not only are they clearly more numerous in English, they are also much more intense, and this intensity is heightened by the sharp contrast with the rather conservative tone of the rest of the dialogue.

If this accentuation in the number and the intensity of the swear words attests to an intention to compensate for the level of the vernacular language in the original, it also produces an altogether different effect. In the case of the "belles-sœurs," whose morality is dictated by religious principles they claim to adhere to and follow to the letter, the act of constant swearing constitutes a contradiction that derides their avowed religious sentiment. The derisive effect engendered by a rewrite favouring the use of profanity could lead an English audience into sensing a duplicity that is not found in the original. The "belles-sœurs" may be dogmatic, often bigoted, and occasionally disrespectful, but the sincerity of their faith is beyond question.

Furthermore, the English version pays particular attention to the effects of religion. For example, Rose says, "Pis a finira pas comme moé, à quarante-quatre ans avec un p'tit gars de quatre ans sur les bras,"[65] which has been translated as, "She won't end up like me, forty-four years old, with a two-year-old kid and another one on the way."[66] The English version underlines the legendary Québécois submission to the Catholic precept prohibiting birth control, and Rose Ouimet is far more a victim of this prohibition in the English version than in the original. In pursuit of its ethnographic mission, the translation becomes more Québécois here than the Québécois version by accentuating the effects of religion in the lives of the "belles-sœurs."

Another element in the previously quoted excerpts contributes to a prominent isotopy in the source text that is absent in the translation. Germaine's expression "Maudite vie" is repeated again in the famous quintet, "Une maudite vie plate," later to be delivered by a chorus of five exasperated women, including Germaine, who endlessly recite the litany of women's household chores. It is one of the play's most eloquent moments, a scene punctuated with the following refrain: "Chus tannée de vivre une maudite vie plate!"[67] In the translation this refrain becomes, "I'm sick to death of this stupid, rotten life!"[68] There is no reference to the expression "maudite vie," which reduces the intensity of the isotopic network that it introduces and to which it contributes.

Other suppressions, substitutions, and additions do not fundamentally alter the message but modify its impact. For example, in the first English version, "A pleurait comme une Madeleine. A m'a même embrassé les mains"[69] has been translated as, "And she was crying... she even tried to kiss my hands."[70] Here, what seemed excessive in the orginal has been toned down. The vulgarity of certain expressions has also been attenuated by translating, for example, "C'est pas plus riche que nous autres pis ça pète plus haut que son trou! J'ai mon verrat de voyage!"[71] as, "You're not fooling us with that shit about being rich. You've got no more money than the rest of us!"[72] The revised version, however, sticks closer to the original with the following equivalents: "She was so happy...weeping with gratitude...she even kissed my hands" and "She's got no more money than the rest of us and she thinks her farts smell like perfume!"[73] Other substitutions are prompted by plays on words and riddles, which are cleverly transposed into the target language. For example, when Des-Neiges Verrette conceives the following slogan for the Hachette bookstore, "Achète bien qui achète chez Hachette," the translation comes up with, "Hachette will help you chop the cost of your books."[74] Lastly, it is worth noting that the translated version is oblivious to the punctuation in the original, which underlines the exclamatory tone of the dialogue. Tremblay is perhaps rather generous in his use of the exclamation mark; nonetheless, the punctuation of the original informs us of the tone and the emotional intention attributed to each line.

The other translations revised by Glassco and Van Burek attest to a desire to move closer to the original text. In the second version of

Hosanna, published in 1991, the place names and the original locations have been reinstated, and the majority of the Quebecisms attributed to Hosanna have disappeared. This means that the numerous Gallicisms that appeared in the 1974 version were removed in favour of their English equivalents. The diglossia found in the first version has therefore disappeared and the character of Hosanna is Anglicized just like his partner Curiette. The linguistic-cultural analogy put forward by the previous translation, in which Hosanna and Cuirette symbolize the confrontation, dialogue, and reconciliation of the French and English cultures, has been eliminated. By 1979, Van Burek had already considered revising the translation of *Hosanna* to make it more accessible.

> There's a good deal that I'd like to change in *Hosanna*. I'd like to open it up more, make it more accessible. It has too much French in it. Also, even though Richard Monette made the accent work, I don't believe anymore that it should be written into the script...I don't want to re-write the play, but the translation can change. Above all, other than being accurate, I want the plays to be accessible. As *Hosanna* stands now, it would be hard for an actor in Idaho or Birmingham, England to take on the role, and I'd like to make it easier for that to happen.[75]

This revised version, however, retains certain passages from the first translated version that deviate from the original. For example, in Hosanna's following dialogue, the passages deleted in the two English translations are underlined.

> **HOSANNA.** Chus ridicule quand chus déguisée en homme, <u>quand j'coiffe mes Juives jewish-renaissance. Des vrais gestes de femmes qu'y me disent que j'ai...</u>"You should work in drags [*sic*], Claude!" <u>Pis si j'irais travailler en femme j'gage qu'y me laisseraient tomber parce qu'y veulent pas se laisser toucher aux cheveux par des femmes...</u>Pis chus ridicule quand chus déguisée en femme <u>parce que j't'obligée de faire la folle pour attirer l'attention parce que chus pas assez belle pour l'attirer autrement...</u>Pis chus t'encore plus ridicule quand chus poignée comme ça, entre les deux, avec

ma tête de femme, mes sous-vêtements de femme, pis mon corps d'homme.[76]

The deleted information might have been shocking or difficult for the target audience to understand. It also contains a line in English, which would pose a challenge for the translation. So it was deemed preferable to remove the markers of alterity that interfered with a smooth transcultural passage.

Another important modification implemented in the first translation of *Hosanna* remained unchanged in the revised version. At the very end of the play, even though he is painfully aware of being a man under his womanly guise, Hosanna is unable to remove the make-up that still identifies him with his borrowed identity. He expresses this dilemma in the following exchange with Cuirette.

> **CUIRETTE.** L'important c'est que tu soyes toé. C'est toute. J'pense que c'est toute. Claude...c'est pas Hosanna que j'aime...(*Silence*) Va te démaquiller...Va te démaquiller...

> HOSANNA *se lève et s'installe à sa table de maquillage. Elle prend un pot de démaquillant, le remet à sa place. Elle se regarde dans le miroir.*

> **HOSANNA.** Cléopâtre est morte, pis le Parc Lafontaine est toute illuminé!

> *Elle se lève lentement, enlève son slip et se retourne, nue, vers* CUIRETTE.

> **HOSANNA.** R'garde, Raymond, chus t'un homme! Chus t'un homme, Raymond! Chus t'un homme! Chus t'un homme! Chus t'un homme...

> RAYMOND *se lève, se dirige vers* CLAUDE *et le prend dans ses bras.*[77]

Where the original sets forth an acknowledged but unresolved conflict of identity, the underlined sentences in the two excerpts indicate how the translation chooses to settle the issue. The signs of the borrowed identity are erased and the dilemma is resolved. Rid of his wig and his make-up, Claude can fully assume his male sexual identity.

> **CUIRETTE.** The important thing...Claude...it's not Hosanna that I love...

> *Silence.*

> **CUIRETTE.** Take off your make-up...go on, take it off...

> *HOSANNA gets up and sits down at her make-up table. She removes her wig, and takes off her make-up. She looks at herself in the mirror.*

> **HOSANNA.** Cleopatra is dead, and the Parc Lafontaine is all lit up!

> *She gets up, takes off her underpants, and turns slowly toward* CUIRETTE.

> Look Raymond, I'm a man...I'm a man, Raymond...I'm a man. I'm a man...I'm a man...

> *RAYMOND gets up, goes toward CLAUDE, and takes him in his arms.*[78]

If, as Tremblay states in the documentary *Backyard Theatre*,[79] the transvestite represents the difficulty for Quebec to affirm its true identity,[80] in this instance the rewriting takes on a symbolic meaning that favours the resolution rather than the recognition of this identity conflict. It could be that the translators closed their eyes to this symbolic aspect or that they were unaware of it, or even that they chose to explicitly affirm the character's masculinity. In any case, the choice was made to end the play with an unequivocal image in which Hosanna rejects his borrowed identity and fully embraces his sexual identity.

The translations of *Bonjour, là, bonjour* also liberally indulge in Gallicisms. So Lucienne can boast about having married an Anglophone by exclaiming, "I got what I wanted, I got my Anglais,"[81] and her father can surprise her in the company of her lover "on la rue Ste-Catherine the other day."[82] Yet the character referred to as l'Anglaise in the original[83] is cleverly rebaptized Lady Westmount in these same translations. Why such a discrepancy?

What is even more surprising in the revised version, however, is that the names of the characters have been changed; Albertine is replaced by Gilberte, and Gabriel by Armand. This substitution is even harder to justify as Tremblay's whole body of work is built around the same circle of characters, whose comings and goings we follow from one fictional tale to another. In several of Tremblay's plays and novels, Albertine and Gabriel are known to be brother and sister, Victoire's only children. Albertine is also the central character in the play *Albertine, en cinq temps* (1984) and, along with Gabriel, appears in the novels that constitute Chroniques du Plateau Mont-Royal published between 1978 and 1985. This revision effectively severs the link that connects this play to other related works.

Resorting to Gallicisms in the translated versions culminated with *La Maison Suspendue*, published in 1991, as can be observed in the following excerpt in which the Gallicisms have been underlined.

VICTOIRE. Josaphat, franchement!

JOSAPHAT. And off we all go to ma tante Blanche, or to ma tante Ozéa! The forest slides away beneath us, Duhamel is tout petit, les Laurentides disappear completely into the darkness...The house sways gently...Me and your mother, we just sit here on the verandah and watch the sky go by. Usually all we see from here is a big black hole where Lac Simon is, but now it's the Big Dipper, the Little Dipper, la planète Mars...The house turns on the end of the rope and we see the whole sky pass before us, like la parade on St-Jean-Baptiste Day. During the whole journey, the house sways gently back and forth, back and forth...Us, we're sitting pretty. It sure is beautiful. (*Silence. The three characters look around them.*) When we get to our relatives, the canoe sets us down next to their place, bonsoir la compagnie, get out your accordéons, push the chairs against the wall, here we are! And then, let me tell you, the party starts in earnest! (*He dances en turlutant, then stops as if at the end of a story.*) And that, mon p'tit gars, is how you've been to Morial [Montreal] without even realizing![84]

One wonders what function, other than emphasizing the alterity of the borrowed text, this confusing linguistic amalgamation fulfills for a unilingual anglophone audience, given that it reflects no actual usage in a context unexposed to the friction and the hybridization of languages.

This analysis of Glassco and Van Burek's translations of Tremblay's plays, particularly those of *Les belles-sœurs*, reveals that the texts undergo numerous manipulations designed to favour their reception within the target context. Even though the anglophone literary institution had yet to develop a tradition of promoting the use of a preface or notes in which the translator presents the work for theatre publications, as it had for novels, the radical novelty of Tremblay's work could have benefitted from such an introduction. All the more so as the audience to which it was addressed did not have the necessary linguistic resources or sociocultural references to grasp the cultural issues embodied in the text.

While it manages to convey the cognitive contents of the dialogue, the translation is unable to account for the reversal of literary and discursive codes instigated through the use of *joual* within the context of Quebec at that time. The original text exhibits a linguistic and cultural alienation stemming from a twofold colonial tradition: that of a Franco-French linguistic norm from which it is isolated and to which it is difficult to correspond, and that of the dominant presence of English within the Canadian and North American context. Symbolic of this double alienation, *joual* sees itself entrusted with a twofold mission: it must denounce the consequences of contact with the English, and distance itself from the Franco-French that, up until then, was considered the only language capable of expressing a true francophone culture on Quebec stages. Unexposed to the sociocultural conditions that shaped the French spoken in Quebec, the Anglo-Canadian language would be hard pressed to convey *joual*'s historical and ideological connotations. Given that translating *joual* into English appears to be an impossible task, the translators must have been faced with some difficult choices regarding how to present Tremblay's texts to an anglophone audience.

A comment made by Van Burek on the nature of *joual* and the pejorative connotations associated with the term throws some light on the translator's position in relation to the source language: "I don't like the word 'joual.' It's like saying 'nigger-talk.' It seems degrading to me. It is simply a way that French is spoken in Quebec. Like American English.

Tremblay's language isn't even 'joual,' it's more an evocation of the quality of language, i.e., self-image, spoken by the people he writes about."[85] Although he makes the case for French spoken in Quebec by maintaining that it is as legitimate as American English, Van Burek nevertheless overlooks the sociolectical and emblematic value of Tremblay's *joual*, particularly in his early plays. Representative of the most disadvantaged social class, this sociolect also emerged as a denunciatory language of a linguistic and cultural alienation, and as a symbol of identity affirmation. More than just a regional variation, it is an iconic language that in this case must be transposed into a linguistic, literary, and social context offering few similarities with that of the original. This reluctance would help to explain the choice to translate *Les belles-sœurs* into what Vivien Bosley calls a "standardized...generic North American,"[86] which has been interspersed with profanities that are sometimes excessive, along with an abundance of Gallicisms that embody all the *québécitude* of Tremblay's texts. This is a nonthreatening *québécitude* as it evokes the reality of a traditional Quebec for which the anglophone public feels nostalgic.

Divested of *joual*, a critical component of the shock induced by Tremblay's writing, the play's subject matter is stripped of its subversive content; Québécois society is depicted through alienated characters who belong to an underprivileged social class that is poorly educated, bigoted, and socially powerless, and that expresses itself in a Standard English whose alterity is confined to numerous swear words and exotic Gallicisms. As a result, a text that originally broke with tradition, and in doing so became the symbol of this rupture, now promotes a traditional image of Quebec. By being translated like this, to borrow the words of Jacques Saint-Pierre, "Michel Tremblay perpétue pour les anglophones un fantasme, celui d'une certaine vision de la société québécoise des années précédant la Révolution tranquille."[87]

It's an effect similar to that which Barbara Godard identifies in the translation of Roch Carrier's novel *L'amour dans la ferraille*. Translated by Sheila Fischman under the title of *Heartbreaks along the Road* and published by Anansi in 1987, the English version of the novel retains the original names of characters and places. According to Godard, "it introduces the 'translation effect,' strangeness within the target language which inscribes difference within language....In the comic context of

Carrier's novel, however, translation might have been a more appropriate choice, since the effect of these French terms is to emphasize Quebec's difference in the context of translation, where the threat of that difference is reduced, as a province that is folklorized as cute and quaint, and hence trivialized."[88]

In this light, the functional equivalence of the English versions of *Les belles-sœurs* seems anchored in a quest for authenticity expressed through an accentuation of specific signs of linguistic alterity that create a certain novelty regarding the matricial and linguistic norms applied to translation within the receptive context. However, at the discursive level, the translated version is the exact opposite of the original inasmuch as it conveys a traditional and reassuring image of a text that, quite to the contrary, decidedly broke with tradition.

Furthermore, if we take into account the political context of the period, integrating French into the English, as artificial as it might be, also promotes bilingualism by offering a model of linguistic cohabitation through the virtues of translation. It must be remembered that the play is one of the very first works supported by the Canada Council for the Arts through the Aid to Translation Program established in 1972, a program that sought to encourage dialogue and exchange between the francophone and anglophone cultures of Canada at a time when relations between the two linguistic communities were particularly tense.

These linguistic borrowings leave us with the impression that the translation strove for maximum adequacy to the original play. The lack of any explanation on the part of the translators does nothing to belie this impression. However, in contrast with Gélinas's previously examined play, which also lacked an introduction, the obstacles encountered by the transposition of Tremblay's language into an Anglo-Canadian context border on the insurmountable due to the sociohistorical conditions that shaped *joual* and the rupture that its consecration brings about within the Québécois cultural discourse. This specific and fundamental alterity in the original text is negated by the translation. The approach adopted in this case attests to a search for adequacy to the original text rooted in the "surconscience"[89] of the difference and an excessive exploitation of certain nonthreatening markers of alterity that in no way reveal the subversive dimension of the original text, thereby ensuring its acceptability within the target context and its insertion into the Anglo-Canadian literary canon.

Why this insistence on translating and producing Tremblay's works in English when faced with such transcultural obstacles? As Richard Plant explains in the *Oxford Companion to Canadian Theatre*, this work presented English Canada with a model of dramatic writing whose novelty lies preeminently in the aesthetic means it deploys: "Tremblay has brought to English-Canada a multi-layered poetic drama, rich in imagery and centred around volatile issues and powerful emotions. His experiments with form, and his use of musical structures, interwoven aria-like monologues, and choruses are among the range of exciting possibilities he has shown to English-Canadian playwrights."[90] The Anglo-Canadian theatrical system imported the Tremblay model for its textual literary norms and use of dramatic techniques. Although this entailed a certain amount of linguistic bartering, the transcultural passage could only be accomplished to the detriment of the discursive content of the original texts.

Beyond the formal novelty offered by Tremblay's plays, it is necessary to acknowledge their important contribution to the creation of the Canadian repertoire at a time when the network of English-Canadian "alternative theatres" was taking shape. Responsible for breaking with the British and American models then dominant within the English-Canadian institution, the goal of the alternative movement was "the development of a distinctive and indigenous Canadian voice in all aspects of theatre."[91] On the periphery of the dominant norm found in the subsidized theatres that serve as its apparatus, the alternative network was made up of companies both young and poor for whom translation had much to offer. Not only did borrowing provide access to a repertoire whose success had already been proven; such success represented a rare model of Canadian accomplishment, and Tremblay's work could fully partake in the creation of a distinct Canadian drama repertoire. With twenty plays produced and published in translation before 1998, thirteen between 1972 and 1979, which is the period when a national Canadian repertoire was created, Tremblay would become the francophone playwright with the greatest number of works translated in English Canada.

If the canonization of *joual* as the language of the Quebec stage played a key role in the drama of the 1970s, its ensuing gradual decline in the theatre does not mean that the language question had been settled and relegated to the background in the establishment of a Franco-Québécois drama repertoire. In this respect, the next two texts provide remarkably eloquent examples of new verbal aesthetics brought to the fore in Québécois dramatic writing of the 1980s.

Jovette, Violette, and Translation "in the Tone"[92]

The production of Jovette Marchessault's *La terre est trop courte, Violette Leduc* was an eagerly awaited event within the milieu of Montreal feminist theatre. Few had forgotten Pol Pelletier's memorable performance in Marchessault's *Les vaches de nuit*, produced in Montreal in 1979 at the Théâtre expérimental des femmes and in Toronto the following year by Atthis Theatre. It must be said that feminist theatre was an increasingly strong presence on Quebec stages, where women's voices were supplanting expressions of a nationalist tenor silenced by the decision on the 1980 Quebec referendum. Feminist theatre was inaugurated with *La nef des sorcières*, an event produced by a feminist collective at the Théâtre du Nouveau Monde in 1975. Then, in April 1981, once again at the Théâtre du Nouveau Monde, Marchessault's *La saga des poules mouillées* garnered a great deal of publicity; the play was then produced at the Tarragon Theatre in an English translation by Linda Gaboriau and published by Talonbooks in 1983.

The production of *La terre est trop courte, Violette Leduc* directed by Pol Pelletier at the Théâtre expérimental des femmes in November 1981, in which Luce Guilbault had the lead role,[93] was a tour de force, enthusiastically received by the critics, in spite of some reservations about the excessively lyrical writing. On this subject, there was a clear divergence in the reaction of francophone and anglophone critics. On one hand, the "pure virtuosité" of Guilbault's work was praised, and "la profusion et le foisonnement"[94] in this "tourbillon baroque," at times puzzling for the audience, was well received: "le théâtre des femmes, le théâtre d'ici, le théâtre tout court accomplit un grandiose pas en avant."[95] On the other hand, there were protests against this "marathon of questionable taste—a masturbatory, expiatory, hermetic, hysterical sea of words."[96] This outrage seems to be due as much to the subject of the play—the exploration of unconventional female sexuality and literary censorship—"so pretentiously shocking" as to the way in which it was depicted, "so burdened with verbiage and vulgarity."[97] It it is interesting to note that, beyond the themes addressed in the text, its use of language incited extreme resistance amongst anglophone critics in Montreal and Toronto alike, as the reception of its English version in Toronto would later indicate. In Quebec, however, the play was well received within the Franco-Québécois drama repertoire and gave rise to another production at the Théâtre d'Aujourd'hui in November of 1992.

According to Marchessault, the writing of *La terre est trop courte, Violette Leduc* emanated from a veritable creative osmosis with her heroine that enabled her to speak with the voice and "dans le ton" of Violette Leduc, the mid-century French writer who inspired this biographical work. Incidentally, journalist Francine Pelletier sees a striking similarity between Marchessault and Leduc. The two of them share a conception of writing as a "narcissisme essentiel, viscéral: une façon de se donner l'ego que les femmes n'ont généralement pas."[98] Representative of this fusion between the two authors, the play is conceived as a collage that includes seventy-three excerpts of varying lengths, from a single sentence to an entire page, borrowed from five of Leduc's novels. Marchessault reproduces Leduc's style remarkably well; the resemblance is astonishing. As explained in the preface of the play published in 1982 by Éditions de la pleine lune, the authors have a great deal in common: "l'amour des femmes...une liaison particulière au monde des objets, le monde tactile, ce qui explique peut-être pourquoi elles ont la métaphore si facile, si aiguë...[et] elles ont les larmes abondantes, particulièrement en écrivant."[99]

Marchessault also states that a chief motivation of the project was to "riposter à la censure, l'histoire de Thérèse et Isabelle en étant un exemple flagrant."[100] In fact, censorship is one of the play's major themes and is the subject of the first short scene, "Le vampire est à son poste," in which Marchessault portrays Leduc shattered by the attitude of publishers who refuse to publish the beginning of her novel *Ravages*, which contains descriptions of the sexual relations between Thérèse and Isabelle, who attend the same boarding school. The ten short scenes that follow present Leduc struggling with a jealous husband and an overly demanding lover, confronted with Jean Genet and abandoned by Maurice Sachs, in conversation with inanimate objects after having escaped from a psychiatric clinic to which she'd been committed, and, finally, taking refuge with Simone de Beauvoir, whom she greatly admires and who encourages her to start writing again. It must be stressed here that, in contrast with the previously studied plays that were preoccupied with Québécois reality, the subject matter of this play is not local, and the action takes place outside of Quebec. As we will see in more detail in the analysis of the next play, this attitude reflects the new openness demonstrated by Québécois theatre of the 1980s. Furthermore, the play is the first of a series of portraits in which Marchessault enables women artists of diverse nationalities to be seen and heard. Her writing is at the junction of the epic and the realistic, with larger-than-life characters expressing themselves in a hyperliterary language. The spelling respects the rules of standard French and exhibits no markers of orality.

When the play was published, it contained a preface taken from an article by Francine Pelletier that appeared in La Vie en rose, an epigraph borrowed from Joan Digby, a dedication, and an introduction in which Marchessault introduces Violette Leduc. Lastly, it included a description of the characters and a short description of the set as well as details concerning the play's creation, with a list of all those who were involved. Several photographs of the production accompanied the text.

The play was translated into English by Susanne de Lotbinière-Harwood, a Montreal translator who stated her translation position in what she called "la traduction comme pratique de réécriture au féminin," the subtitle of her work Re-belle et infidel / The Body Bilingual: Translation as a Rewriting in the Feminine published in 1991. At the time, de Lotbinière-Harwood was already known in feminist literary circles, and she had recently won the 1981 John Glassco Translation Prize for her translation of Neons in the Night, a collection of poems by Louis Francoeur. Produced by Nightwood Theatre at Toronto's Theatre Centre in May 1986, The Edge of Earth is Too Near, Violette Leduc was not published. However, the library at Montreal's National Theatre School has had a copy of the manuscript of the English version since 1985.

This translation retains the eleven-scene structure of the original and contains three preliminary pages that provide the play's English title, the name of the author and the translator, and even the date the translation was completed. The second page is an English version of Marchessault's introductory text in which certain French expressions deemed untranslatable have been kept in French. As in the original publication, there is also a description of the characters and the set. The following page contains a translator's note informing us that the play includes several excerpts borrowed from the works of Leduc that have been placed in quotation marks in the translation. Lastly, the translator thanks her collaborators, Linda Gaboriau and Elaine Lalande. The original title of the play is not mentioned, nothing is said about the French and English productions, and there is no indication of what approach the translator adopted. There are no longer any cross-references to Leduc's books from which the excerpts have been borrowed, such as those that appeared in an appendix to the original play.

On the microstructural level, the translation reproduces the hyperbolic and metaphorical style as well as the lyricism of the original text, which is no mean feat, even if occasionally sacrificing a certain economy of means. Accordingly, in the third short scene, Marchessault provides Leduc with a line borrowed from her book *La bâtarde*,[101] which appears here in italics.

> **VIOLETTE.** *J'ai une mère bleu azur, je l'aime à travers la tragédie, je l'aime après la tragédie. Ma mère, c'est le vent du large parce qu'elle ne passera pas le seuil d'un bourbier.*[102]

Here is the English version:

> **VIOLETTE.** "My mother is azure blue. I love her in times of tragedy, I love her after the tragedy. My mother is the offshore breeze, she'll never set foot on the threshold of a dung-heap."[103]

It must be pointed out that the translation of the excerpts of Leduc's work does not reproduce the existing translated versions. Moreover, in her book *Re-belle et infidèle / The Body Bilingual*, de Lotbinière-Harwood vigorously criticizes Derek Coltman's translation of *La Bâtarde*, which was first published by Peter Owen in 1965, then by Panther Books in 1967 and by Virago Press in 1985. She decries certain translative choices where the specificity of the female gender is ignored and deplores the damage done "to women's bodies and meaning(s) by 'androcentric posture' translations,"[104] as in the following example: "Violette Leduc (1907–1972) in her celebrated 1964 autobiography *La bâtarde*, writes: 'Je suis née brisée. Je suis le malheur d'une autre. Une bâtarde, quoi!'[105] Translator Derek Coltman's 1965 version reads: 'I was born broken. I am someone else's misfortune. A bastard!'[106] Where Leduc specifically refers to herself as her mother's bastard, indicated textually by the feminine form '*une* autre,' Coltman's vague 'someone else' masks the mother-daughter bond central to Leduc's life and work."[107] De Lotbinière-Harwood proposes instead: "I was born broken, I am another woman's sorrow, a bastard," and recommends that all of Leduc's work be retranslated "ideally by a feminist."[108] What's expressed here is an important element of the translation position adopted by the translator. The translating subject advances a feminist approach aimed at accentuating the female gender in the rewriting of the play in English. So, in place of "Go and screw yourself then" offered up by Coltman as an equivalent to "Va te faire foutre, mocheté," a passerby's insult to Violette, de Lotbinière-Harwood proposes the equivalent, "Get stuffed you old bag."[109] This is how she explains her choice: "To screw is male-speak for what a man does to a woman during intercourse. The man insulting Violette Leduc is speaking from that dominant position (on top)....In addition, this American slang is unsuitable in this book's context: Paris in the forties....[My] rendering stays close to Leduc's explicit language, unusually daring for a woman writing twenty-five years ago. It also retains the image of the female sex as a hole or bag, passively needing to be filled by the male member."[110] It is rare to have such a detailed account of certain aspects of the translation project, which is to say, the way in which the subject negotiates her translation position regarding the specific requirements of the work to be translated. Insisting as it does on the visibility of the female subject in the act of translation, feminist practice offers up an ideal field of observation for the study of the translating subject.

Still at the level of microstructural analysis, other than some minor substitutions and additions, the translation is conspicuous for its numerous deletions of various passages deemed inappropriate for an anglophone audience. Ironically, the passages underlined in the following excerpt, wherein Violette rages against censorship and defends the beginning of her novel *Ravages* that the editors wanted to delete, were cut out. (The passages in italics are borrowed literally from Violette Leduc.)

> **VIOLETTE.** *Genet, je ne comprends plus. Je ne comprends pas.* Ils disent qu'ils craignent la censure. Mon éditeur craint la censure. <u>Où se perche-t-elle la censure? Quels sont ses tics, ses manies? Je ne la situe pas.</u> La censure? C'est Paris insensible. <u>La censure?</u> C'est ma ville en Alaska. On ne dérange pas la censure, on ne frappe pas à sa porte, on n'entre pas chez elle <u>sur la pointe des pieds. On ne peut pas l'aborder.</u> Elle tranche vos feuillets, elle part sans être venue. C'est une guillotine cachée. <u>Je construisais un dortoir...un collège... un réfectoire...une salle de solfège...une cour de récréation... chaque pierre une émotion. Ma truelle aux souvenirs. Mon mortier pour sceller les sensations. Ma construction était solide. Ma construction s'écroule. La censure a fait tomber ma maison du bout des doigts.</u> Si je pouvais me jeter à ses pieds je m'y jetterais. Je m'expliquerais.[111]

Cuts were also made when the markers of cultural alterity were deemed excessive for an anglophone public, for example when Violette refers to the titles of her other books in French, *L'asphyxie* and *L'affamée*, or when it comes to the writers that surround her, such as Maurice Sachs, Jean Cocteau, Jean Genet, Jean-Paul Sartre, Nathalie Sarraute, Clara Malraux, and Simone de Beauvoir.[112]

However, certain omissions are difficult to explain as they shorten passages that serve to illustrate the dynamics that connect Leduc to writers, both men and women, to whom she is attached, particularly to Simone de Beauvoir. For example, in the following reply addressed to Simone de Beauvoir by Nathalie Sarraute, the English translation deleted the underlined text.

NATHALIE. Vous avez tenté l'impossible pour RAVAGES, Simone de Beauvoir. Votre révolte, vos colères, toutes vos démarches auprès de tous les éditeurs parisiens. Violette est extraordinaire, inouïe. L'AFFAMÉE m'a fait un effet de choc. Après l'avoir lu je suis revenue un peu honteuse à mes enfants, à mon mari. (À Simone): Ce livre est une lettre d'amour. Quel hommage elle vous rend! Quelle passion elle a pour vous![113]

This deletion, apparently driven by the reference to a book that the spectators would not know—when *Ravages* has already been mentioned at the beginning of the play—contradicts the translating position adopted by the translator when she deplores the erasure of the bonds uniting women in the translations subjected to a male symbolic order: "Some feminists (Daly, Lorde) contend that female bonding—between mother and daughter, between sisters, friends or lovers—is the most threatening bond of all for heterosexist patriarchy. This female bonding is erased from our memories and consciousness by countless strategies."[114] However, it is this type of bond that is highlighted in the passage shortened by the translation. One can see in this discordance the result of a conflict between two objectives; the desire to facilitate the text's transcultural passage interferes with the translation's feminist aim. Favouring the text's acceptability within the receptive context therefore impinges upon the translation project.

As for the play's reception in Toronto, Robert Wallace raises the question of the critics' indifference towards the mediative function of the translation, an oversight that, in his opinion, reflects "a general insensitivity to the issues surrounding translation that permeate [sic] Canadian culture."[115] In the case of *La terre est trop courte, Violette Leduc*, where Marchessault's writing overlays that of Leduc, this oversight is doubly dangerous. So when the *Toronto Star*'s Henry Mietkiewicz criticizes the text without mentioning that it is a translation, "he not only criticized Jovette Marchessault, but devalued the work of Violette Leduc."[116] Here is an excerpt from Mietkiewicz's review: "Presumably examples of Leduc's writing have been incorporated into the script. If so, they have not been properly showcased and sound like shrill, relentless ranting...Indeed, when it comes to use of language, it's difficult to determine where Leduc leaves off and Marchessault begins. Whoever is responsible, we can do without the gratuitous scatology and the abundance of nonsensical images."[117] Yet this was one of the first times that the *Globe and Mail*'s Ray Conlogue would attempt to consider the role played by translation in his perception of a play: "Marchessault is not completely at ease about certain aspects of theatre writing. Her commitment to legitimizing lesbianism leads to the writing of awkward and maudlin scenes about Leduc's relationship with her lover, Hermine, that do not play well theatrically. Part of the problem is a French lyrical verbosity that does not work in English—at least, not in Suzanne [sic] de Lotbinière-Harwood's overwrought translation."[118]

This is a case of history repeating itself, as anglophone critics directed the same reproach towards the production of Marchessault's play, *Saga of the Wet Hens*, translated by Linda Gaboriau. According to the *Globe and Mail*'s Norma Harris, the play's magic had disappeared as the result of confusing direction and a "poor translation of shameless literary pretension [that] drowns the *Wet Hens* in a flow of classy prose."[119] Gaboriau attributes this reaction to the different theatrical traditions in English Canada and Quebec.

Actors in English Canada receive training which is distinctly North American and which is often, in terms of contemporary theatre, more psychological than it is in Quebec. They're not as comfortable, for instance, with flights of language, with poetry, or lyrical, rhetorical material. These are precisely the elements which have been most characteristic of Quebec theatre in the last two decades [1975-1995]....[T]he results on stage can be quite awful, something like the effects of a dubbed movie, when the gestures don't always match the intonations of the language.[120]

Gaboriau goes on to describe the experience she had in 1992 during the Victoria production of her translation of Marchessault's *The Magnificent Voyage of Emily Carr*: "I had not made Jovette's dialogue any more conversational than it is in French. It is often very lyrical, sometimes philosophical....What happened is that the delivery, the acting style, especially from the actors playing the other characters, had the feeling of psychological drama, and the text sounded as if it were coming from somewhere else....I just felt as if my translation, and indirectly Jovette's play, sounded very pretentious, very abstract and very wordy."[121] According to Gaboriau, this is the reproach most often directed towards contemporary Québécois theatre by anglophone critics: "the plays are verbose, Quebec playwrights use theatre as a forum."[122] Conlogue also underlined this verbosity in Michel Garneau's dialogue in *Les guerriers* and Normand Chaurette's in *Le passage de l'Indiana*.[123]

In *The Edge of Earth is Too Near, Violette Leduc*, there is a divergence in the reactions elicited by the play's use of language within each literary system. Even though it disturbed Québécois theatre's then current linguistic code and engendered certain reservations, it is a lyrical and hyperliterary style of writing that echoes a certain literary tradition. In that respect, it benefits from an acknowledgement that facilitates its reception within the original context. This hyperliterariness and this lyricism, which the English translation does not seek to temper and occasionally even highlights, does not seem rooted in any present or past norm that could facilitate its insertion within the drama repertoire of the target context. It upsets this system's playwriting codes and creates an incompatibility between the dialogue and the actors' style of acting.

Even though she must respect the unique artistry of this feminist-inspired play, de Lotbinière-Harwood is not impervious to the expectations of the target audience. She therefore makes short shrift of numerous passages deemed unacceptable for her intended anglophone audience, unfamiliar with the books, the artists, and the cultural references alluded to in the play. This concern for acceptability, however, interferes with the translation project's feminist aim inasmuch as it requires the deletion of passages that feature bonds linking Leduc to other women and other female writers of her time.

The resistance to the translation of Marchessault's text resides on the level of the discursive codes conveyed by the text and a dramatic work's specific linguistic norms. Although the theme of lesbian love and certain sexually-risqué scenes had evoked reservations, it seems to be the literary codes determining the parameters of theatrical language that impede the transcultural passage.

Once again, the pertinence of the Anglo-Canadian literary system borrowing this Franco-Québécois play can be questioned. Despite the incompatibility of the text's linguistic and textual norms, the novelty of the feminist discourse apparently justified the borrowing. As Louise Forsyth states, within the Canadian context, "feminist playwriting in Quebec developed out of a climate of ferment during the Quiet Revolution of the 1960s and was consequently more radical."[124] In 1989, Forsyth wrote, "Jovette Marchessault has written the most significant body of radical feminist theatre work yet produced in Canada."[125] In 1986, when the play was presented in Toronto, Marchessault had already completed five plays, some of which had a significant effect on the Québécois theatre scene, and two of which had been produced in English in Toronto. The English versions included the monologue, "Night Cows," produced in 1980 and published in 1985 in the collection *Lesbian Triptych*, and the play, *Saga of the Wet Hens*, produced in 1982 and published in 1983. English Canada thus sought to fill a gap by borrowing from a figurehead of Québécois feminist theatre. Moreover, this borrowing was facilitated by the prevailing climate of collaboration between the francophone and anglophone feminist communities. It is interesting to note that, after Marchessault's *Saga of the Wet Hens*, the only other of her biographical works to be produced and published in English was the one that she based on the Canadian painter Emily Carr, which Gaboriau translated in 1992 under the title *The Magnificent Voyage of Emily Carr*.[126] Here, not only is the subject rooted in the receptive context, but the translator in question had also developed a solid reputation within the English-Canadian theatre milieu. These elements combine to promote the value of the borrowing in the cultural marketplace within the target context. However, the literariness of Marchessault's language posed a problem, once again, in the English transposition of a Québécois text.

The work on language and the dismantling of the dramatic structures, characteristic of theatrical research on aesthetics throughout the 1980s, are particularly evident in the works of playwrights such as René-Daniel Dubois and Normand Chaurette. While the former distinguishes himself through an extreme volubility that multiples the range of voices and the references in plays in which he pulls out all the stops, the latter stands out for the remarkable intricacy of voices and narrative threads with which he fashions hauntingly beautiful texts.

Amongst his plays, *Provincetown Playhouse, juillet 1919, j'avais 19 ans* is a "classic" of the Québécois theatre repertoire, where it has acquired "le statut d'un chef-d'oeuvre."[127]

Chaurette: When the Audience Is Unaware of What it Doesn't Know

Chaurette's third play, *Provincetown Playhouse, juillet 1919, j'avais 19 ans*, is the work of a playwright who distinguishes himself through a verbal aesthetic at once sober and intense, and by his skillful handling of polyphony, polysemy, and *mise en abyme* to multiply possible meanings. The play was first produced at Montreal's Café-théâtre Nelligan in September 1982, remounted at Chicoutimi's Maison Carrée in 1983, and presented the following year at the Festival de théâtre des Amériques in a solo performance by Larry Tremblay. It was subsequently staged in 1992 at Montreal's Espace Go and in 1994 at the University of Ottawa's Studio Léonard Beaulne.

Resulting from a theatrical exchange program developed by Montreal's CEAD and New York's Ubu Repertory Theater, William Boulet's translation, *Provincetown Playhouse, July 1919*, was presented at a public reading in New York in 1984 before being produced in English by Toronto's Buddies in Bad Times Theatre in 1986. This first English translation of one of Chaurette's works was published in 1986 as well by Toronto's Coach House Press in the anthology *Quebec Voices: Three Plays*, edited by Robert Wallace, which also included *Breaks* by René Gingras, translated by Linda Gaboriau, and *Don't Blame the Bedouins*, Martin Kevin's translation of a play by René-Daniel Dubois.

This anthology opens with a presentation by Wallace and an introduction by Paul Lefebvre translated by Barbara Kerslake, who was also responsible for the translations of the prefaces that precede each text. It appears that these prefaces, written by the directors of the Québécois productions of each of the plays, were taken from the programs that accompanied the original productions. The volume concludes with biographical notes and bibliographies for each playwright. In the case of *Provincetown Playhouse*, Gilles Chagnon's introduction "La scène cautérisée," which accompanied the 1981 edition of the play published by

Éditions Leméac, was not included. The translated version provides a list of the casts, dates, and sites of the Québécois productions along with a list of the characters and a description of the set, both taken from the original publication. Yet it fails to mention that the play is composed of nineteen short scenes and omits the variations on scene six and scene eleven included in an appendix to the original. Lastly, there is no indication of a translation strategy.

In his introduction, Lefebvre provides several highly instructive remarks on the evolution of Québécois theatre and the choice of plays included in this anthology.

> Quebec theatre is no longer nationalistic....From 1965 to 1975, there was complete agreement, not only on both sides of the footlights but in Quebec society as a whole, as to the meaning of the pronoun "we": without question it meant "we, as a nation" or "we, Quebecers." Since then that sense of group identity has been eroded. Already by 1978, the lives of individuals were becoming a favourite topic for exploration....Although the relation between Quebec and its theatre was becoming more diffuse, playwrights were dealing with a greater variety of concerns....What has been lost in unity and cohesion has been gained in greater breadth and variety, and a greater willingness to experiment with new forms.[128]

Provincetown Playhouse illustrates what preoccupied the theatre of the 1980s through certain characteristics that Lefebvre describes as "self-consciously literary writing," "a setting that is foreign...and an examination of the private."[129] Resolutely modern in its aesthetic, the play is conceived as a mathematical exercise in *mise en abyme* aimed at dissecting the mechanics of the illusion. Through a series of incantatory scenes composing a self-referential ritual, we learn that for nineteen years Charles Charles has been confined to a Chicago clinic, where he is celebrating his thirty-eighth birthday by replaying in his head the play that he wrote for himself and two friends, one of whom was his lover, and that they performed on July 19, 1919, the night he turned nineteen. The play sets out to sacrifice beauty by stabbing— nineteen times—a bag that supposedly contains a child, but which in fact contains cotton soaked in pig's blood. After it is discovered that the bag actually contains the body of a young black boy, the three men are charged with murder. During the trial, Charles Charles pleads insanity and is confined while his friends are sentenced to be hanged because of a gap that exists in their memories: they no longer remember what they were doing during the hour preceding the play. We will later learn that Charles Charles has come upon them asleep in one another's arms and that he is the one who put the child in the bag.

In his review of *Quebec Voices: Three Plays*, Jean-Cléo Godin regards the original play as "one of the finest pieces of writing in Québécois theatre, and this English translation conveys the same sober beauty of this play about beauty, death, and madness."[130] In fact, the English version faithfully reflects the verbal mechanics of the source text, but it slightly accentuates the orality of the language, making it more idiomatic. In the translation, the syntax has been corrected, and the text contains numerous elisions drawn from the spoken language. These characteristics of the translated text are in sharp contrast with the austerity of the original, which adopted an unconventional syntax and, except for omitting the first part of the negation, makes little concession to the spoken language. To illustrate this, here is an excerpt from the opening lines of the play in which we meet two characters, Charles Charles 38 and Charles Charles 19, who represent the play's main character at two moments of his life.

> **CHARLES CHARLES 38.** Charles Charles, 38 ans, auteur dramatique et comédien, leur dire que je suis fou. Autrefois l'acteur l'un des plus prometteurs de la Nouvelle-Angleterre. Ma fin de carrière: l'une des plus prématurées et des plus éblouissantes de l'histoire. Depuis je suis seul. Depuis, c'est un one-man-show. Mesdames et Messieurs.[131]

Here is the same excerpt from the translation:

> **CHARLES CHARLES 38.** Before you this evening, you see Charles Charles, thirty-eight-year-old actor, playwright—and madman. Formerly one of the most promising actors in all New England, my career met a startling and untimely end. Since then, ladies and gentlemen, I have been a one-man show.[132]

The desire to render the text more idiomatic is also apparent in the punctuation, which is sometimes rather lax or completely absent in the original when the character is in the throes of a verbal delirium. This makes it an important textual sign in a play that is based on the opaqueness of words and the difficulty in connecting with the senses that they conceal, as can be seen in this part of the play where Charles Charles 38 speaks about his birthday.

CHARLES CHARLES 38. Aujourd'hui c'est mon anniversaire j'aimerais qu'on me fasse un gâteau avec dix-neuf chandelles une pour chaque année de mon séjour ici c'est pas trop demander j'ai jamais rien demandé je pourrais en demander trente-huit j'ai trente-huit ans mais dix-neuf je m'en contente on dira à ceux qui poseront des questions 19 plus 19 ça fait 38 tes 19 ans plus les miens ça fait 38 on partagera le gâteau puisque tu es revenu 19 ans tu es revenu avec tes 19...Ils ont dit non qu'ils ont dit...ils ont dit vous êtes plus un enfant qu'ils ont dit.[133]

Here is the same excerpt from the translation:

CHARLES CHARLES 38. I told them it's my birthday today. I'd like a cake with nineteen candles. One for every year I've spent in this place. It's not too much to ask. I've never asked for anything. I could've asked for thirty-eight candles but I'll settle for nineteen. I'll tell whoever asks that nineteen and nineteen makes thirty-eight. Your nineteen and my nineteen years make thirty-eight. We'll share the cake now that you're back and you're nineteen...you're back. Do you know what they said? They said no, that's what they said. They said you're not a child anymore. That's what they said.[134]

Besides the changes in the punctuation, this passage exhibits numerous changes in the written form of the English. The idiomatization of the English text goes hand in hand with the desire to explain the message in order to render it more accessible. This frequent tendency in translation is one of the "universals of translational behaviour" that Gideon Toury defines as "an almost general tendency—irrespective of the translator's identity, language, genre, period and the like—to explicitate [sic] in the translation information that is only implicit in the original text."[135] Here, this desire to explain is exacerbated by a convoluted style of writing that takes pleasure in diverting us, as illustrated in the following excerpt from which the title of this section is borrowed. A particularly convoluted passage in the original and its equivalent in the translations have been underlined.

> **ALVAN.** Voyez comme c'est curieux; il y a un enfant dans le sac, nous on le sait pas. Or, on dit au public qu'il y a un enfant dans le sac, donc le public le sait. <u>Alors le public ignore que nous on sait pas. Alors nous tout ce qu'on sait c'est que le public ignore. Mais comme le public sait pas qu'il ignore</u>, une fois qu'on saura tout le public pensera qu'on le savait...Alors on s'est pris à notre propre jeu.[136]

> **ALVAN.** Don't you see how odd this whole thing is? There is a child in the bag, but we don't know. Nevertheless, we tell the audience there's a child in the bag. So they know. <u>But what the audience doesn't know is that we don't know there's a child in the bag</u>. And when this whole thing comes out, they think we knew. We got caught in our own trap.[137]

To facilitate understanding of this exceedingly tortuous logic, the translator has simplified and clarified the utterance. Thus, the self-referential and playful aspect of a dramatic text caught up in its own game of illusions has been sacrificed for a certain semantic linearity.

Still concerned with clarification, the translation has redistributed certain lines and added stage directions to clarify what is intended. Other changes have been effected through the elimination of all the excerpts from Charles Charles's *Mémoires* preceding the fifth, sixth, eleventh, twelfth, and thirteenth scenes in the original. They would have been deemed superfluous or redundant in a play in which the dialogue is already subject to a complex ritual.

There are also substitutions that indicate a concern to appropriate the text into the target context. For example, when Alvan is describing what he was doing before the show, "j'ai fait de la méditation" has been replaced by "I read."[138] Also, when Winslow follows suit with, "j'ai fait un peu de gymnastique," it has been replaced by "doing my voice exercises."[139] Because this translation was originally intended for a New York audience, the change in these cultural references seems movitated by the translator's concern for the play's reception within the American target context. This may explain why "I had a fight with a nigger" was chosen as an equivalent for "je m'étais battu avec un Noir"[140] when the author could have certainly used the word "negre" in the original if he had wanted to. It is however a choice in keeping with the context of Provincetown in 1919. In translating, "Je les déteste, c'est vrai, j'ai toujours eu horreur du noir" as, "I hate them. It's true. I've always had an absolute horror of coloureds,"[141] a play on words has been eliminated in order to once again underscore Winslow's racism.

Another interesting substitution in the English text occurs when "Si j'étais vous, j'irais interroger ceux qui ont écrit qu'on faisait du théâtre bestial. Quand on sait pas ce qu'on écrit, on sait pas ce qu'on fait" is translated as, "If I were you, I'd question those who wrote that what we were performing was Bestial Theatre. How can you know what you're doing if you don't know what you are saying?"[142] Taken from Alvan's indictment of the theatre critics, this sentence alludes to the weight of the written word and, as a result, contributes to the self-referential dimension of Chaurette's writing. This dimension is absent in the translation, replaced by a more idiomatic formulation that favours the word and thus orality. Lastly, there is an occasional mix-up between the lines attributed to Charles Charles 38 and Charles Charles 19, as is the case at the beginning of the second scene, which opens with dialogue attributed to Charles Charles 38 in the original and to Charles Charles 19 in the translation.[143]

Although the translation had been conceived for an American audience and was originally presented in a public reading in New York, it was very well received in English Canada, where it was produced at Theatre Passe Muraille by the Buddies in Bad Times Theatre. One critic described the play as "bizarre but fascinating" and was captivated by Chaurette's writing, which he compared to that of Pirandello and Tremblay: "The writing is evocative, exploring the impulses that trigger art, genius and madness and tinged with sardonic humor. Like Pirandello, Chaurette juggles illusion within the context of theatre. Like his Quebec colleague Michel Tremblay, he daringly bends time, allowing characters from different decades to interact."[144] When it was remounted at the University of Ottawa's Studio Léonard Beaulne, another critic appreciated the play as a "lovely layered piece of writing...a spare script...where visceral reality is poised against the worship of Beauty."[145]

The translation as a whole appears to be motivated by a search for adequacy to the discourse of the original text, which incidentally offers little impediment to the cultural transposition into the American target context. The hospital in which Charles Charles 38 resides is located in Chicago and the events described unfold in Provincetown. However, the highly literary style of the original play requires several adjustments that contribute to facilitating the translation's reception within the target context. The syntax has become much more normative and more closely follows that of everyday spoken language, while the highly complex structure of the original has been simplified, and passages deemed too difficult to understand have been clarified.

As was the case with Marchessault's text, the highly inventive linguistic resources and the literariness of expression pose problems for the translation of Chaurette's text into English. However, unlike *La terre est trop courte, Violette Leduc*, these attributes of Chaurette's writing have been moderated to facilitate the work's reception. While this literariness broke new ground within the source context and helped to give these texts a central value within the Québécois institution, it was also an impediment to their reception in translation. In the case of Marchessault, where this literariness was pushed to the extreme, the reaction was negative. Despite the play's innovative discourse, the lyricism of the writing was an obstacle, and the translation was never published. In contrast, the literariness and complexity of Chaurette's text has been moderated and was therefore well received within the receptive context, where the emphasis was placed on the newness of form that it brought to the dramatic structure. It must be said that the play depicted homosexual characters and contributed to a discourse that, much like that of the feminists, grew considerably throughout a decade where dramatic writing, deprived of its "national" mission, opened up to diverse themes and realities.

Consequently, the first of Chaurette's texts to be produced in English was sought out by the Anglo-Canadian theatre system more for what it offered in terms of narrative structure and the discourse it contained than for the novelty of the poetic resources it harnessed.

It was the textual and discursive codes that motivated the borrowing, while the linguistic codes, such as those in Marchessault's text, were subject to a norm that moderated the literariness of the language to make the text acceptable first within the American and then within the Canadian receptive context.

The exploration of linguistic resources would continue in Québécois playwriting during the 1980s, to the point where the text would be stripped of its primary signifying function. Certain companies specializing in visual theatre would undertake a veritable visual odyssey through performances in which dialogue was sparse, multilingual, and, most often, incidental. This visual theatre must be viewed as another example of the dismantling of the verbal and narrative structures that characterized this period. Alongside *théâtre de l'image*, textual theatre continued to develop with Franco-Québécois playwrights who were very successful on anglophone stages. Such was the case for René-Daniel Dubois with the play *Being at Home with Claude*, translated by Linda Gaboriau and produced at Toronto's Tarragon Theatre in 1987. It was also the case for Michel Marc Bouchard, whose play *Lilies or The Revival of a Romantic Drama*, also translated by Linda Gaboriau, was acclaimed at the Factory Theatre in 1988, and which Robert Wallace described as "une expérience émotionnelle plus intense que la production originale de la pièce à la salle Fred-Barry de Montréal."[146] Bouchard quickly made a name for himself on anglophone stages, and, with ten plays produced or published in English between 1991 and 2004, is currently second only to Michel Tremblay as the francophone playwright with the most plays translated into English. The next analysis will focus on two plays that were very successful in English Canada: *Lilies or The Revival of a Romantic Drama* and *The Orphan Muses*, both translated by Linda Gaboriau.

Michel Marc Bouchard, a New Version

As it states on the back cover, *Les feluettes ou la répétition d'un drame romantique*, published by Éditions Leméac in 1987, "marque le coup d'un nouvel âge théâtral: celui du retour de l'âme. Et de l'émotion,"[147] an emotion that proved fascinating on anglophone stages that were normally reluctant to display such emotion in acting or in words. Gaboriau translated the play into English, and it was published by Coach House Press in 1990, produced at Toronto's Theatre Passe Muraille in 1991, and again in 1994 at Vancouver's Touchstone Theatre, where it won several awards. It was subsequently brought to the screen by Toronto director John Grayson and received the 1996 Genie Award for best Canadian film. Thanks to its exceptional success, Bouchard was introduced to English Canada through a work that displays the narrow-mindedness and religious dogmatism prevalent in Roberval in 1912. Are we to think that English Canada remained nostalgic for a bygone era?

Following the success of *Lilies*, Touchstone Theatre produced another of Bouchard's plays: *The Orphan Muses*. In this work, the author conjures up and exorcises a bleak vision of the family before concluding that "the most beautiful thing about a family is knowing how to leave it!"[148] The play reunites three sisters and a brother, Catherine, Martine, Isabelle, and Luc, abandoned by their mother twenty years earlier and whose father died in the war after having left his unfaithful wife. While awaiting their mother's purported return the following day, the children recall the past. But there will be no reunion as announcing their mother's return was part of a staged event worked out by Isabelle to say goodbye to her family and to the past.

First produced at the Théâtre d'Aujourd'hui in September 1988 and remounted there in 1994 in a version revised and corrected by the author, the play was first published by Éditions Leméac in 1989, then republished in a "new version" by the same publisher in 1995. In this second edition, Bouchard mentions that he had made some "cuts and small changes" before the play was restaged in the fall of 1994. Dominique Lafon compared the two versions, in which "seul le rôle de Luc a fait l'objet de coupures significatives," and these cuts were less concerned with the role itself than with "la part du texte dont le personnage est l'auteur, c'est-à-dire ce livre sans cesse récrit, en gestation."[149] The scene where Luc wears a dress that belonged to his mother is missing in the new version and some passages from the book that Luc reads to his sisters have been cut.

Gaboriau's English version was published in 1995 by Victoria's Scirocco Drama (since relocated to Winnipeg), and, in an introductory note, the translator explains that the translation "includes the revisions made to the script by the playwright, prior to the second production at the Théâtre d'Aujourd'hui in 1994."[150] Therefore, it appears that she worked from the revised edition published the same year. In any case, both versions of the original will be taken into account in the analysis of the translation in order to reveal the discrepancies in the original texts that could have influenced the translated version. The dates that accompany the following excepts correspond to each of these publications, either the original versions published in 1989 and 1995 or the translation that also appeared in 1995.

The original publication in 1989 included a presentation of the three previous plays in the series that focussed on the Tanguay family, acknowledgements, a biographical note in which Paul Lefebvre introduces the author, information on the play's creation, a description of the characters and the set, as well as a dedication. In the revised version, the acknowledgements and the dedication have been eliminated, the biographical note shortened, and there is now information on the creation of the revised version as well as a note from the author in which he introduces this new text. The list of characters from the first version is retained, while the description of the set has been simplified. The revised text has been divided into three acts composed of eight scenes, five scenes, and one scene respectively, whereas the first version contained three acts of eight, eight, and three scenes.

The translation reproduces the dedication and the short introduction of the first edition. Indeed, it is unnecessary to introduce the "new" version of the play in this first English publication. The descriptions of the characters and the set are also borrowed from the 1989 edition. Next, the picture of the author is accompanied by a list of his plays, their translations into various languages as well as the awards they have garnered. For the first time in the corpus under study, a picture of the translator appears in conjunction with a biographical note containing the names of the most celebrated playwrights she has translated and the awards that her translation of Bouchard's play *Les feluettes* has received. Here we learn that the translator has been nominated for the Governor General's Award and has received the "Dora Mavor Moore, Chalmers and Jesse Awards."[151] This is a notable development in valuing the contribution of the translator, who receives the same treatment as the author in the pages that introduce the work. The profile of the translator is followed by a list of the play's productions, including the initial American production in 1993, and the Canadian productions at the Western Canada Theatre Company in Kamloops and at Victoria's Belfry Theatre in 1995. Other than the aforementioned comments, there are no other observations concerning the translation. However, the translator publicly expressed her translating position in an article that appeared in 1995: "For me, there is no doubt—my loyalty is to the playwright....I'm trying to capture the originality of this work, and to convey not only what these artists are talking about but how they are talking about it....Because I've made the decision to try to capture the distinctive theatrical voices of the playwrights I translate, I rarely adapt their work."[152] Her extensive experience in theatre translation has also led her to confront a characteristic of Franco-Québécois playwriting that she describes as follows: "In all Quebec theatre, there is an omnipresent, invisible character and that is the Québécois language. The presence of that spoken language, whatever level the playwright has chosen, is a statement in itself, a statement of cultural survival, aspiration and communion....The underlying difficulty I find in translating Quebec theatre is dealing with this preoccupation with language, the constant awareness of the importance of speaking French."[153] One can indeed note this insistence on the language and on the exploration of linguistic resources in the plays previously studied. After the revolution brought about by the recourse to *joual*, authors such as Marchessault, Dubois, Chaurette, and now Bouchard, strove to develop an exuberant and unconstrained dramatic idiom that distanced itself from both the everyday language of *joual* and normative French. It is an idiom that, aligning itself with neither, must invent ways to circumvent them both.

Though, on a macrostructural level, the English text has retained the original's three acts, they are no longer divided into scenes. While visible in the written text, this modification goes unnoticed in the performance, as was the case in the translation of Gélinas's *Bousille et les justes*.

The microstructural analysis reveals that the original text employs a vernacular bearing the markers of a local idiom, which is not however the *joual* of the urban settings that Tremblay depicts. The action unfolds at Saint-Ludger-de-Milot in the author's native region of

Lac-Saint-Jean, and some dialectal forms are reflected in the spelling. Thus we find terms such as "à cause" (pourquoi), "meman" (maman), and "quecque" (quelque). Certain attributes of *joual* are also on display, such as the Anglicisms "pitcher," "trucker," or "chum," the elision of pronouns, the addition of the pronoun "tu" after a verb, and certain markers of orality such as "ousque" (où), "icitte" (ici), or "beu" (boeuf). It's a vernacular language that is nevertheless interspersed with very elaborate terms, and the book that Luc is writing uses a hyperliterary language that often borders on preciosity. The juxtaposition of the levels of language and the integration of hyperliterary expressions into a local vernacular creates ironic effects through a contrast of extreme states of language. These characteristics are also to be found in *Les feluettes*, where the local dialect of the residents of Roberval mixes with the beautiful language of a French countess still very much attached to her aristocratic roots and that of an elegant young woman from Paris vacationing in Roberval. There is, thus, a range of languages that calls upon a wide variety of resources, which poses a problem for the English translation, as Gaboriau has pointed out: "These language choices are very difficult to translate. If you were to read the original plays by Michel Marc Bouchard and by René-Daniel Dubois, and then read my translations, I'm quite sure you'd see more variety in colour and level of language than I was able to capture in co-called Standard North American English. There is a range of differences available within English, but it is difficult to capture the striking variety of hues of the original."[154]

The language used in the translation is indeed more normative and homogenous than that of the original. Although there are some elisions drawn from the oral language and dialectal specificities such as "Ma," "Mama," or "retard," as a whole, this is less in evidence than in the French, as can be noted in the translated version of the following excerpt, in which markers indicating a deviation from the normative language have been underlined.

CATHERINE. Quand? Ça fait <u>ben</u> une dizaine d'années qu'<u>yl</u>'a commencé! Plus que ça...<u>y</u> avait onze ans quand j'<u>y</u> ai dit que c'était mieux d'écrire <u>c</u>'qui <u>y</u> passait par la tête que de se déguiser comme meman. J'aurais <u>donc</u> dû être moins compréhensive. Une claque en arrière de la tête <u>pis</u> la valise aux pauvres! Vas-y avant qu'<u>y</u> revienne. Vas-y![155]

CATHERINE. When? He'<u>s</u> been working on it for ten years now! Longer...He was eleven years old when I told him he'<u>d</u> do better to write what was going on in his head, instead of dressing up like <u>Ma</u>. God, I should<u>n't</u> have been so understanding. A good slap in the face, that'<u>s</u> what, then dump the suitcase at the thrift shop! Get going, before he comes back. Go on![156]

The English version gives the impression of a slightly higher level of language due more to the nature of these markers than to their quantity. With the exception of "Ma," all the elisions noted in the above excerpt are markers of spoken language frequently found in written texts. In this way, they conform to the usual spelling of theatre dialogue. The original text, however, proposes new spellings for certain expressions, such as "qu'yl'a" and "c'qui," as well as "ben," "y," and "pis," which are characteristic of Franco-Québécois colloquial language. So, vernacular markers are less prominent in the translation.

The same levelling-off strategy has been employed when the language veers towards a more pronounced literariness. Gaboriau illustrates this in an anecdote about how *The Orphan Muses* was received in New York: "At one point in the play one of the sisters says, '*Si tu penses que tu vas nous jouer l'apothéose du pardon, tu te trompes.*' I found 'apotheosis of pardon' a bit over the top and I called it 'the epitome of pardon.'"[157] The *New York Times* theatre critic took exception to the baroque treatment of the play and condemned the expression: "Who would ever say 'epitome of pardon'? And it was a line I had already watered down."[158] It goes without saying that reducing the gap between the spoken and the literary language of the translation facilitates the play's reception in a cultural context unaccustomed to this type of theatrical language. Nonetheless, one also runs the risk of homogenizing the levels of language to the point where they merge, thus rendering incongruous the use of overly marked terms from one side or the other. Every translator confronts these difficult choices when faced with the task of creating texts that are "both 'true' to their original sources and effective in their new incarnations."[159]

In addition to reducing language gaps, the dialogue from which the following excerpt is taken contains fewer terms of endearment and certain substitutions. Here is the 1995 original version:

MARTINE. Non, on ne se tapera pas l'apothéose du pardon! "Apothéose," ça veut dire la cerise sus l'sundae! Prends ton dictionnaire!.

LUC. (Lisant) "21 juillet 1944. Cher fils adoré. J'ai reçu une lettre des Forces armées canadiennes. Votre père est mort lors du débarquement de Normandie. Ses amis l'avaient surnommé 'Le suicidaire.' À l'annonce de la nouvelle, Martine a cassé la statuette du matador."[160]

In the translation of this same excerpt, the underlined passages are borrowed from the 1989 original version—they had been replaced or eliminated in the 1995 revised version—and the sentence in italics did not appear in either of the original versions.

MARTINE. She's not going to put us through the epitome of pardon! "Epitome" means the cherry on the sundae! Use your dictionary, for chrissakes!

LUC. (Returning to his book.) "21 September 1944. My Beloved Son. The autumn winds are sweeping over the hill and there's no escaping the sand. Federico has recovered from his wounds. I received an official letter from the Canadian Armed Forces. Your father is dead. He died in the Normandy landing. His soldier friends had nicknamed him 'the suicide case.' When I announced the news, Martine smashed the matador statue."[161]

In this excerpt, certain additions result from a practice common to theatre translation: the practice of including passages in the translated text that are borrowed from different versions of the original.

This textual patchwork is made possible by a singular attribute of the theatre text, which is that it can be circulated in various manuscript versions, sometimes differing greatly, before being published. Also, it is not unusual for a previously published theatre text to be revised to meet a new production's needs and for these revisions to be incorporated into subsequent publications.

This same strategy can be used elsewhere to intensify certain dramatic effects. For example, in the first version of the play, the first two of the three excerpts from the mother's letters to her eldest daughter bear the signature "J.T." (for Jacqueline Tremblay), while the third is signed "Jacqueline Rosas." In the 1995 version, they were all signed "Maman." The translation adopts the latest version for the first and third letter, which are signed "Mama" and "Ma," but adheres to the first version's "Jacqueline Rosas" for the second letter. This strategy succeeds in revealing that the mother is now married to the man for whom she left her children. It is a dramatic effect and a piece of information that had disappeared in the second version of the original, but a decision was made to retain it in the translation.

Still at the macrostructural level, several of the stage directions have been removed, added, or modified. Comments have sometimes been added to explain movements or intent, such as the following stage directions that do not appear in either of the original versions and are all found on the same page of the translated version: "Heading for the door," "Catherine starts arranging the chairs," "The three sisters are obviously excited," and "Luc re-enters."[162] One can detect in these additions the effect of a previously discussed universal of translation that consists of rendering something explicit in a translation that was implicit in the original. There is, however, a stage direction added to the very end of the translated version whose function goes beyond the desire to clarify and considerably modifies our reading of the end of the play as a consequence.

Having announced that she is pregnant with the child of a man she recently met and who has explained to her the truth about her mother, the youngest child, Isabelle, leaves the family home. The only indication of this included in the two original versions is the following stage direction: "*Isabelle sort.*"[163] In each of the originals, Martine follows her out. In the translation, this stage direction is preceded by the following statement: "*We hear a trailer truck pull up outside and honk.*"[164] In addition, Martine's departure has been deleted. This modification resolves the play in a much more calculated fashion, and whatever is gained pragmatically comes at a cost to Isabelle's freedom and her courage. To a certain extent, this framework is incompatible with the quest for independence that marks the end of the play. This strategy for ending the play is reminiscent of the conclusion of Tremblay's *Hosanna*, in which any ambiguity is resolved by eliminating the conflict of identity. There appears to be a similar need here to concretize an ending, to frame an outcome that in the original gave free rein to the imagination.

Other deletions also resulted in condensing the dramatic effect of certain lines, such as when the underlined sentence in the following passage, which appeared in both the versions of the original, was deleted. Perhaps it was deemed redundant or unnecessary.

> **CATHERINE.** J'me suis sentie tellement ben. Tellement ben. J'me suis sentie libre. J'avais pus de secret. J'me vengeais d'eux autres. (*Elle prend la valise.*) Je m'en vas faire un autre plaisir. (*Elle va dehors, entre à nouveau.*) Y s'en vient un char que je connais pas. (*Martine l'a rejoint* [sic].) J'en ai douté jusqu'à la dernière seconde.[165]

Other changes seem motivated by a desire to render an utterance more accessible for the recipient, such as the following addition that links a known reference to what might be an unfamiliar religious practice. When Catherine emphasizes that her mother "s'est dévouée à toucher l'orgue à toutes les messes saintes pendant des années,"[166] she is alluding to services that occur in the week leading up to Easter. The translated version has expanded and accentuated this statement as follows: "Ma never missed a chance to play the organ, every Sunday, every holy day, year in and year out."[167]

As for onomastic and toponymic references, the translation has kept the names of the characters and of the village where the play is set, which it nevertheless simplifies by referring to it several times as "Saint-Ludger,"[168] whereas the original used "Saint-Ludger-de-Milot," and by opting for "Quebec City" as an equivalent for "Limoilou." The translation has also retained the French forms of address "Madame Tessier," "Madame Giroux," and "Madame Tanguay."[169] This last form of address, however, was changed a few lines further on to "Mrs [*sic*] Lucien Tanguay,"[170] which leads to some confusion regarding the codes used in naming the characters.

Elsewhere in the text, certain statements whose metalinguistic function requires a transposition are adapted according to the resources of the English language, such as the lyrics to Isabelle's song and the descriptions of the terms from the dictionary that Isabelle is learning. Accordingly, the French dictionary, "avec les noms communs pis les noms propres,"[171] that Catherine gives to Isabelle has been very cleverly transposed as "A dictionary...It's even got illustrations."[172] However, considering Isabelle's fascination with words, it would have been possible to retain the reference by alluding to "proper nouns" or "names of places and people."

When the English version of the play opened in Vancouver in March 1996, the press praised the production and lauded the universal quality of the play's subject matter, as is illustrated by the titles of the following reviews that appeared in the *Vancouver Sun* and the *Georgia Straight*. In an article entitled "Vancouver Production of a Quebec Play Shows a Universal Symbol for Survival," Barbara Crook contends that the "emotional truths that Quebec playwright Michel Marc Bouchard tackles in his bold, highly theatrical and wonderfully extreme dramatic adventure are instantly recognizable and richly resonant."[173] Here, the universality of the play lies in the ease with which one can identify with the emotions expressed in this "extreme dramatic adventure." This last description is moreover very interesting as it could, in some fashion, represent an acceptable version of excess. Describing the same production, Colin Thomas also emphasizes the universal character of the play in an article entitled "*The Orphan Muses* Strikes a Universal Chord."[174] Notably, these reviews make no mention of the translation process, a process that once again remains invisible.

As for the notion of universality, it is interesting to recall Wallace's comment that "the assumption, all too prevalent, in Canadian criticism, [is] that the best theatre reveals universal truths."[175] However, if one acknowledges that all criticism is historically defined and informed by the position that it occupies within the context from which it comes, the very notion of universality is problematic, as it presupposes a network of absolute norms and representations that are shared by all. As

Linda Hutcheon explains in *The Canadian Postmodern*, the "eternal universal Truth I was taught to find has turned out to be constructed not found—and anything but eternal and universal."[176] Just as Ann Wilson does, one could ask oneself, "who determines what constitute this essential humanity which is beyond gender, class and race?"[177] The notion of universality is an ideological construct designed to affirm certain dominant values.

That the so-called universal qualities of Bouchard's play are underlined in this manner is reminiscent of the critical reception of Tremblay's works some twenty years earlier. Indeed, according to Koustas, the Toronto reviews devoted to Tremblay "indicate that he triumphed as a Canadian, not Quebec, playwright due primarily to the universality, not *québécitude* of his plays."[178] A comparison of Tremblay's plays with Bouchard's reveals common themes borrowed from Quebec history prior to the end of the 1960s. The settling of scores that occurs in *Les feluettes* takes place in 1952 and describes events that unfolded in Roberval in 1912. The action in *Les muses orphelines* unfolds in Saint-Ludger-de-Milot in 1965 and concerns events that took place twenty years earlier. Is this because the period preceding Quebec's Quiet Revolution was more suitable to the expression of universality?

In the same vein, it is interesting to examine Michel Bélair's remarks concerning the playwrights of the period that preceded the birth of the new Québécois theatre in 1968. In his opinion, the dramatic texts of Gratien Gélinas, Marcel Dubé, Francoise Loranger, Jacques Ferron, and Jacques Languirand exhibit "une constante de non-incarnation dans le milieu québécois se manifestant surtout par des préoccupations de type universel."[179] According to Bélair, it is by escaping this concern for universality that theatre written in Quebec could become truly Québécois, that is to say, "voué à la transcription des tensions et des lignes de force qui agitent la société québécoise."[180] From this perspective, Michel Tremblay would champion a typically Québécois specificity, while being acclaimed in English Canada for the virtues of his plays' universality.

The term universality is also used to serve strongly divergent interests according to the discourse into which it is inserted. This brings to mind the *Montreal Star* critic who appreciated the universal theme of Gélinas's *Bousille and the Just*, while a Toronto critic applauded its typically Québécois nature. It is clear that the use of this term, Québécois, is highly relative and that it represents criticism or praise depending on the position it occupies and the intended objective.

While the English translation of *Les muses orphelines* attests to a volition for adequacy to the original, as expressed elsewhere by the translator in her translating position, it is not immune to strategies of appropriation that make it acceptable to the recipient. Accordingly, sociocultural references that could prove unfamiliar have been modified, while the gaps between the levels of language have been reduced, and statements have been fleshed out or clarified to render them more easily understood. In addition, certain changes in the play seem to result from a desire "to improve" the dramatic dynamics by selecting from elements contained in the two original versions and by creating new dramatic effects when necessary, as illustrated by the final stage direction describing Isabelle's departure at the end of the play.

It must be acknowledged that the desire to reveal the original work is replaced here with an evident concern to improve it. While certain intercessions seem intended to facilitate the reception of the play within the target context, others are the result of personal aesthetic judgements. In this instance, the particular poetics of the translating subject and that individual's relationship to the writing have a decided affect on the translated work.

The 1980s saw the development of a Canadian francophone drama in which Franco-Ontarian Jean Marc Dalpé had acquired a highly enviable popularity. A three-time recipient of the Governor General's Award, the first of which was in 1988 for his play *Le chien*, he also received the Prix du Nouvel-Ontario. Dalpé has written six short texts for the stage and eight plays, four of them created in collaboration with various Franco-Ontarian artists. In 1995, *Lucky Lady* was nominated for the Governor General's Award, and the English version of the play was produced in translation in Ottawa and in Vancouver in 1997. These two plays will be the subject of the next analysis.

Jean Marc Dalpé and the Hybridity of Language

Jean Marc Dalpé co-founded Ottawa's Théâtre de la Vieille 17 in 1979 and was the artist in residence at the Théâtre du Nouvel-Ontario, "le premier théâtre de création en Ontario français et le seul théâtre professionnel d'expression française dans le Nord de l'Ontario,"[181] which was founded in Sudbury in 1971. This company produced his play *Le chien* at the Théâtre français du Centre national des Arts in February 1988.[182] This play was a resounding success in Canada and abroad and, as mentioned, went on to win the Governor General's Award. It was translated into English the same year by Maureen Labonté and the author himself, and produced in November at Toronto's Factory Theatre.

Following *Le chien*, three of Dalpé's plays, *Eddy* (1994), *Lucky Lady* (1995), and *Trick or Treat* (1999) were translated into English by Robert Dickson, a bilingual author from Sudbury with whom Dalpé worked closely. Although none of the translations were published, they are all available in manuscript form at the Centre des auteurs dramatiques and at the library of the National Theatre School of Canada. The translated versions of *Le chien* and *Lucky Lady* both provide the name of the author, the translators, and the title of the translation. The second play also includes the original title, information on the French publication, and the date of the translation. In each case, there is a list of the characters as well as a description of the set and of the play's location. Faithful to the originals, *Le Chien* is set "on the outskirts of town," while *Lucky Lady* takes place "[in a] small industrial city on the decline near Montreal."[183] It is worth underlining that in both cases the translations retained the original titles. If this goes without saying for the second play, *Lucky Lady*, which is named after the horse on which everything has been wagered, it is more difficult to explain why the first work, *Le Chien*, would retain the French title, if not to underline the origins of a play whose success contributed to the discovery of an author and, as a result, Ontario francophone theatre. This Gallicism, however, is hardly representative of the translative strategies employed, inasmuch as French is nowhere to be found in the text, with the exception of the name of one character, Céline, and other individuals who are mentioned in passing, "Bouchard, Briand, Paquette...Dieudonné St-Cyr."[184]

On the macrostructural level, the divisions into acts and scenes remain the same, as do the names of the characters in both plays, except for Mireille, who becomes Mimi in the English version of *Lucky Lady*. In this play, the note "comédie en trois actes" that accompanied the original title has disappeared in the translation.

In *Le chien*, we are witness to the painful reunion of Jay and his family, which he left seven years earlier to distance himself from a violent and authoritarian father. The play is set in a small Northern Ontario town near Timmins, and the characters express themselves in a convoluted French that reflects the difficult reality of linguistic minorities. French-English code-switching is a distinctive trait of this speech. Such hybridity is the result of the French language's constant exposure to the dominance of English. It is a French interspersed with expressions and entire sentences in English, as the following excerpts illustrate.

> **JAY.** J'travaille quatre, six semaines, deux mois; douze, quatorze heures par jour; pis j'me ramasse du cash, pis j'sacre mon camp, pis j'vire une brosse ou deux; pis j'suis lucky pour les jobs, ça pas d'bon sens, quand j'commence à manquer d'argent, y'a toujours quequ'chose de payant qui s'pointe. L'Amérique Tabarnak! Free Spirit ostie! James Dean Easy Rider Sacrament! Le bicycle à gaz au Texas câlice![185]

> **PÈRE.** Fait que j'les laisse entrer. "Was tryin' to get to the hospital, ya see." J'ai amené la femme tu-suite sur not'lit. "Goddamn car swerved in front of us, we went down into the ditch just over here. Fuckin asshole didn't even stop!" Là, à lumière pis proche d'elle, j'ai vu que la femme, ben c'était vraiment une fille. J'veux dire, elle avait l'air d'avoir dix-huit ou dix-neuf ans, même pas. J'sais pas trop.[186]

The English translation also calls upon a highly-accentuated vernacular, but the code-switching has been erased in favour of a unililingual English text, as the English versions of these same excerpts illustrate.

JAY. I work four, six weeks, maybe two months, doin' twelve, fourteen hour days; I pick up good money, and then, I fuck off somewhere else, and get good and pissed for a while: but I'm really lucky, cause when the money runs low, bang, there's always a good payin' job that comes along. Never misses. America! The Free Fuckin' Spirit! James Dean Easy Rider! Shit! Flyin' wild down a stretch of highway in Texas on a suped up bike![187]

FATHER. So I let them in. "Was tryin' to get to the hospital, ya see." So right away, I lead the woman into our bedroom so she can lay down. "Goddamn car swerved in front of us, we went into the ditch just over there. Fuckin' asshole didn't even stop!" Then, in the light, and close up, I could see that the woman was really just a girl. I mean, she looked eighteen or nineteen, maybe not even that old. I wasn't too sure.[188]

It must be added that this erasure was the result of a consensus inasmuch as the author collaborated on the English translation of his play with Labonté, a seasoned theatre translator living and working in Montreal who had completed several translations as part of the exchange programs for translations established by Gaboriau at the Centre d'essai des auteurs dramatiques in 1985.

These programs brought about an important change of direction regarding the English translation of the francophone repertoire. Under the exchange programs translation became the responsibility of the Québécois theatre institution, which presided over the selection of the works to translate and their translation before exporting them outside the province. Rather than responding to an external need, in this case that of the polysystem that borrows the play, here the borrowing results from an internal desire to promote Franco-Québécois and Franco-Canadian theatre to an anglophone audience in Canada and abroad. The works were henceforth translated locally by anglophone translators who were attuned to the delicate question of language and all that it entails for Canadian theatre written in French. So there is a reticence to employ linguistic strategies that result in a false-sounding or exotic translation aimed at a unilingual anglophone audience unexposed to the friction with a dominant language, an audience for whom the code-switching would rob dialogue of any verisimilitude. While it avoids the trap of exoticism, this strategy does however cancel out the linguistic duality inherent to the source text, which is at the very heart of the problematics of identity and culture facing Canada'a francophone-minority communities.

According to Kathy Mezei, the recourse to English in francophone texts is invested with considerable symbolic meaning, and erasing it subverts the text by assimilating it into a unilingual anglophone reality.[189] She suggests that we draw on italics, parentheses, translator's notes, paraphrases, or any other textual devices to indicate to the reader the code interferences present in the original text. Though they might be suitable for a written text meant to be read, such devices are moot in a text intended to be performed, as the performance dynamic requires the recipient to immediately understand the message expressed on stage without access to explanatory notes or other strictly textual devices. The linguistic code-switching in the theatre text thus presents translation with a sizeable challenge, as its transposition is possible only insofar as it does not hinder the reception of the text in performance. If unilingualism is necessary in *Le Chien* to retain the verisimilitude of the dialogue, it results paradoxically in the affirmation of the supremacy of English, which remains impervious to French.

Lucky Lady presents us with five misfits, including a "country singer," a "small-time dealer," a taxi driver, and two young delinquent parents, who end up placing all their money and all their dreams on a horse race. Here again, they speak a basic, convoluted French interspersed with English expressions. In the translation, this code-switching gives way to a unilingual English text. The text does, however, contain the French version of some dialogue uttered by the racetrack announcer as he describes the horse race in question, dialogue that appeared in English in the original French text. This particular translation was intended for an Ottawa audience; thus, the public bilingualism is completely plausible. Here is an example:

> **VOICE.** And it's...a photo finish at the wire! Too close to call. We'll have to wait for the judges'decision. Quelle belle course! What a race! Gardez vos billets, s'il vous plaît! Keep your tickets, please![190]

Living in a francophone-minority community in Ontario, the translator was aware of the language issues at stake and could resort to translative strategies that avoided the pitfall of exoticism in a play intended for an audience unaccustomed to code-switching in the everyday vernacular, although it was completely acceptable in the vehicular public language. Thus, the text was adapted for the target audience in a way that managed to avoid unwanted strangeness. After all, a realistic linguistic aesthetic is an essential proviso of the play. As Rémy Charest points out in his review of the original production: "Ce que Dalpé saisit à merveille, c'est que, au-delà du rythme, il faut absolument que l'on croie à ces cinq personnes et qu'elles aient tout à perdre ou tout à gagner pour que l'édifice tienne."[191] There is an evident search for appropriation for the intended audience without any attempt at improving the text or arranging it to comply with the expectations of the anglophone spectator. Although it is indicated that the play is situated in a francophone context, with characters bearing French names, a reproduction of the code-switching or a linguistic hybridity that would have distorted the text has been avoided. In this sense, the translation attests to a search for adequation to the source text's intent, which above all is aiming for verisimilitude with the target audience.

The production of *Le Chien* at the Factory Theatre in 1988 received a lukewarm reception. According to the *Toronto Star* critic, one didn't know whether to blame the translation or the fact that the original production's actors had to speak a second language in which they were not comfortable. Although it obviated the need to recast the play, thus reducing costs, the choice to present the same production in English with actors who lacked a complete mastery of the language is somewhat surprising, particularly in a play in which the dialogue results from a decidedly naturalistic aesthetic. This brings to mind the initial English productions of Tremblay's plays that also suffered from this type of linguistic ambiguity. In any case, the review was harsh: "It is raw, angry and occasionally quite powerful. But it is also messy, unfocussed and overwritten....People shout a lot. The emotions are overdrawn and have a melodramatic, soap-opera feel. There's some stumbling over words and the timing of the dialogue is not sharp."[192]

Lucky Lady also received a rather chilly reception in Ottawa in 1997. The *Ottawa Citizen* theatre critic questioned certain choices in the staging that may have been detrimental to the production's credibility and concluded that the characters were superficial: "The play, in its English-language premiere...never moves beyond that dog-eared snapshot phase....The humour is erratic and only occasionally biting. And the characters remain as superficially clichéd throughout as they were in the opening, despite Robert Dickson's fluid translation."[193] Despite the considerable success that Dalpé has enjoyed with the Canadian francophone public and the prestigious awards his plays have garnered, he remains unknown in English translation. The productions were not as successful as they were expected to be, and none of the English versions of his plays have been published.

This concludes the descriptive analysis of the English versions of French-language plays included in the corpus. This analysis reveals various strategies that appear with a certain regularity, which makes it possible to measure the primary, secondary, or idiosyncratic character of the norm from which they result.

Norms at Work in the Corpus

With regards to preliminary data, the title of the translation, the names of the author and translator as well as the literary genre are considered primary norms, as they apply to each of the translated works. The original title and details concerning the creation of the play are included in Tremblay's text and are later present in the works that have been published. This information is missing in Gélinas's text, which attests to the indifference towards the process of translation and the Canadian indifference towards the subject of translation in the early 1960s, which Wallace would subsequently deplore.[194] However, from the 1960s on, the title of the original play as well as information on its creation and any subsequent productions were readily provided—an indication of the growing interest in the social context from which a play originates and in turn represents.

Similarly, three of the six English translations under study were accompanied by introductions: the publications of the plays by Chaurette and Bouchard, and the manuscript of Marchessault's work. Marchessault's and Bouchard's plays were translated between 1986 and

1993 and included the prefaces that accompanied the original publications. Chaurette's text, published in an anthology in 1986, is well served inasmuch as it is preceded by a presentation by the publisher, an introduction by a well-known Québécois theatre critic, and a preface taken from the program of one of the original productions. However, it did not include Gilles Chagnon's introductory essay to the original publication of the play. Lastly, Tremblay's play, *Les Belles-Soeurs*, was published a third time, appearing in the 1993 anthology *Modern Canadian Plays*, in which the editor provides a history of Canadian theatre before introducing the authors and their works. It was deemed unnecessary to introduce Gélinas's text, published in 1961, nor any other translated version of Tremblay's plays mentioned in this study, although they were all accompanied by numerous prefaces or introductions in their original publications. As a result, there was no mention of the difficulties involved in the translation of Tremblay's language, a language that attested to the ideological rupture occurring in Quebec at the time and to the sought-after cultural autonomy. Such translations lead the English reader to believe that the translated text is an exact reproduction that presupposes a complete compatibility of the two cultures. Yet, as we have observed, the work on language and its symbolic representations in Quebec constitute an insurmountable obstacle to the English translation's transcultural passage. The primary function of the language as a cultural and discursive motor within the Franco-Québécois context is quite simply foreign to the receptive system.

Moreover, what is remarkable in all the published translations examined here, many of which include explanatory metatexts that are at times numerous, is that there is never any mention of the mediative effect of translation. Clearly, this is a primary norm that implies that the work of the translation, and the changes it generates in the text, remain invisible. Furthermore, by putting the emphasis on the final product, to the detriment of the process employed, the work of the translation, and the differences between the original and the translated versions are somewhat concealed. However, in the case of Bouchard's play, republished in a revised version, Gaboriau indicates which version she used. This attests to her awareness of questions surrounding the translation process; of course, Gaboriau is an experienced translator who contributes to the dissemination of the English versions of francophone plays within a Québécois organization dedicated to the development of francophone drama. It is also notable that not a single one of these Québécois plays translated into English was adapted and the action transposed into the target context, whereas adaptation would greatly influence the translation of English-Canadian theatre into French up until 1990.

In addition, all but two of the plays were published, and two others appeared in anthology form, one of which was Tremblay's, first published in 1974 and then again in 1992 in a revised edition before being anthologized in 1993. The publication of Québécois plays in translation thus represents a primary norm and these plays occupy a choice position within the marketplace of English-Canadian theatre publishing. Tremblay's plays have generated twenty-three English-language publications, yet in not a single case was it deemed necessary to include an explanation of the translation strategies involved.

Still within the preliminary data, the note concerning the original language used by Gélinas was deleted, as were scenes six and eleven in Chaurette's text. These changes allowed the Gélinas text to avoid the question of the specificity of the source language and enabled the Chaurette text, the structure of which has been simplified to render it more accessible, to avoid the question of the lack of closure. The fact that the English version of Marchessault's play was never published could explain why the refererences to Violette Leduc's books were never provided.

At the macrostructural level, with regard to the works of Gélinas and Bouchard, the division into acts and scenes has been modified. Sporadic in occurrence, this strategy constitutes a secondary norm in the English translation of the Québécois text. For Gélinas's play, the redistribution of the acts and scenes seems motivated by a search for symmetry within the temporal framework of the action. The disappearance of the scenes in Bouchard's play results, instead, from a desire to eliminate divisions that were deemed superfluous.

As for the stage directions, there is a primary norm that requires that the description and the original names of the characters be retained in the translation. However, Gélinas's text is an exception; it gives rise to a considerable onomastic and toponymic revision that results in the substitution of the French names in the original by French names assumed to be more familiar to an anglophone audience. In this instance, these changes render the play suitable for the anglophone imagination, a process most often apparent on the microstructural level. In the case of Gélinas's text, however, this effect occurs at the macrostructural level, which makes it easy to observe. Thus, in this instance, the modes of cultural appropriation are readily apparent. However, at the beginning of the 1970s, a new norm required that the original names be retained in the translation. In the case of Tremblay, even the French forms of address and the titles of the original plays were retained. Thus, there was a break in the mediation of the Québécois product in English translation; from the 1970s on, Québécois theatre accentuated certain marks of cultural alterity in order to promote its "Quebecness."

Within this corpus, another primary norm exists regarding the revision of stage directions; stage directions may be removed, added, or modified according to what the translator deems preferable. Most of these revisions are aimed at clarifying an intention or a movement and have only a minute effect on the play's dynamics. This is, however, not the case for the stage direction added at the end of Bouchard's text, which results in a substantial change in the resolution of the conflict, as was the case with *Hosanna*. These revisions reveal the effect of a secondary norm that favours a more definite closure for the text, where the original chose to leave things unresolved. Similarly, the excerpts of Charles Charles's journal and the variants to scenes six and eleven that were included in the appendix to Chaurette's original text were also discarded.

The microstructural analysis reveals the effect of a primary norm that dictates the use of an everyday target language; the everyday target language is heightened when the original employs a vulgar or vernacular language and is tempered or oralized when the original language is too literary. Reducing the language gaps in the Québécois texts in this manner facilitates their reception within a theatre system that elects not to cross certain well-determined linguistic parameters. Accordingly, Marchessault's lyrical flights or the "overwritten" nature of Dalpé's text are deplored and the translation carefully tempers what is perceived as excessive in the vulgarity of Tremblay's *joual*, in Chaurette's verbal delirium, and in the extreme disparity between the levels of language employed by Bouchard. However, this levelling off divests the language of its cultural and discursive iconic function, bringing about a shift that sees the referential aspect of the language in the source text give way to a more vehicular use of language in the translation.

This standardization of the language is accompanied by a homogenization of the linguistic codes, given that the code-switching and the numerous Anglicisms of the original plays disappear in the consistently unilingual translated versions, except in Tremblay's plays, which exhibit Gallicisms that do not correspond to any actual usage. This effectively accentuates the exoticism of both the subject matter and its inherent criticism, thereby preventing the anglophone public from identifying with it. Furthermore, whereas the Anglicisms of the original text expose a friction within the codes and a contamination of the French language by English, the Gallicisms in the English translations serve only to underscore the play's origins.

While certain practices discerned through the analysis of the microstructures were foreseen through the study of the macrostructure, there are others that it fails to reveal. The deletion or replacement of any utterances deemed unnecessary or unacceptable occurs in all the texts under study, with the exception of Dalpé's, and constitutes a primary norm aimed at accentuating the translated product's acceptability within the target context. Also contributing to this is the secondary norm aimed at clarifying passages deemed obscure or situations considered unclear, as in the texts by both Chaurette and Bouchard. The aim of another secondary norm is to intensify the dramatic effects in order to heighten the dramatic dynamic of the translated play, as can be observed in the texts by Gélinas, Tremblay, and Bouchard.

Finally, in most of the translations, certain sociocultural references that could have proved awkward have been appropriated to the target audience, even in the case of Chaurette's play that takes place in the United States and was translated in New York. All the place names in Gélinas's play and some of those in the plays by Tremblay and Bouchard have been changed. Lastly, the references to authors and works unknown to anglophone audiences were eliminated from Marchessault's play. This is indicative of a primary norm that seeks to facilitate the anglophone public's identification with the play's subject matter either through elimination or by appropriating certain information with which it is unfamiliar.

Comparison with the Systemic Context

Let us now return to the extratextual norms formulated in the discourse dedicated to literature and literary translation. The inventory of emblems devoted to translation is dominated on the anglophone side by the metaphor that sees in this activity "a possible bridge over the gap of language between English and French Canadian writing," "a bridge of sorts," or "a bridge between two solitudes."[195] This rhetoric, which developed at the end of the 1960s and became prominent during the 1970s, the time when francophones were affirming their presence and laying claim to their rights, culminated in the creation of the Aid to Translation Program by the Canada Council for the Arts. If translation henceforth enabled a bridge to span the linguistic gap, what about the social, cultural, and ideological differences confronting it? The translation of Tremblay's plays in particular illustrates the extent to which the ideological aspect associated with the use of a language could elude the translation process, especially since the silence surrounding the loss of this dimension of the text suggests a complete adequacy between the source and target texts. Thus, not a single obstacle seems to hinder the meeting between the two cultures through the agency of the bridge provided by the translation, particularly if certain marks of familiar and nonmenacing alterity are highlighted, as was the case in the plays by Gélinas and Tremblay. Moreover, Van Burek's expressed reticence regarding the pejorative connotations associated with the term "joual," which he conceives as a French variant comparable to "American English," could have contributed to his translation position and promoted a raising of the level of language.

However, left untouched in the translation of the texts by Marchessault and Dalpé, the use of language in Quebec drama would create a problem and bring to light another important norm in English-Canadian theatre: its attachment to naturalist dialogue. This norm would prove to be a major obstacle to the efficient crossing of the translation bridge. Marchessault's and Dalpé's plays were deemed artificial and verbose as their verbal aesthetics were not tempered by the translations. In the case of Marchessault's plays, the feminist translator had to remain faithful to the lyrical quotient of the original language since this lyricism bore the distinct marks of a feminist writing. In Dalpé's case, a bilingual author, intimately involved in the English translation of his plays, decided to retain a coarse and crude vernacular. However, it was deemed appropriate to naturalize Chaurette's text, which would then be readily welcomed within the receptive drama system, as was the case for Bouchard's text in which the gaps in the levels of language had been reduced.

It is interesting to note that, upon the production of Chaurette's *Passage de l'Indiana* at the Théâtre du Nouveau Monde in November 1996, Conlogue published a review entitled "Fuelled by Long Monologues, Play's Verbosity Is Its Engine." Representative of a norm belonging to English-Canadian theatre tradition, the *Globe and Mail* critic went on to confess, "I have to admit to a limited taste for this sort of thing, no matter how brilliantly it is done." However, for the benefit of his readers, he hastened to acknowledge that, "the French, of course, love this kind of literary theatre, especially if it is witty."[196] This is an instance of a fundamental difference in the verbal aesthetics favoured by each drama system.

Noticeably present in the borrowing of the original proper names found in all of the translated texts, and by the French forms of address in the plays by Bouchard and Tremblay, the ethnographic norm identified by Simon is most apparent in the translations of Tremblay's plays wherein numerous Gallicisms result in an accentuation of a nonthreatening alterity. The mission of revealing Quebec to English Canada, with which the ethnographic translation is entrusted, is paired here with a desire to reassure the anglophone public by favouring a familar aspect of "Quebecness."

The high number of translated works in publication attests to the fact that English Canada grants francophone drama, especially that of Quebec, a prime position within its repertoire, despite the sometimes insurmountable difficulties facing the translation. What are the functions these numerous translations are asked to fulfill? This question will be examined in the last chapter wherein we will look more closely at the position occupied by the translated drama repertoire within the evolution of the English-Canadian literary polysystem. It is necessary beforehand, however, to analyze English-Canadian plays translated into French so as to be able to compare the subsequent findings. Chapter 5 is devoted to just such an analysis.

5

DESCRIPTIVE ANALYSIS

The English Repertoire
Translated into French

AS IN THE PREVIOUS CHAPTER, this analysis will first present the work in translation and the circumstances relating to its transcultural passage before examining the preliminary data, the metatexts, the macrostructural components that frame the text, and the microstructures that constitute the smallest integral unit of the translation. It will then be possible to identify the norms that govern the translation and the type of equivalence that they establish. Lastly, having analyzed all the texts belonging to the same repertoire, representing various moments in its evolution, we will be able to evaluate the intensity and value of the observed norms as well as the function assigned to the translated texts within the target context.

Herbert and Adaptation "à la Québécoise"

Aux yeux des hommes, the Québécois adaptation of Torontonian John Herbert's *Fortune and Men's Eyes*, was published in 1971 by Éditions Leméac and was the second play in their collection Traduction et adaptation.

This collection had been launched the previous year by *L'effet des rayons gamma sur les vieux-garçons*, Michel Tremblay's adaptation of Paul Zindel's acclaimed play, which signalled the emergence of an intensely active translation practice in Quebec. Herbert's play had created a stir in New York in 1967 before being translated into several languages and brought to the screen in a 1970 American/Canadian co-production that was filmed in a Quebec City prison. That same year, René Dionne's adaptation of the play was staged at Montreal's Théâtre de Quat'Sous. Between 1970 and 1990, Dionne was responsible for more than fifteen Québécois translations and adaptations of primarily American and British plays. *Aux yeux des hommes* would be remounted by the Théâtre du Vieux-Québec in 1978 and by the Théâtre du Trident in 1985.

The 1970 production of this play was enthusiastically acclaimed by the critics. While acknowledging the attraction of a new theme, they sang the praises of Dionne's translation into *joual* and the direction of André Brassard, now well-known following the recent success of Tremblay's plays. In fact, according to critic Jean-Paul Brousseau, "le sujet (l'homosexualité) est dans l'air à Montréal, tant au théâtre qu'au cinéma."[1] The reviews that appeared in *Le Devoir, La Presse,* and the *Montreal Star* following publication of the Québécois version of the text mentioned the author's name, but provided no further information about him. The introductory pages to this work published by Éditions Leméac gave the names of the author, the translator, the original play, the initial production, the collection it was part of, and the editor. The program accompanying the Québécois production stated that the text was "l'adaptation en 'québécois' de la pièce du 'Torontois' John Herbert," later adding that the play "a connu un succès à New York, Londres et Los Angeles" before being presented in Quebec.

It is worth noting that in this brief introduction of the author, both the indication of his origins and the target language of the translation are placed in quotation marks, as if they somehow constitute an equation in which one compensates for the other. Also, this indication of a translative strategy is not exactly representative, as it only alludes to the choice of the target language and fails to mention the other changes the text has undergone. Here it is necessary to examine the meaning of the term "adaptation" because this inherently unstable translative strategy calls upon various processes that are applied indiscriminately.

In some cases, the term is used to designate versions where the recourse to a Franco-Québécois language is the only modification brought to the text. For example, in his 1977 "adaptation québécoise" of Edward Albee's *Who's Afraid of Virginia Woolf*, Dionne retains the New England setting as well as the names and occupations of the characters in the original play; the only change is the use of a target language meant to be specifically Québécois. Eleven years later in his "translation" of the same play, Michel Tremblay, who also retains the original setting and the characters' names and occupations, cuts various lines from the text and modifies and adds dialogue when deemed appropriate; in short, Tremblay makes numerous and major alterations to the source text.

In addition to the choice of a Franco-Québécois target language, the adaptation can also affect the setting or the period in which the action of the plays unfolds. While certain Québécois adaptations retain the setting and the period of the original play, many only transpose the setting of the action. So in the adaptation of Arnold Wesker's *La cuisine*, produced in 1985 at the Théâtre du Nouveau Monde, Dionne retains the temporal context of the play, but moves it from London to Montreal and has an inexperienced young Gaspesian arriving there, whereas the original dealt with a young Irishman. An adaptation can also operate on two levels, as in the case of *Le gars de Québec*, where, in the hands of Tremblay, the nineteenth-century Russia of Gogol's *Revizor* becomes the north shore of the St. Lawrence River in the time of Duplessis. Lastly, and more rarely, the adaptation affects only the period in which the action takes place, as in the case of Jean-Claude Germain's *Les Faux Brillants de Félix-Gabriel Marchand*, an adaptation of Félix-Gabriel Marchand's *Les Faux Brillants*, wherein Quebec vaudeville at the turn of the last century is updated to 1977.

The extensive borrowing of contemporary American plays explains the popularity of the first two modes of transposition, as a North American affinity between the two cultures facilitates the adequation of the original play's setting to the Québécois context. Sometimes, deleting the place names, while retaining the contextual ambiance of the original play, is enough to create the illusion that the action takes place within the receptive context. Although transposition of the spatial or temporal axis frequently occurs in adaptation, it is not an essential strategy. Nor is it exclusive to adaptation. Such transposition can be found, albeit rarely, in texts that are classified as translations. The Québécois version of Norm Foster's *Melville Boys*, which will be examined later, provides an example of such transposition.

It appears that the transposition of the target language, of the spatial and temporal contexts, as well as of their sociocultural corollaries, is not always enough to completely acclimate the foreign work. As Paul Lefebvre and Pierre Ostiguy explain, it is sometimes still necessary to eliminate "[des] personnages sans grande importance" and occasionally to "raccourcir certains passages trop longs" by deleting dialogue or scenes deemed unnecessary.[2] In contrast, it is sometimes preferable to "étoffer non seulement les dialogues mais aussi la situation."[3] In this respect, the adaptation of Wesker's *La cuisine* offers a striking example of a redistribution of the text through an amalgamation of elements borrowed from each of two versions of the original published in 1964 and 1981. In this adaptation, the setting, the nationalities, and the names of the characters are changed, their number reduced, hockey replaces soccer as chicken does cod, certain lines are uttered by different characters or disappear altogether, while others are added. These examples illustrate the extent to which the adapter can take the place of the author when it comes to judging the pertinence of whether to modify certain traits of the work in translation, and thereby ensure that it corresponds to its new receptive context.

Furthermore, to avoid distorting the original work and to convey the author's intentions more effectively, the symbolic or ideological connotative value of certain utterances is transposed by calling upon "un réseau de connotations connu du spectateur."[4] Hence, in *La cuisine*, the image of the Virgin Mary, hanging in the only room where the young Irishman Kevin will feel at home, becomes in Dionne's adaptation "un calendrier de la Sainte Enfance," a symbolic equivalent for the young Gaspesian newly arrived in Montreal. Even though the object mentioned in the source text is completely familiar to the Québécois public, it seems that the translator gave it a particular symbolic value that necessitated this transposition.

The numerous applications encompassed by the term "adaptation" imbue it with an ambivalence that maintains the invisibility of the translative process. In the case of *Aux yeux des hommes*, the spectators are presented with sociocultural references that invite them to situate the action within the target context. So Queenie is renamed Alice, and the city of Timmins turns into Thetford Mines, the Matachewan Reserve becomes a North Shore Reserve, Pocahontas is replaced by Kateri Tekakwitha, Florence Nightingale by Jeanne Mance, and Saint Joan by Madeleine de Verchères, while Bob Hope and Bette Davis, though well-known by Canadian francophone and anglophone audiences, must give way to their Québécois counterparts Claude Blanchard and Yvette Brind'amour. The action is relocated to Quebec, and all allusions to anglophone cultural realities are erased in favour of Franco-Québécois cultural references.

The play is a naturalistic, psychological character study, with a linear development that respects the unity of time and place and aims for a sense of verisimilitude. It brings to the stage four young prisoners caught up in the plots and intrigues of the power struggles within a prison environment and the sexual benefits at stake. Smitty, recently arrived and still inexperienced, quickly learns the rules of the game and succeeds in dethroning Rocky, who runs things in the cell they share with the effervescent Queenie and Mona. Mona is passively uncooperative with the milieu's implicit rules. Published in 1967 by New York's Grove Press, this biting critique of the prison system is divided into two acts, the first of which contains two scenes, and is accompanied by an introduction of the characters and a prologue to the first scene, which provides information on the context and the set.

On the macrostructural level, the translated version respects the original format of the acts and scenes, but deletes the description of the characters that precedes the text. The prologue to the first scene is retained, as is the information on the context and the set, but the titles of the opening songs are not included. The description of the context in which the action unfolds refers to a "maison de redressement, au Canada," thereby literally reproducing the initial formulation situating the play in "[a] Canadian reformatory."[5] So there is no indication that the play has been transposed into a Quebec setting. Lastly, the text is followed by an index of terms borrowed from prison jargon and a compilation of excerpts from newspaper reviews devoted to the production. Many photographs of the play also appear in the publication.

On the microstructural level, the language in use is a *joual*, containing numerous English expressions and slang specific to the prison environment. Just as in the source text, the written form exhibits very pronounced markers of orality. Numerous deletions and various substitutions attest to the change in the play's location. However, some of the changes remain difficult to justify other than by a desire to prune the text of passages deemed superfluous, too vulgar, or untranslatable, such as the passage underlined in the following excerpt, which is accompanied by its translation.

> **ROCKY.** All Indians is screwin' finks an' stoolies, an' I woulden trust 'em with a bottle o' cheap shavin lotion; <u>and that Blackfeet bum probably slugged some ol' fairy in a public crapper, t'git a bottle o' wine</u>.[6]

> **ROCKY.** Les sauvages, c'est tout des hosties d'tabernacles de stool. Pis en plus j'les trusterais même pas avec une bouteille de Branvin.[7]

The following excerpt finds the underlined portion of Queenie's dialogue deleted and replaced in the Québécois translation by a line delivered entirely in English.

> **QUEENIE.** <u>Well...I lifted my left leg and then my right, and between the two of them, I rose right to the top</u>.[8]

◊◊◊

> **ALICE.** My husband and I say: "Fuck you."[9]

The descriptions of characters' appearances and their body language as articulated in the stage directions continue to be significantly cut. For example, in the following stage direction from the beginning of the second act, the underlined text was deleted.

> The GUARD <u>crosses to</u> reset the record, and QUEENIE enters, looking like a combination of Gorgeous George, <u>Sophie Tucker</u> and Mae West. He wears a platinum-blonde wig, spangled sequin dress, long black gloves, large rhinestone jewelry on ears, neck and wrists, heavy make-up and is carrying a large feather fan. <u>There is</u>

no self-consciousness or lack of confidence: movements are large, controlled, voluptuous and sure. He throws open the fan, as ROCKY, SMITTY and the GUARD watch, bending his knees in a slow dip, so the tight gown pulls across his heavy, rounded body, giving the look of an overweight strip teaser beginning the act; slowly he undulates the hips forward and upward in a series of professionally controlled bumps and grinds, the meat and muscle of burlesque dancing. As the record plays the opening to a song, an old night-club favorite, QUEENIE prepares the way with these bold, sex-conscious movements.[10]

Many cuts have also been made to passages that feature songs that are either heard or sung in the play. Not only do most of these songs belong to the English repertoire, they are also rewritten by Queenie and thus pose a real translation challenge. Therefore, they have been eliminated when deemed unnecessary to the unfolding action of the play.

The translative strategies deployed in this adaptation seem to be aimed at attaining the greatest possible acceptability of the translated product through a total appropriation to the receptive sociocultural context. What is surprising, however, is that the source text contains no insurmountable obstacle that could have hindered the Québécois public's understanding of the play. Is the reality of an Ontario penitentiary so different from a comparable Quebec institution that this setting needs to be adapted? While conceding that certain cultural references may have necessitated an adaptation, such as the allusions to Florence Nightingale and Pocahontas, there are certainly many others that are very well-known to the Québécois public, such as the allusions to Jeanne d'Arc, the cities of Timmins and Ottawa, and the American movie stars Bob Hope and Bette Davis. Here, the decision to adapt everything that does not specifically refer to the target context indicates a desire to insist upon the unbridgeable cultural distance separating the original text and its translation. This desire justifies the need to conceal the initial context and to entirely identify the play with a Québécois reality and system of references.

This purely Québécois system of references is not however to be confused with the actual knowlege of a Québécois public that is well acquainted with the characters and the cities in question. But these characters and these cities allude to anglophone realities, and the English factor, omnipresent in spoken French within the Canadian context, must be banished from a purely Québécois system of references, as if resistance to this overwhelming presence entails denial of its representation. To achieve this, the translative operation takes a solipsistic turn by relegating the source text to the position of pretext and erasing its origins in order to provide exclusively local references.

It must be noted that the play's linguistic and discursive codes lend themselves particularly well to this task. Since the language on display is a vernacular, it could be easily replaced by *joual*, the newly-canonized emblematic language of Québécois theatre. Moreover, the play's subject matter certainly is very well-suited to the new discourse on identity, singling out an alienation that must now be overcome: the young protagonist's innocence and honesty gives way to anger and violence once he has fallen victim to the oppressive forces represented by the prison. Following the success of *La Duchesse de Langeais*, which had just been presented on the same stage by the duo of Tremblay and Brassard, the play's homosexual subject matter was far from being a hindrance. Thus, not only did the original play's popularity add to its borrowed value, the linguistic and discursive codes that it deploys were perfectly suited to the linguistic and discursive norms established by the new Québécois theatre that was eager to affirm its identity in the 1970s.

At the same time, the Québécois society's interest in its own history greatly contributed to the enormous success of John McDonough's play *Charbonneau and Le Chef*, which details two men's confrontation during the 1949 Asbestos strike. In examining one of this period's darkest chapters, this play brings about a collective catharsis, in the sense that, according to Aristotle, tragedy engenders *katharsis*, or a purification of passions.

McDonough and the Success of "Docudrama"

John Thomas McDonough joined the Dominican Order in 1950, attracted by their interest in the life of the intellect and social justice. Then, in 1968, during a stay in a small northern mining town, he abandoned the church and spent long evenings writing a play. Based on the conflict between the premier of Quebec, Maurice Duplessis, nicknamed Le Chef, and Monsignor Charbonneau, the bishop of Montreal, it takes place during the 140-day strike that beset Asbestos in 1949. The original manuscript in four acts and an epilogue was submitted in 1967 to Jean-Louis Roux, then artistic director of the Théâtre du Nouveau Monde, who suggested some revisions. In 1968, a revised version in three acts and an epilogue bearing the title *Charbonneau and Le Chef* was published by McClelland & Stewart, and the following year a radio adaptation was broadcast by the Canadian Broadcasting Corporation. For this radio version of the play, McDonough "cut it down to radio size. It was an editing job, not an adaptation."[11]

In 1971, the Québécois poet Pierre Morency, and Paul Hébert, then artistic director of Quebec City's Théâtre du Trident, fashioned an adaption of the play based on the original text, the publication, and the radio version. The play was produced at the Trident in 1971 and 1972, then in Montreal the following year in a co-production with the Compagnie Jean-Duceppe, which purchased the rights and which, after the eighty-nine performances already staged in Quebec City, presented it more than 128 times in Montreal and a further seventy-six times on tour, always to sold-out houses. Published in 1974, *Charbonneau et le Chef* was the fourth play in Éditions Leméac's collection Traduction et adaptation. The play was revived by Jean-Duceppe in 1986 and was such a success that it was held over twice.

The program that accompanied Jean-Duceppe's 1973 production made little mention of the author. It mainly strove to introduce the company, which had just been founded, and its members. There was a synopsis of the play, and the director provided the introduction and part of McDonough's prologue. For the 1986 revival, there was a greater insistence on the play's historical aspect in the program, supported by numerous photographs and newspaper articles depicting the significant events of the Asbestos conflict. In the program, the author is briefly introduced as "un ancien dominicain, [qui] était étudiant à l'Université Laval en 1949, lorsqu'éclata la grève d'Asbestos," and the play's development is outlined. The program also states that, in the author's opinion, the actual subject of the play is neither the Asbestos strike, nor the trial of Duplessis or Monsignor Charbonneau's apology, but rather the denunciation of the injustice committed by the church in the name of God, "la plus grave des injustices" according to McDonough. In the director's message, Paul Hébert, who also helmed the 1986 revival, described the producers' anxiety when the play was first produced in 1971: how would the political and religious circles react to the stage depictions and the disclosure of facts that had up until then been shrouded in silence? Despite disapproving letters and controversial statements in the newspapers, the production went on to enjoy considerable success. Fifteen years later, in the 1986 production's program, Hébert considered the play's subject matter all the more pertinent, stripped as it was "des attributs politico-folkloriques dont on pouvait complaisamment l'affubler au début des années 70."

In the original version of *Charbonneau and Le Chef* published in 1968, the text is preceded by a dedication, a biblical epigraph from the Book of Jeremiah, an introduction in which the author comments on the play's subject matter, and a list of the ten characters, which does not include the extras who portrayed journalists, police officers, and strikers. The text itself is divided into three acts and an epilogue. The first act, entitled "The Conflict" and subtitled "What is truth? / Pontius Pilate," is preceded by a lengthy prologue that describes the beginning of the strike. It contains six scenes that depict the founding of the union, the company's refusal to give in to its demands, Le Chef's determination to use force to prevent the strike, and the opposition of Monsignor Charbonneau, who delivers the famous sermon in which he supports the strikers and comes to their aid by organizing a fundraiser. The second act, entitled "The Conspiracy" and subtitled "An Enemy of the People / Henrik Ibsen," is divided into four scenes that portray how Le Chef, furious at having to give in to the strikers' demands and recognize their union, supports the steps undertaken by the bishop of Rimouski to destroy Monsignor Charbonneau's reputation with the pope and force him to resign from his functions. The third and last act, entitled "The Condemnation" and subtitled "It is better for one man to die for the people—Caiaphas / John 18:14," contains two scenes in which Monsignor Charbonneau is forced to resign and exiled to Victoria, which shakes the confidence of the head of the Asbestos union towards a church that would thus betray its most charitable members. The epilogue presents Duplessis's electoral victory two years later as he is returned to power despite his flagrantly unjust treatment of the workers and the unions.

Documentary in nature and inspired by historical events, the play could be categorized as a "docudrama," a genre aimed at dramatizing and potentially demythifying segments of Canadian history. Docudrama was popularized in the early 1970s by alternative theatre companies such as Theatre Passe Muraille. At the beginning of each act or scene, the playwright provides extensive descriptions of the historic events and the characters that they depict. The stage·directions are numerous and often redundant. Surprisingly, they are placed in italics and within French quotation marks. In this naturalistic play, based on the verisimilitude of the actors and the unfolding action, the tone is oratorical, and the sometimes cumbersome tropes cannot avoid certain stereotypes concerning the French-Canadian "soul." A particularly eloquent example of one such trope can be found in the following exchange between Monsignor Charbonneau and Father Georges-Henri Lévesque, who advises him to travel to Rome to plead his case.

> **CHARBONNEAU.** It's useless, I tell you, useless. How can I ever hope to understand the Roman mind? I'm the son of a pioneer, my ancestors were coureurs de bois. I don't understand subtleties and nuances. I like straight-forward answers, frankness...I prefer the direct approach to problems, I...

> **DOMINICAN.** You are inflexible and proud, like the tall pine trees of your forests.

> **CHARBONNEAU.** Well why not? I come from the old French-Canadian stock.

> **DOMINICAN.** You allow yourself to be governed too much by your heart and your emotions.[12]

To add to this portrait, on four occasions the author insists on the strong French-Canadian accent of the protagonists, especially in the case of the union head René La Roche, his wife, and, finally, Le Chef.

The dialogue, in Standard English without markers of orality, is generously seasoned with borrowings from the French, imbuing the text with a strong ethnographic flavour.

The 1974 adaptation by Hébert and Morency published by Éditions Leméac thoroughly reworked the text: complete scenes were deleted and others added or combined, while dialogue was cut, expanded, or redistributed, and new characters were added. The play has actually been rewritten, leaving only the central subject matter and the basic structure. As in the original, the action still unfolds in Asbestos and Montreal, which indicates that the adaptation did not affect the spatial or temporal axes. There was, in fact, no need to relocate the action, which was already situated within the boundaries of Quebec. The publication was fleshed out with numerous photographs taken from the 1971, 1972, and 1973 productions.

The introduction that appears in this 1974 publication mentions the playwright's name without providing any information about him. The designation "translation and adaptation" constitutes the only indication of a translative strategy. This is followed by the date and place of the first production and the revivals in 1972 and 1973, accompanied by a list of the characters and all those who contributed to the productions. The list of the characters varies from one production to the other, which indicates that revisions were made along the way. What is surprising, however, is the disparity between the number of characters in the translated version and in the original play. In the 1971 production, there are twenty-five characters, not including the extras representing the strikers or the police, whereas the original contained but ten. These new characters include Jean Marchand, general secretary of the Confédération des travailleurs catholiques du Canada; Pierre Laporte, a journalist with the newspaper Le Devoir; L'abbé Camirand, the union's chaplain, who replaces the Dominican, Georges-Henri Lévesque, found in the original; lastly, several extras in the original, strikers, police officers, and journalists, have been transformed into secondary roles in the translation, including Paquet, Rainville, Ruel, O'Brien, Ti-Rouge, Rosaire, M. Gagnon, Marcoux, Drouin, Latendresse, and Jean Thivierge. The translation also contains a new element that remains unmentioned in the list of the characters: a narrator's voice that informs the audience of what was originally intended for the reader in the introduction and before the last scene.

On the macrostructural level, the introduction found in the original has been combined with the prologue to the first scene and is read by the narrator. The acts have been stripped of their titles and subtitles, and the play has been restructured into two acts consisting of six and seven scenes respectively. Many of the stage directions have been deleted, as has the beginning of each scene that describes the historical situation. The following analysis details the most prominent changes.

In the introduction that has been transformed into a narration, McDonough comments on his choice of subject matter and how it is developed in the play. Where he sees this historic event as a tragedy that "engaged the consciences of all the people of Canada," the translated version envisions a drama "qui engagea la conscience de tous les Canadiens français"; where the author views the object of the play as "to awaken the Canadian conscience to its own poetry and drama," the translators want to "inciter les Québécois à prendre conscience de leur propre drame et de leur propre poésie."[13] As a result, the translation has the author addressing the people of Quebec exclusively. A part of the prologue to the first act, with its first scene deleted, is grafted onto this narration.

The second scene is retained. This scene features Le Chef and Mr. McDonald, the director of Johns Manville, the American company that runs the mine in Asbestos. Folkloric or overly pious scenes are deleted, such as the one in which, at the sound of the Angelus bell, Le Chef removes his hat, kneels, and recites a prayer. The translation adopts a more direct tone, less descriptive than the original text, and the dialogue is limited to what is strictly applicable to the situation. The lines are shortened, the pace is quickened, and Le Chef's cynicism is accentuated.

The following scene is a creation of the translators, who present the strikers gathered around Jean Marchand to discuss working conditions before deciding to go on strike. The third scene retains elements of the initial version that are substantially expanded. Emphasis is placed on the fact that academics, much like the clergy, opposed Le Chef's methods, while an unflattering reference to Camillien Houde, then mayor of

Montreal, is deleted. In the next scene, wherein the police confront the strikers in a brutal conflict that ends in a burst of machine-gun fire, the translation tempers the brutality of the situation. As was previously the case with the deletion of the radio broadcast describing the deployment of the police force in Asbestos and the violence of the ensuing confrontations, the scene where the recently arrested La Roche is savagely beaten has been deleted, as has the scene in which the pregnant Simone is brutally manhandled by the police and risks losing the child she is carrying. The translators add a reference to the presence of Pierre Elliott Trudeau and Gérard Pelletier in Asbestos in the subsequent scene wherein the union's chaplain meets Monsignor Charbonneau and informs him of the situation. Finally, in the last scene of the first act, there is a softening in the tone and in the reproaches that Monsignor Charbonneau directs towards the government and the foreign employers from the height of his pulpit. Then, the last scene of the first act in the original is deleted, the one in which the strikers, delighted with how things have turned out, sing "Auprès de ma blonde."

The second act opens with the confrontation between the bishop of Montreal and the bishop of Rimouski, Monsignor Courchesne, who frowns upon the position adopted by his colleague, accuses him of heresy and threatens to denounce him to the pope. Here again, the tone is less violent than in the original. Where Charbonneau foresees "a violent rebellion" of the Québécois society, the translation refers to "de grands bouleversements."[14] The reference to some of the church's privileges that the bishop of Rimouski would like to protect at any price is also tempered: "If our government ever begins to tax our Church properties, all is lost" becomes "Qu'allons-nous devenir si les octrois accordés à nos institutions sont coupés?"[15]

The second scene of the original text has been deleted. In this scene, the Dominican priest gives us a guided tour of Quebec City's Avenue Grande-Allée, during which he delivers the following remark: "Perhaps the British victory was providential....Under British rule, our people were able to preserve their identity. What would have happened to us under Napoleon or George Washington?"[16] The scenes that follow portray Monsignor Charbonneau in discussions with the haunting image of Le Chef and subsequently present us with the press conference organized by Duplessis to describe the settlement of the strike. In the translation, this scene includes specific references to the allegiance of certain news-papers, including *Le Soleil*, *L'Action catholique*, and especially *Le Devoir*, which Le Chef cheerfully castigates and describes as "communiste." The next scene to be deleted is the one in which Monsignor Charbonneau is about to leave on a hunting trip when Father Lévesque informs him of the intrigues targeting him and bids him to travel to Rome to defend his cause at the Vatican.

In the following scene, Le Chef expresses his support for the bishop of Rimouski, to whom he proposes that the state finance his trip to Rome to denounce Monsignor Charbonneau to the pope. Finally, the last scene of the adaptation is drawn from the first scene of the third act of the original, wherein Monsignor Charbonneau is compelled by the pope to resign and is exiled to Victoria. Thus, the second scene of this final act, where La Roche questions his attachment to a church that mistreats someone like Monsignor Charbonneau, is deleted, as is the epilogue that portrays a widely popular, recently elected Duplessis.

Amongst the numerous modifications to the original play carried out by the translators, it seems that the author was most vehemently opposed to the deletion of this epilogue. In Lawrence Sabbath's *Montreal Star* article on the adapted version of the play, McDonough remarked, "The epilogue is symbolic. It's my way of saying the public re-elected him in 1952 with one of the greatest majorities in Quebec his-tory, despite what he did to Charbonneau and what he tried to do to the workers and unions. I guess the epilogue cuts too close to the bone. But what is drama if it doesn't? I meant it to cut close to the bone."[17] In this same article McDonough deplored the fact that "the radio play was stronger than the French stage play" and offered up this remark on the translators' approach: "I guess M. Hébert didn't want to offend any Quebec sensibilities."[18] In effect, the adaptation attests to a desire to spare the concerned parties, particularly the government, the police forces, and certain ecclesiastics, and to modify the dramatic struc-ture of the text. Governed by a search for acceptibility, the translation retains the original subject matter but profoundly changes the play in order to utilize dramatic methods deemed more efficient and more per-tinent within the receptive context. Furthermore, the subject matter could not be better suited to the Québécois public; after all, the play presents a page from Quebec's own history. However, beyond the formal modifications and attenuated tone, there must also be a discursive appropriation of the play. This is achieved by eliminating the folkloric commentary on nature, the remarks on the advantages of the British conquest for French-Canadian survival, and the emotion "toute québécoise"; these elements do not correspond to what was at the time the dominant social discourse in Quebec. The October Crisis had just brutally brought an end to the Quiet Revolution, and the Québécois were seeking an identity free from a colonial past and anglophone domination. This explains why the producers and the francophone journalists do not dwell upon the play's origins or on the irony that one of Quebec drama's greatest successes was borrowed from the English-Canadian repertoire.

Finally, in order to correspond to the linguistic norm favouring the use of *joual* on the Québécois stages of the day, the standard language of the original is replaced with a colloquial level of language that bears more pronounced markers of orality in the dialogue of Le Chef, the strikers, and the police, as can be seen in the following excerpts from the original and the translated versions, in which the markers of the colloquial language are underlined.

LA ROCHE. (*Solemn*) Take care, gentlemen, take care...that could have grave consequences for the town of Asbestos.

LE CHEF. (*Rising on his toes, his fists in the air*) Is that a threat?

LA ROCHE. We are French Canadians...we will defend our homes and our jobs. (*They stare at each other*)

LE CHEF. (*Suddenly, with anger in his voice*) I am the Prime Minister of Quebec, I will defend the rights of the people and the laws of the people from the illegalities of your crazy strike.

LA ROCHE. (*Calm*) Our union is holding a meeting tonight, in front of the Parish Church, Saint Aimée. (*He points to the Church*) If you free me, I will tell the others what you have in mind.

LE CHEF. (*Rapidly*) You are free to go. But remember (*He shakes his long finger in La Roche's face*), remember, La Roche, I will not tolerate any violence or scorn of the laws. <u>You</u> be sure to tell that to your comrades, <u>you hear</u>! Otherwise I will throw <u>the lot of</u> you in jail. I mean it, I mean it, I mean it.[19]

◊◊◊

LAROCHE. <u>Moé</u>, à <u>vot'</u>place, <u>j'frais</u> attention à mes paroles, Monsieur.

DIRECTEUR. Pourquoi?

LAROCHE. Vous parlez des <u>scabs, hein</u>? Ça pourrait avoir des conséquences pas mal graves pour la ville d'Asbestos.

LE CHEF. <u>C'est-y</u> une menace ça, Laroche?

LAROCHE. On est des Canadiens français, on va défendre nos foyers et nos <u>jobs...au coton</u>...

LE CHEF. (*En colère*) Moi, <u>j'suis</u> le Premier Ministre <u>d'la</u> province, <u>mon gars, pis j'vas</u> défendre les droits du peuple, <u>j'vas</u> défendre les lois du citoyen contre l'illégalité <u>pis</u> contre vos maudites grèves de fous! Vous avez une assemblée <u>à</u> soir?

LAROCHE. <u>Ouais</u>, on <u>d'vait</u> se réunir...

LE CHEF. Avertis ta <u>gang</u>, sans oublier ton aumônier, que le mépris des lois, <u>j'tolère</u> pas ça!

LAROCHE. Mais monsieur, <u>comment que j'vas leu</u> dire ça? <u>Chus</u> arrêté.

LE CHEF. <u>T'es</u> libéré! Envoye! (*Laroche ne bouge pas.*) Envoye! <u>Scram!</u> <u>Pis t'es</u> mieux de dire tout ça à tes amis, compris! Autrement, je <u>sacre</u> tout <u>l'monde</u> en prison![20]

Here, as in the previous play, *Aux yeux des hommes*, the borrowed text addresses the collective Québécois conscience and is reflective of its own image. Nevertheless, there was a need to modify certain discursive codes that were deemed inacceptable for the target audience, one of which was the criticism contained in the epilogue to the original. Though the level of language has generally been lowered, the clerics continue to employ a standard language, while elisions and familiar turns of phrase inserted into Le Chef's dialogue, and rendered slightly more pronounced in the case of the strikers and the police, are sufficient to endow them with local colour. It is left to the actors to decide whether to accentuate this identifying detail. Thus, one observes here a hierarchical organization of language levels according to the protagonists' social rank, with the evident exception of a "Chef" whose contempt for decorum was legendary.

In this period of theatrical revival, considerable creative enthusiasm was exhibited in translations whose function was not to represent the other, but rather oneself through a medium that played a leading role in the affirmation of a specific identity. Accordingly, the trend towards adaptation would sweep through the 1970s and the 1980s, at the end of which the systematic recourse to this mode of translation in Quebec would be questioned. The next work to be analyzed implements another variation on adaptation. This play is David Freeman's *Battering Ram* presented in January 1984 at Montreal's Théâtre d'Aujourd'hui.

Freeman and *Le bélier*, Revised and Corrected

Freeman, a Toronto playwright with cerebral palsy, became famous with the 1971 production of his play *Creeps* at Toronto's Factory Theatre. Presented off Broadway in New York in 1973, the play received a Chalmers Award and a New York Drama Desk Award then toured Canada, the United States, and Great Britain. Ten years later in April 1981, *Les tout-croches*, Louison Danis and Pierre Collin's Québécois version of the play, enjoyed a successful run in Montreal's Salle Fred-Barry. In this translation of a play featuring disabled young people unhappy with the treatment they receive and confronting their dreams and ambitions, the sociocultural references and the characters' names have been transposed into a Québécois context, and there is nothing that reveals the English-Canadian origin of the text.

The Québécois adaptation of the second of Freeman's plays, *Battering Ram*, produced in workshop at the Factory Theatre Lab in Toronto in 1972 before being mounted in a revised version in 1973 at the Tarragon Theatre, was also translated by Louison Danis under the title *Le bélier.* It was presented at the Théâtre d'Aujourd'hui in January 1984, twelve years after it first appeared in English. On that occasion, Freeman, who had relocated to Quebec in 1976, was described as an "auteur anglo-montréalais" in the newspaper *La Presse*, where the critic praised the quality of an adaptation that manages to leave the spectator with "la conviction d'assister à une véritable création originale."[21]

It must be noted that the production did in fact resemble an original creation as the author was asked to rewrite the text by including a number of changes. Danis then translated a text that had been previously revised and corrected by the playwright, which means that many of the changes could have occurred before the translation. Whatever the case, these changes are representative of the constraints inherent in the play's target context. According to Marie Laurier of *Le Devoir*, the translator acquitted herself "avec beaucoup de succès, en québécisant le langage, en insérant nos jurons dans les répliques parfois intempestives et dures des comédiens. Et cela passe bien."[22] Despite her laudatory review, Laurier had one reservation concerning "la fin heureuse de la pièce, qui arrive de façon un peu trop abrupte, dans une espèce de hâte d'en finir avec cet imbroglio où la mère, la fille et l'infirme, après avoir connu de violents affrontements, redeviennent tout doux et tout miel pour continuer leur vie commune."[23] This allusion to the play's happy ending is enough to surprise anyone familiar with the original, given that it involves a major change in the translated text, as we will see later.

After the Playwrights Co-op reissued the play in 1972 and 1973 in editions that included the changes made to the text during the productions at the Factory Theatre Lab and at the Tarragon Theatre, a definitive version of the text was published by Talonbooks in 1974 following a production at Vancouver's Arts Club Theatre that same year. This edition, which is the one we will analyze, begins by listing the previous productions, the theatres and the artists who were involved in them, and provides a short description of the scenography. The text is naturalistic, as were its earlier versions, and is divided into two acts, which contain four and two scenes respectively. The spelling of the informal level of language in use occasionally reproduces the elisions of oral language.

The first act in this version introduces Irene, a woman in her forties who is volunteering in a residence for the disabled and informs her seventeen-year-old daughter, Nora, that she has invited Virgil, a paraplegic, to come and live with them after he threatened to commit suicide. We will later sense that this act of charity also furthers Irene's sexual interest in the young man. Wanting to prove his virility, Virgil first attempts to seduce Nora, but is rebuffed. He then turns to Irene, who desperately attempts to monopolize his attention, and they end up sleeping together. In the second act, we discover that Virgil has not abandoned the idea of seducing Nora. He almost succeeds before being interrupted by the arrival of Irene, who is furious and throws him out of the house. However, as the young man points out, he doesn't leave without having experienced the sexual adventure they were both seeking.

The Québécois adaptation remains unpublished, but a manuscript version has been submitted to the library at the National Theatre School, and this is the version that will be analyzed. Although any last minute changes may be missing, it is nonetheless representative of the processes deemed necessary for the adaptation.

In this version, the period of time in which the play is set remains the same, but it now takes place within the context of Quebec. Consequently, the names have been modified: Corinne (Irene) and her daughter Laura (Nora) open their door to Gabriel (Virgil), who has just left the Ville-Joie (Sunnyville) residence where Dr. Grisé (Griffin) works. Corinne's favourite movie star, Glenn Ford, gives way to Jean Gabin, and the American actor Kirk Douglas, who is alluded to in the play, is dislodged by Jean-Paul Belmondo, a favourite with all audiences, including those for Van Burek and Glassco's *Les Belles-Soeurs*. The allusions to "Buckingham Palace" and the "Royal Winnipeg Ballet" are deleted, and the play's origins are never revealed. The characters speak a Franco-Québécois vernacular that exhibits very pronounced markers of orality in the spelling. So, without specifying the exact site where the action unfolds, the translation has replaced any onomastic, toponymic, and sociocultural marks indicative of English with references that encourage an audience to situate the play in their own context.

On the level of preliminary data, both the translated and the original titles are provided, as are the names of the author and the translator-adapter, as well as a description of the set and the action. The first scene is significantly reworked, and in it we discover Corinne doing aerobic exercises. Although this activity is completely absent in the English text, the translation finds her doing it regularly, sometimes in the most absurd fashion; in one scene, for example, we surprise her training in the middle of the night with a flashlight in her hand after trying in vain to exercise in the closet during the day so as not to bother her guest. These aerobic workouts, while further underlying the young man's disability, seem chiefly intended to inject a comic element into a play that the translation aims to turn into a tragicomedy. So, gleefully gesticulating, Corinne announces Gabriel's imminent arrival to her daughter Laura, who reacts to this intrusion with an ironic petulance that the translated version turns into sarcasm. Right after her mother introduces her to Gabriel, she says, "Pis! Ça t'amusait pas, la foire aux infirmes."[24] Later, in a line added to the translated text in which Gabriel asks her to help him take off his boots, she answers, "T'es t'un cas d'bonne à plein temps, toi! C'tait qui ton esclave l'an passé?"[25] From the very beginning of the translation, then, through the introduction of comic effects, the relationship between the characters is presented as being much more aggressive and conflictual in nature than in the original. This is comedy that accentuates the violence and critical content in the dialogue. This type of sarcastic comedy also involves an accentuation of the vernacular and of the language's vulgarity.

In the following dialogue, Laura gives into Gabriel's entreaties to attend a modern dance recital in which she will participate. As this scene is the one that most nearly reproduces the original play, it is possible to compare the levels of language attributed to the same dialogue in each version.

IRENE. You know, you sound just like my husband, (VIRGIL *throws his hands in the air in disgust.*) Always putting the onus on me. Always trying to get me to make the decisions for him, and then if things turned out wrong, he'd always blame me.[26]

◇◇◇

CORINNE. Sais-tu quoi? Plus j't'écoute, plus tu m'rappelles
mon mari.

(GABRIEL, *exaspéré, lève les bras au ciel.*) Y m'mettait toute su l'dos.
Tout l'temps. Y voulait que j'prenne toutes ses décisions pour lui.
Pis après, si ça virait mal, y blâmait toujours ça su'moi.[27]

There is an evident lowering of the level of language when it comes to
the vocabulary, syntax, and grammar, as well as a systematic recourse
to the elisions of spoken language.

The third scene is completely reworked. On their return from
rehearsal, a violent argument erupts between Laura and Gabriel while
Corinne is hidden in the kitchen, "d'où elle écoute derrière la porte."[28]
Here again, a comic element has been added to the translated version.
The beginning of this scene is joined to the fourth scene of the original
text and the intervening text is deleted. Then, the end of the first act
and all of the second act of the English play, which ends with Virgil's
departure, are compressed in order to end the first act of the translated
version with a new scene in which Laura is sexually assaulted after she
has provoked Gabriel.

The second act is completely new. It depicts Corinne doing her
utmost to please Gabriel, who has become her lover. Fussing over the
young man, she is not overly concerned about her daughter's depres-
sive tendency, which leads a critic to comment that she appears to "lui
soutirer sa fille, en prime."[29] The tension increases between the daughter, the mother, and her lover, and, several weeks later, Laura informs
them that she is about to move out. Corinne then tries to get Gabriel to
leave, but he refuses. Laura dares him to kill himself, since he threatens to do so each time that events do not work out the way he wants,
but he is unable to do it. In what appears to be a strategy developed
by Corinne and Laura to get rid of him, Gabriel agrees to temporarily
move out to give them time to sell the house and buy a more spacious
one in which the three of them can live together harmoniously. If one is
to believe Laurier's review, the play's staging has approached this last
scene as a "happy ending" rather than a sly betrayal to get rid of Gabriel,

who is no longer welcome. Whatever the case, this ambivalent ending is a clear departure from the resolution of the conflict in the original. Furthermore, in this additional second act, there is a greater insistence on Gabriel's manipulation and blackmail of the two women, which results in increasing the rift between the mother and the daughter.

The adaptation thus appears to be largely governed by a search for acceptability aimed at presenting the play as a local product in which the theatricality has been linguistically and textually enhanced. To accomplish this, the rewritten play strives to intensify the dramatic effects by combining an almost farcical comedy with a heightened verbal and gestural violence. The combination is then delivered in a vernacular that is hardly lacking in vulgarity. To endow the characters like this with an excessively Quebecicized spoken vernacular, their social status had to be slightly lowered. As Annie Brisset suggests, the need to use a distinct Québécois French as a stage language requires a proletarianization of the protagonists: "la representation théâtrale de la québécité passe par un abaissement social des protagonists de l'oeuvre originale."[30]

Commenting on her choice to utilize a markedly vernacular spoken language, Danis describes her way to translate thus: "Comme je fais de la traduction contemporaine, je le fais dans le langage qu'on entend dans la rue....Je suis d'ailleurs un peu allergique au langage ampoulé, à cette langue qui ne se dit pas. J'adore lire, mais j'ai horreur, quand je joue, de réciter....Il y a dix ou quinze ans, j'ai l'impression que la hantise que la traduction d'ici soit comparée à celle d'ailleurs faisait qu'on traduisait de façon littéraire."[31] The translator and actor expresses her aversion to the former norm of promoting the use of normative French as a stage language and her preference for the language "qu'on entend dans la rue." This linguistic position is certainly apparent in the translation of Freeman's text and explains the accentuation of the markers of orality present in the adaptation.

Faced with a text so extensively altered, one wonders why this play was borrowed. What this translation essentially retains from the original is a situation involving a disabled young man and the people around him, a theme that Freeman brought to Canadian stages with *Creeps* and one that had yet to be explored within the Québécois drama repertoire. Thus, it is the newness of the text's subject matter that is of interest, but this novelty must be adapted to the linguistic and dramatic codes of the target context. Moreover, this novel subject matter does not clash with any dominant discursive code. On the contrary, at a time of increased awareness to what were once hidden realities, the play's theme is looked upon favourably. Besides, in the uncertain time that followed the 1980 referendum, it was easy to identify with a disadvantaged hero who refuses to be brought down by his disability. The play thus reveals a reality that is easily rendered Québécois while exploring an appealing new theme at a time when the theatre had lost its nationalist drive and was looking to invest in new discursive areas.

The post-1980-referendum period was gloomy, and the public needed cheering up. Comedy enjoyed a certain popularity, which grew to the point of becoming a veritable industry within the performing arts in Quebec. Comedies were then borrowed from the English-Canadian repertoire, including Bernard Slade's *Chapeau* and *Deux à dos*, which were produced in 1981 and 1982–1983 respectively, followed by John Palmer's *Hystérie bleu banane* in 1983. Subsequently, four of Norm Foster's comedies were translated, one of which, *The Melville Boys*, had enjoyed enormous success in 1984. The Québécois version of this play, presented in Hull in 1989, is the next translation to be analyzed.

Foster or Comedy at Any Price

Foster's plays *Sinners* and *The Melville Boys* were created at Theatre New Brunswick in Fredericton in 1983 and 1984 respectively. These comedies were enormously successful on Canadian stages, where the latter gave rise to more than twenty productions that took the play from Fredericton to Victoria between 1984 and 1988. Québécois versions of the two texts were subsequently presented at Hull's Théâtre de l'Île in 1989. The first was translated by Robert Marinier under the title *Péché mortel*, while the second, *Les frères Mainville*, was the work of Paul Latreille. Two of Foster's other plays were translated by Josée Labossière and presented at the same theatre in 1992 and 1994: *L'amour compte double* from *The Affections of May*, created at Theatre New Brunswick in 1990, and *Une chance sur un million* from *Wrong for Each Other*, created at the same theatre in 1993. With these last two plays, the gap in time

between the creation and the translation had considerably narrowed—
a case of hastening to produce a successful playwright for an audience
that had embraced him.

Following the initial success of the comedy *Péché mortel*, Foster
once again graced the stage of the Théâtre de l'Île in 1989 with a new
play, *Les frères Mainville*, which, like those previously examined, was
decidedly naturalistic. Latreille's "juste et sensible"[32] translation in
which he "captures all the nuances of the original and transposes it
to a Quebec context with a delicate touch" was extolled in a production whose premiere "was one of those magical evenings that happen
all too rarely."[33] When Colette Godin of the magazine ARTicles asked
the theatre's artistic director, Gilles Provost, who also directed the
play, "s'il y a eu adaptation de la pièce pour la rendre plus accessible au
public francophone," he replied that "cela n'a pas été nécessaire."[34] He
went on to explain: "Lorsque j'ai reçu le texte, j'ai trouvé que cela cou-
lait de source...le milieu ouvrier qui y est décrit existe aussi au Québec,
le contexte est familier."[35] In the manuscript version available at the
National Theatre School library, which serves as the basis for this analysis, the play is described as the French version and a translation. There
is, however, no other indication of a translative strategy. This manuscript version's two preliminary pages provide the play's original title,
the name of the author and the translator, as well as information concerning the Québécois production and the producer. It also mentions
that Foster wrote *Péché mortel*, but there is no other information on the
original play or its creation.

On the macrostructural level, the characters' names have been
Gallicized, their descriptions retained, and the indication that the two
brothers "smoke throughout the action" has been deleted. The characters have been renamed Léo Mainville (Lee Melville), Yvon Mainville
(Owen Melville), Marie (Mary), and Simone (Loretta). The extensive
description of the set and the play's division into two acts, containing
three and two scenes respectively, remain the same. To clarify the setting, the translation contains a floor plan of the inside of the cabin in
which the action takes place. The cabin in question belongs to "mononc'
Thomas" and "matante Rose."[36] The two brothers spend several days in
the country at this cabin. Leo, the eldest, would like to use this *tête-
à-tête* to discuss certain things with his younger brother Yvon, who is

rather childish. Set on enjoying himself and avoiding any serious conversations, Yvon invites Marie and Simone to join them, much to Leo's displeasure. However, the latter finds Marie to be an attentive and compassionate listener when he reveals to her that he has been stricken with cancer. After an eventful night, the two men end up broaching the subject that Yvon has been trying at all costs to avoid: Leo's imminent death. The two brothers assess the situation and decide that together they will be able to face the dreadful reality.

Although there is no exact mention of where the play takes place, the microstructural analysis reveals that there has been a Quebecicization of the sociocultural and toponymic references in the play. Thus, the factory "Hudson Plastic," where the Mainville brothers work, is renamed "Bellehumeur Plastique," and the K-Mart hardware stores are replaced by their Québécois counterparts, "Pascal pis Rona."[37] Simone, an aspiring actress who "acte dans les annonces à la television," imitates her performance in a commercial for "Chez Roger Latourelle Voitures Usagées: l'aut'bord d'la track sur Saint-Jean Baptiste, en face du 'Drumstick and Doughnut' et à côté de Fern Patate,"[38] whereas the source text indicates "Harry Farmer's Used Car Showroom. Just below the tracks on St. Charles."[39] Not only is there an onomastic and toponymic repatriation of the location here, one also notes the effect of a "universal of translational behaviour," which states that the necessity to transpose triggers the addition of further commentary by the translator. The modification of the name and location of the original site to transpose it to Quebec also presents an opportune moment to add jokes to the comedy or additional remarks aimed at creating laughter. Accordingly, numerous passages of this Foster comedy are enlarged, accentuated, or explained, and privileged themes emerge from these substitutions.

In the excerpt quoted above, there is a discernible comic effect obtained through juxtaposing evocative French and English names. This comic effect through the juxtaposition of linguistic codes, resulting from different languages or different levels of language, is very popular within a bilingual context, especially in border regions where francophone minorities are exposed to an intense "traffic" in languages. Various juxtapositions of French and English codes, which go beyond the current usage of Anglicisms, were added to the text, as illustrated by the following excerpt where Simone re-enacts her role in this particular commercial.

> **SIMONE.** Bonjour! Ici Simone Simonet chez Roger Latourelle Voitures Usagées. (*À part, à Yvon*) Simonet, c'est pas mon vrai nom, c'est Roger qui trouvait que ça faisait plusse "showbiz."

> **YVON.** Ah, j'comprends—ça fait très sexé.[40]

Here is the English version of this excerpt:

> **LORETTA.** This is Loretta Starr, for Harry Farmer's Used Car Showroom. (*To Owen*) Starr isn't my real name. Harry thinks it sounds better.

> **OWEN.** I like it. Sounds great.[41]

Several strategies accentuate the comic effects in this instance. To begin with, the choice was made not to translate literally the family name of the aspiring young actress, who could easily have been named Simone Star or Simone L'Étoile, and this loss is compensated for by the reference to "showbiz." This results in a juxtaposition of linguistic codes that is even funnier, as the name Simone Simonet alludes to a French actress, Simone Signoret, who is known for her roles in prominent dramatic films that have become classics of French cinema. Therefore, the reference to "showbiz" and to the sexy nature of her name is completely misplaced and constitutes an addition to the original message. This is an example of a highly efficient operation in which there is a superimposition of several translative processes aimed at creating the maximum comic effect. This intention is apparent throughout the text and motivates several translative choices.

Another isotopy at work in the modifications made to the text proposes a critique of the translations that appear on Québécois television. When, in the English version, Owen answers his brother, "(*with his best John Wayne voice*) I've been out checkin' the grounds, cap'n," the translation has Yvon reply, "(*imitant une mauvaise post-synchro de John Wayne*) J'inspectais les lieux, mec!"[42] The use of this last term, "mec," which strays from the military vocabulary to borrow from French slang clearly indicates that the poor translation is French and not Québécois. This criticism, triggered by the transposition, is continued several pages further on when Yvon enters the cabin where his brother is waiting for him and says, "(*Imitant une mauvaise post-synchro de Robert Young dans* Papa a raison) C'est moi, chérie!"[43] In the English version, Owen's line, "Honey, I'm home!" appears without any stage direction.[44] The need to intervene in the text in order to transpose the action allows for the addition of critical comments concerning a situation that is frowned upon in Quebec: the French monopoly in the dubbing of American television series.

Other additions allude to certain Québécois cultural products, which are also criticized, as in the following line where Simone observes the two brothers arguing and exclaims, "Heille, c'est l'fonne ça. Pareil comme un bon téléroman cheap"; the original text reads, "Oh, they're really going at it!"[45] In the same way, the dream that Lee harbours to play "professional football one day...in one of those big stadiums" is adapted to a more typically Québécois reality and becomes, "j'ai toujours pensé que j'pourrais jouer au hockey un jour—j'veux dire dans la ligue nationale...au forum."[46]

However, the most consistent contribution to situating the play within the context of Quebec is the constant recourse to the idioms borrowed from the Québécois vernacular that recur throughout the text. Here are some examples: "veux-tu bein m'dire," "C'est bein simple," "J't'aussi bin," "Ça, c'est l'boutte," "M'a te dire quèque chose moé," "mes snaurauds," "Ah bein, ça parle au yabbe!" "enwoye donc," "pour l'amour du bon yeu?" "Heille...menute," "Ben, c'est quoi d'abord," "M'a t'dire une affaire, moi," "Et pis j'te gage que," "Quelle affaire que t'as à...," "en train de nous monter un bateau," "C'tait déjà assez plate," "Je l'sais-tu moé?" "envoye don'," "Attends-menute, là," "Bein, 'garde don' ça," "Bein, laisse-moi te dire une affaire, bonhomme," "au plus sacrant," "y'a pas d'danger," "c'est ça, han?" "Bon, bein," "Bein quiens," "P'is à part de ça," "T'es malade, cou'don," "Bein voyons don'," and "P'is m'a t'dire un' aut' affaire."[47] These numerous regional expressions display the varied spelling of words such as "bien," that is written as "bein," "ben," or "bin," and "puis," which results in "pis" ou "p'is." The exclamation "hein" also appears as "han," and the expression "enwoye donc" later on becomes "envoye don.'" Similarly, we find "ici" and "icitte," "contre-maître" and "forman," "jobbe" and "job," and "fun" and "fonne."[48] This lack of cohesion in the spelling of the regional expressions attests to a very pronounced oralization.

Throughout the text, the language and the cultural or topnymic references have been adapted to the context of Quebec, except when it comes to a trip to Disneyland. Whereas the translation eliminates the line in which Lee explains to his brother his wish to travel and take his family to Disneyland before he dies, a little further on, it retains his brother's line in which he answers, "C'est ça qu'i' t'as dit d'faire ton médecin? D'aller à Disneyland?"[49] The urge to remove any reference to a context outside of Quebec results in an incoherence in the translation project, since Yvon can hardly comment on a trip he has never heard about and that has never been mentioned in the text.

As was the case in Le bélier, there is a pronounced oralization in the spelling, which contains numerous elisions and words in dialect in conjunction with a lowering of the level of language. Comic linguis-tic effects are accentuated and new ones formed through frequent recourse to decidedly familiar expressions. For example, when Yvon utters an unpleasant remark about an elderly lady, unaware that she is the mother of the two women, he says, "j'pense qu'è't'un peu Alzheimer," where the original reads, "I think her mind's starting to go."[50] Or again, "eat all day" is translated as "se bourrer 'a face à longueur de journée," and "that stupid boat" is translated as "c'te crisse de chaloupe."[51] Most of the excerpts already cited attest to this lowering of the language and the frequent recourse to decidedly vernacular expressions.

Lastly, several deletions occur when a line, most often a joke, con-stitutes an insurmountable difficulty for the translation. For example, the underlined passage in the following excerpt is cut. Owen is answer-ing Lee who suggests that he take night courses after his wedding: "And when am I supposed to see Patty? I mean, I'd say 'I do' at the wedding, and then I never would."[52] Lines deemed unnecessary are also cut, as is the case for the underlined sentence in this example of Owen's dia-logue: "Yeah. She said she had a good time last night. And, she said to tell you she was going to buy a new car."[53]

The analysis of this translation reveals that, just like the other plays studied, Foster's comedy is completely transposed to Quebec and never once betrays its origins. However, this version is not described as an "adaptation," which demonstrates the semantic vagueness of the term, since the strategies utilized in the transposition of this play do not differ from those at work in the preceding versions that are described as adaptations. It must be noted that the play was presented in 1989, at a time when the systematic use of adaptation was being challenged. As Jean-Luc Denis observed in 1990, "L'adaptation n'est pas en soi quelque chose d'illégitime; c'est lorsqu'elle est érigée en système qu'elle fait problème....Elle doit être reléguée le plus vite possible au territoire qu'elle n'aurait jamais dû quitter: celui du phénomène épisodique."[54]

Foster's text is characterized by a search for maximal comic effects that results in an "overtranslation" of the text. Every occasion is ripe for exaggeration, whether it be the juxtaposition of usually incompatible linguistic codes, a proletariazation of the text by means of abundant vernacular local expressions, a reworking of dialogue to include jokes, criticisms, or any other type of interjections, or an accentuation of the text's existing comic effects. If the translation project at work is to create laughter at any price, one can only conclude: mission accomplished.

Though the linguistic codes, levels of language, and comic value of the dialogue are rearranged, the original structure of the text and its distribution are respected. In this sense, the translation approach indicates a concern for adequacy to the original text, which distinguishes this translation from that of the two previous plays and is similar to that of the first translation examined in this chapter, René Dionne's adaptation of John Herbert's text.

As the legitimacy of theatrical adaptation is questioned, the concern for adequacy is more noticeable. At the outset of the 1990s, Franco-Québécois theatre began to exhibit an openness towards English-Canadian theatre; one of the results was that, between 1990 and 1993, a record number of thirteen Anglo-Canadian plays were produced in French translation. It must be noted that English-Canadian theatre was then exploring new directions that were were far removed from the once dominant naturalistic aesthetic. Judith Thompson, who had already been praised for the audacity of the dramatic resources she brought to the stage, lead this new movement with *Je suis à toi*, the

French version of *I Am Yours*, translated by Robert Vézina and presented by Théâtre de la Manufacture in 1990 at a Montreal restaurant theatre, La Licorne.[55]

As would also be the case for the works of Brad Fraser, *Je suis à toi* is notable for its staunchly modern, nonrealistic aesthetic and flamboyant writing similar to that found in Quebec at the time. As director Claude Poissant expressed, "I am surprised she's English...Canadian English....It's like she wrote our energy...this excess, this energy, it's more Latin, it's Italian, it's more like Quebec."[56] Although it did not lead to an adaptation, this translation totally relied on *joual*, thereby eliminating the class conflict upon which the plot was based. This linguistic levelling down also affected the play's reception in Quebec, as it contributed to the "plat déterminisme" for which the playwright was criticized.[57] It should be pointed out that the choice of *joual* as the translation's only language was somewhat anachronistic at a time when dramatic writing had resolutely freed itself from this constraint. As Denis underlines, although *joual* had been a dominant norm in theatre written and translated between 1968 and the end of the 1980s, the Franco-Québécois language had considerably evolved, and, in 1990, one could say that it "parcourt aujourd'hui tout le registre des niveaux de langue."[58] Besides, from 1980 onwards, there were several explorations into an aesthetic that involved the elaboration of decidedly sophisticated stage languages, as can be seen in the preceding chapter. Perhaps this attachment to *joual* as the language for translation should be seen as an attempt to anchor the play within the receptive context at a time when adaptation had been set aside. Inasmuch as the original onomastic and toponymic references are no longer transposed, the use of a highly accentuated vernacular thus constitutes a compensatory strategy of appropriation into the Québécois context.

The setting aside of adaptation as a model and the exploration of new modes of translation continued through the borrowings of the work of an Albertan playwright who was wildly popular on the Quebec scene before the onset of scandal. The outrageous playwright in question is Brad Fraser, who provokes controversy wherever he goes and leaves no one indifferent in either English or French. Following the success of his play *Unidentified Human Remains and the True Nature of Love*, created by Alberta Theatre Projects in 1988 and produced in translation at Montreal's Théâtre de Quat'Sous in 1991, Fraser returned to Quebec in 1993 with *The Ugly Man*, the next play to be analyzed.

Fraser, English Canada's *Enfant Terrible*

Winner of the Alberta Culture Playwriting Competition in 1989 and workshopped at Alberta Theatre Projects' PlayRites in 1990, Fraser's play *The Ugly Man* was first officially produced at Calgary's Martha Cohen Theatre in February 1992. Some were caught off guard by the resolutely outrageous aesthetic of the play, which is "a cluttered, campy, sometimes startlingly funny exercise in arch schlock, a series of allusions to popular pulp fiction and B-movies juiced up by dead-pan, snappy dialogue," according to Liam Lacey of the *Globe and Mail*.[59] Despite the spectacular aspect of the play, reviews remained reserved in front of what the *Edmonton Journal*'s Liz Nicholls describes as "thin, kitschy comedy, straight of face but bent of everything else. Safely dangerous, I guess you'd say."[60]

Situated in some indeterminate time in the future, the play can be described as a horror story, bedecked with ghosts, animated skulls, magic potions, illicit sex, carnage, and blood spilled in abundance from bodies cut by knives, axes, or a chainsaw. Forest, a man with a horribly burnt face who has just found work on an extremely prosperous ranch in the West, in fact, uses a chainsaw to get rid of a prospective husband who has become troublesome for Veronica, the young woman whose virginity he has been encharged with protecting. He does, however, keep the young man's skull, after having cut up the body, and offers it to Veronica. Hungry for power and incapable of love, the young woman is seduced by the sadomasochistic sexual games to which the ugly man introduces her, and, together, they commit the most violent of acts, including a second crime intended to rid them of an inconvenient witness. As the plot unfolds, we learn that Forest is the sole survivor of a family of servants that Vernonica's father has burned alive while they slept in order to protect the secret to his fortune: drug smuggling. Finally, the truth is revealed about Forest and Veronica's crimes, and, driven by jealousy and the desire for revenge, the brother of the first victim, who has also given in to the brutal advances of the ugly man, kills the young woman, injures her lover, and prepares to chop his legs off with an axe.

The Ugly Man is the second of Fraser's plays to be presented in translation in Quebec. *Des restes humains non identifiés et la véritable nature de l'amour* had been produced at the Théâtre de Quat'Sous in 1991, in a translation by André Brassard, who also directed the play. At the time, there was praise for the appropriateness of the translation into the vernacular, which did not disorient the spectator since "la langue qu'il entendait était la sienne,"[61] despite the fact that the action took place in Edmonton and the characters all had English names. *Des restes humains non identifiés* met with a great deal of controversy-ridden critical success in Quebec, a success attributed as much to the playwright's black humour and trenchant cynicism as to the talent of translator and director Brassard.

In this translation, the references to Edmonton, where the action takes place, and to Tofield, a suburb of Edmonton, have been retained. Nevertheless, names of streets, such as "Jasper Avenue," of businesses such as "La Ronde," or of a neighbourhood, "Beverly," have been eliminated, as have cultural references such as the allusion to the television series "the Munsters," the rock group "The Village People," and the Canadian painter Danby.[62] Thus, the spectators are not bothered by allusions to an unfamiliar context and to sociocultural references that might have escaped them. In the interview provided in the appendix to the translated text, André Brassard explains that he had been tempted to transpose the action to Montreal, but the author disagreed because what was needed was "cette idée d'une ville qui a connu un essor subit, une brève exaltation, et qui a décliné ensuite."[63] In the same interview, Brassard also explains that he had to modify the distribution of the text because he wanted to get rid of the intermission and because spatial constraints prevented the presentation of parallel scenes. As we can see in the following excerpt, the French version enlists a vernacular that contains Anglicisms and elisions characteristic of the spoken language, yet it does not fall into the heavily accentuated *joual* previously favoured for translation.

DAVID. (*Seul*) C'est toujours pareil. Toujours la même chose. Au Club—toujours la même musique—toujours les mêmes faces— toujours les mêmes drinks toujours au même prix. Russ dit qu'il a déjà couché avec tout ce qui valait la peine dans la place. Rod haït toujours autant notre maudite ville. John serait donc heureux à Toronto. Moi, je joue aux machines, pis je bois toujours plus de bière.[64]

Following the resounding success of *Des restes humains non identifiés*, Fraser returned to the stage in March 1993 at the Théâtre de Quat'Sous with the play *L'homme laid*, translated by Maryse Warda and directed by Derek Goldby. The show provoked outrage. "*L'homme laid* est la pièce la plus violente, la plus vulgaire, la plus horrible que j'ai vue," wrote the critic from *La Presse*.[65] In *Le Devoir*, the play was described as a "carnaval sanguinolent...spectaculaire plus que tragique, grossière plus qu'étrange."[66] And the *Mirror* warned, "The juxtaposition of sex and violence in the piece is such that if you wish to survive the evening you better check your PC [politically correct] sensibilities at the door."[67] Be that as it may, the production enjoyed a scandal-ridden success. According to the review in *Voir*, the show is "tout sauf ennuyant" inasmuch as it lapses into "une surenchère de sexe, de violence et d'horreur digne des films les plus sensationnalistes."[68]

The Québécois version of the play was published by Éditions Boréal in 1993 at the same time as the original. This translation was done from the 1989 manuscript version,[69] which was also used for the production at Calgary's Martha Cohen Theatre in February 1992. Some minor revisions were made to this version when the play was published in 1993 by NeWest Press, a publication that included essays by Paula Simons and Gerry Potter. This is, therefore, a text that attracted a great deal of critical attention in its original incarnation. In Quebec, the alacrity with which Fraser's second play was published attests to the privileged position he occupied within the target system. He's a first-rate playwright who exhibits an extremely original model of writing. In a frenzied succession of very brief scenes, scathing repartee is marked with a black humour that leans increasingly towards the "camp." A phenomenon described by a neologism, "camp" could be defined as a semiotic system originating in homosexual culture, where a statement most often serving to glorify the character is arbitrarily injected into the discourse.[70] It's a hard-hitting style that calls upon often unfamiliar references, a style that Fraser further refined in his play *Poor Super Man*.

The back cover of the published edition of *L'homme laid* presents the playwright as "l'enfant terrible de 'l'establishment' théâtral canadien" and offers a brief summary of the play. The preliminary pages provide the translated title, the names of the playwright and the translator, and the dedication that accompanied the original, as well as information concerning the Québécois production. Yet, there is no mention of the original creation. The preliminary pages also provide a description of the characters and the set, which is also borrowed from the manuscript version of the original. There is also a section entitled "Dossier" annexed to the end of the volume that contains an essay by Robert Claing that stems from a meeting with the director Derek Golby. The translation remains faithful to the structure of the source text with its forty-five scenes and retains the original names of all the characters. There is, however, no indication of where the action is situated or of any translative strategies adopted.

While the only references to location in the original play refer to the cardinal points that situate the action in a rather vague "west,"[71] the translation stipulates that it is the Canadian West. It must be noted that since the success of *Des restes humains non identifiés*, not only were English-Canadian plays more readily borrowed, but even the origins of the borrowed text were underlined. Thus, in the essay included in the published version of *L'homme laid*, Claing locates the play in "l'enfer des plaines de l'Ouest canadien,"[72] and the program that accompanies the production states that "la dramaturgie contemporaine canadienne-anglaise suscite de plus en plus d'intérêt dans le milieu théâtral québécois." In *Poor Super Man*, a third Brad Fraser play that was presented in translation in 1995 at the Théâtre de Quat'Sous, not only do the original character names and the site of the action, namely Calgary, remain the same, but the original English title is also retained. Although borrowing the name of the famous comic strip character was necessary, the adjective could have easily been translated into French. This is a recurrence of the strategy previously observed in the translations of Michel Tremblay's plays into English, where the recourse to the calque results in accentuating the origins of the borrowed work. This strategy attests to a new attitude in the perception of English-Canadian theatre within the Québécois theatre institution.

The language adopted in the French version of *L'homme laid* is very representative of that in the source text. It is an informal language that displays some markers of orality and a considerable economy of means. On the microstructural level, the translation remains decidedly faithful to the original text, with some slight adjustments most often aimed at clarifying the meaning. The text strays farthest from the original in regards to the place where the action unfolds. Though the play's origins are underlined in the metatext framing the translated work, there is a vagueness in the text itself, as was the case for *Des restes humains non identifiés*. Hence, the first allusions to the site of the action are retained in the third scene when Veronica's mother Sabina welcomes Cole, the handsome and licentious best man.

COLE. J'avais oublié que votre ranch était si beau.

SABINA. Merci, Cole. J'espère que vous ne trouvez pas le climat de l'Ouest trop chaud?

COLE. Non madame. Dans l'Est aussi il fait chaud.

SABINA. Oui, je sais. Mais c'est beaucoup plus humide là-bas.

COLE. En fait, j'aime bien l'humidité.

SABINA. C'est bien ce que je pensais. C'est l'impression que vous donnez.[73]

Whereas the geographical references were retained in this excerpt from the third scene, they disappear in the sixth scene when Leslie, who wants to get the wedding over as soon as possible, says, "Then we can go back east and everything'll be all right."[74] The geographic reference has been neutralized by translating the sentence thus: "On va pouvoir retourner chez nous puis tout va redevenir correct."[75] In the twelfth scene, when Cole announces he is leaving—"Something's come up in the east. It can't wait"—the geographical reference is once again erased in the translation: "Il est arrivé quelque chose à la maison. Ça peut pas attendre."[76] On the microstructural level, this demonstrates an inclination to delete the allusion to a geographical polarity deemed unnecessary and inappropriate for a public who might perceive "l'est" altogether differently. In the same vein, a few modifications were made when the text included unwanted or untranslatable toponymic references. So, the reference to the "Brooklyn Bridge" becomes "pont," and the reference to the neighbouring "five counties" is changed to "la région."[77]

Several other minor changes were made. For example, a line that Sabrina uses to comfort her daughter was judged excessive and tempered from, "You know I would never let anything that could harm you within a hundred miles of this place" to, "Tu sais que je laisserais jamais personne te faire du mal."[78] Or an explanatory phrase is occasionally added, such as the underlined statement in Acker's reaction to helping out with an artificial insemination of a bull: "Ah oui, OK. On a des chevaux, on comprend ça."[79] The equivalents proposed for the swear words in the original text are indicative of the current use of Anglicisms in this specific area of the spoken Franco-Québécois language. The "Damn!" uttered by Veronica when Cole pushes her away is translated as "Shit!"[80] The "You little slut" that Veronica hurls at the servant Lottie is replaced by "P'tite bitch,"[81] and the "Jesus!" that Cole lets slip three times in scene forty-five become "Shit!" and "Crisse!"[82] Lastly, some adjustments such as the following have been made: "Where's your other partner in crime?" is replaced by an allusion to a classic of French literature, "Où est le troisième mousquetaire?"[83]

Therefore, even though the geographical and cultural references of the original play have been neutralized, the translation of Fraser's *The Ugly Man* rather faithfully reproduces the play's linguistic, textual, and discursive codes. In its aim for adequacy to the source text, the translation project stands in sharp contrast with the rule that insists upon adaptation and the recourse to *joual*, which previously governed the translation of English-Canadian theatre. As was the case for Fraser's first text and those of Thompson, the translation's transposition of the action into the context of Quebec did not result in an adaptation. Nevertheless, while the Anglo-Canadian origins of these plays are underlined in the metatext and the surrounding publicity, they remain inconspicuous within the translated text itself. Whereas the English names of the characters and references to cities or to the geographical location where the play is set remain intact, allusions to a context or to cultural realities that could prove foreign to the intended audience have been neutralized.

With this translation, the recourse to *joual* has decidedly been abandoned in favour of an informal language that no longer bears the numerous dialectical markers of a vernacular once entrusted with affirming a specific cultural identity. Freed from its identity function, the language can set out to reveal a voice whose alterity is no longer an obstacle. Must one see here an isolated case attributable to the particular theatricality of Fraser's works or the emergence of a new Québécois conception of translation vis-à-vis the English-Canadian repertoire? With this question in mind, we will see how the same translator has given voice to George F. Walker, who has recently and rapidly become the English-Canadian playwright with the most plays translated and produced in French in Canada.

George F. Walker: Theatre without Borders

Walker's initial foray into Quebec theatre occurred in 1986 with the public reading of *Zastrozzi, maître de discipline* at the National Arts Centre in Ottawa in a translation by René Gingras. That same year, still in Ontario, the Théâtre d'la Corvée presented Louise Ringuet's translation of *Theatre of the Film Noir* under the title of *Le théâtre du film noir*. Then it was *Amours passibles d'amendes*, Louison Danis's translation of *Criminals in Love*, which was presented in 1989 at Montreal's Théâtre Denise-Pelletier. Nine years later, four other plays from the series *Suburban Motel* were translated by Maryse Warda and produced one after the other at Théâtre de Quat'Sous: *L'enfant-problème* in October 1998, *Pour adultes seulement* and *Le génie du crime* in April 1999, and *La fin de la civilisation* in October 1999. Also in 1999, *L'enfant-problème* shared the award given by the Académie québécoise du théâtre for the best production of Montreal's season with Claude Gauvreau's *Les oranges sont vertes* presented at the Théâtre du Nouveau Monde. To be in such illustrious company in the pantheon of Québécois theatre was quite an honour. Maryse Warda received the Governor General's Award for translation for the series Motel de passage presented at the Théâtre de Quat'Sous. Several plays from this series were subsequently produced in different francophone theatres in Canada and elsewhere. Indeed, 1998 marked a sensational return for Walker to francophone stages, where he received praise, glory, and institutional legitimacy. Does a greater receptiveness to Anglo-Canadian theatre since 1990 explain such an infatuation? We shall try to understand this phenomenon by comparing the translation and the reception of the productions in 1989, 1998, and 1999.

Amours passibles d'amendes is the French version of Criminals in Love, the first of three plays that make up the series East End Plays, Part 1. It was directed by Gilbert Lepage and produced in 1989 at the Théâtre Denise-Pelletier, for an audience largely made up of adolescents. Unfortunately, the production received very poor reviews. The producers were criticized for having "fait l'erreur de prendre la pièce au premier niveau. De la faire plus réaliste qu'elle n'était. Et plus grave aussi."[84] The fact that the lyricism of the acting deliberately contrasted with the unfolding of the action was deplored and it was underlined "qu'il aurait fallu à toutes forces [se] tenir très, très loin du réalisme."[85] Furthermore, there were questions concerning "l'absence d'humour et de fantaisie" in a work that seems "manifestement inspirée de Shakespeare" and "s'achemine vers la tragédie pure."[86] It is difficult to recognize in these comments the tone and style of Walker, whose verbal aesthetic borrows from parody and black humour in a resolutely non-realistic manner. It is interesting to note that, in the program accompanying the production, the director effectively introduces the play as a Shakespearean-inspired work. We should also recall that Walker's Amours passibles d'amendes was produced in 1989—before Thompson and Fraser landed in Quebec to spread the good news that English-Canadian theatre is not always blandly naturalistic. Perhaps the production fell victim to a reading that still believed in the obligatory naturalism of English-Canadian theatre.

A comparison of the original and the translation reveals that the two texts have adopted similar linguistic strategies. The language is at once colloquial and inventive with a simple syntax, several markers of orality, short snappy dialogue, and a reduced vocabulary where gaps between the levels of language serve to create parodic effects. In keeping with the model of the day, the translation insists more on the markers of orality. The characters' names have been Gallicized, but the rare cultural or geographical references in the original have been faithfully reproduced, except when Wineva reveals that she did "Chicago in 68" and the French version refers instead to "Paris en 68," a reference that speaks much more eloquently to a francophone audience.[87] The action has not been relocated to adapt to the receptive context because this play contains no indication of belonging to any specific context, as is the case with all the other Walker plays that were subsequently translated. There are allusions to Al Capone, The Salvation Army, Che Guevara, South Africa, Chile, Barbados, and Chicago, but there is nothing that would situate the play in Canada, which renders it easily exportable in English or in translation, given that it takes place in an unspecified location and alludes to realities well-known in North America and elsewhere. *Escape from Happiness*, the third play of the East End Plays, Part 1, was incidentally first produced in New York, as were three of the plays that make up the series Suburban Motel. It was the first play of this series, *Problem Child*, that established Walker as part of the francophone scene in Montreal.

The translations of the three plays that constitute the series *Motel de Passage, tome 1*, were published in 2001 by VLB Éditeur. They are *L'enfant-problème*, *Pour adultes seulement*, and *Le génie du crime*. The book's back cover features a short presentation of the series, the author, and the translator, which attests to the growing importance accorded to the work of translation. The name of the playwright, the translated title, and the name of the translator are provided, but the introduction, which preceded the English text in Talonbooks' 1997 publication, is deleted. In this introduction Daniel de Raey, the director of *Problem Child*, which premiered in New York in 1997, explains that three of the six plays that constitute Suburban Motel were created in New York and he describes the author's style thus: "Walker is a master of humour without an attitude, of laughter honestly earned from situations and never at the expense of the characters."[88] The translation then provides details on the initial production of the play in Quebec, the list of characters, and the site of the action. The texts of the three plays follow. Their dramatic structure is faithfully preserved, as are the original character names and the description of where the action unfolds. There is no indication of any translative strategies.

In *L'enfant-problème*, RJ and Denise come up against Helen, the social worker who will decide whether the state will return their little girl, taken from them after they were deemed unfit to look after her. While RJ is mesmerized by the "reality shows" that he avidly watches on television, which have come to be more real for him than his own life, Denise struggles to make it without drugs, but loses control when confronted with Helen's well-meaning dogmatism. She knows that she will no longer see her child, as the behaviours being imposed upon her are exactly those her family and her background have taught her to hate. Like all the plays in the series Motel de passage, the play is set in a rundown suburban motel room frequented by a series of crooks and assorted losers. This motel is located "on the outskirts of a large city," a city that will remain anonymous, as there is not a single place name mentioned in the stage directions or the dialogue. There is nothing accidental about this anonymity since Walker tries to depict a reality in his play that is more North American than typically Canadian, as he explained to journalists before the premiere of *L'enfant-problème*: "Si vous vivez dans une grande ville canadienne ou américaine de nos jours, vous vivez un peu la même chose. Et cela, c'est plus important que les questions relatives à l'identité distincte. Vous n'aurez aucun impact si vous parlez de choses que les autres ne ressentent pas. Moi, je préfère m'intéresser à ce qui passe aujourd'hui dans notre monde urbain."[89] The referential nonspecificity resulting from the lack of place names is conserved in allusions to social or cultural realities that are most often designated by a generic form, not identified with a specific context. For example, in *L'enfant-problème*, the social worker responsible for deciding the fate of Denise and RJ's child sees herself as "a representative of our government," without us ever knowing what government this is and which agency she works for.[90]

In this contextually anchorless play, the rare identifiable sociocultural references are to American television celebrities who appear on the talk shows and the reality shows that RJ avidly watches. Oprah Winfrey, Jerry Springer, Montel Williams, Ricky Lake, and Geraldo Rivera are mentioned in the play's first lines.[91] From the outset, this has the effect of favouring American cultural references very familiar to the

Canadian public. So without hindering the understanding of the text in Canada, the reference to successful American television programs in a play devoid of geographic markers is a ready invitation to situate the play in an unspecified North American location.

This is facilitated in the translation through the recourse to a carefully calibrated Québécois French that allows the audience to identify with the characters even if their language is not the heavily accentuated *joual* one would expect from these societal outcasts. It's a choice completely in keeping with the approach described by the translator in this newspaper article by Hervé Guay.

> Selon elle, il est inutile d'adapter le texte à la réalité québécoise.
> "Au Quat'Sous, on se dit que les gens sont assez intelligents pour
> accepter d'autres réalités que la leur. Ils sont capables de faire
> l'exercice intellectuel de se projeter ailleurs." Pour elle, quand les
> enjeux d'une pièce sont universels, il importe peu que l'action
> se déroule à New York ou à Toronto. Par contre, Maryse Warda
> n'hésite pas à recourir à des expressions bien québécoises lorsque
> la pièce se passe dans un milieu populaire. L'essentiel, à son
> avis, c'est que le spectateur puisse comprendre ce à quoi il aurait
> normalement accès dans le texte original. On peut donc, selon
> elle, garder tous les référents extérieurs du texte tout en procurant
> au public la possibilité de s'identifier à une langue qui lui est
> familière.[92]

Here is an excerpt from the translated text:

DENISE. Je le sais pas, mon gars. La vie est juste en train de te
passer sur le corps, pis toi tu dépenses toute ton énergie sur la
marde qui sort de c'te petite boîte là. Ça fait que je me dis que t'est
peut-être pas capable de comprendre ce que j'ai à te dire sauf...je
sais pas, peut-être que je devrais aller à la TV pis m'asseoir sur une
de leurs petites maudites chaises. Pis brailler. Pis peut-être que là,
tu me verrais, pis t'entendrais mon histoire, pis tu m'ouvrirais ton
coeur pis tu comprendrais. Mais si je fais juste te dire comment ça
c'est passé, pis que je suis juste moi, pis que toi, t'es juste toi, je sais
pas, je suis pas sûre...

RJ. C'est-tu ben grave?

DENISE. Elle est morte.

RJ. Qui ça qui est morte?

DENISE. Helen.

RJ. Helen? Helen, la travailleuse sociale?

DENISE. Ouais. Elle est morte. Elle est tombée pis elle s'est cogné la tête sur la toilette.

RJ. La toilette...Notre toilette?

DENISE. Oui...sur le bol...t'sais.

RJ entre dans la salle de bain. Il en ressort.

RJ. Y a personne.

DENISE. Non. Elle est...partie.[93]

As a review of *Le génie du crime* pointed out, "si ce n'était des prénoms anglais qu'elle a gardés, on pourrait croire que la pièce a été écrite par un auteur québécois francophone."[94] In fact, though all the cultural markers in the original text were retained, the impression is given that the action could take place anywhere in North America. Far from expressing a specificity meant to be typically Canadian, the references contained in the text belong instead to an American popular culture that people know well and in which they recognize themselves, regardless of whether they are Anglophones or Francophones.

Add Walker's style to this referential nonspecificity, a style that distinguishes itself by the incisive humour of the rejoinders rapidly exchanged between characters who, in spite of themselves, are caught up in a spiral of absurd situations that they attempt to understand. There is an edginess in this writing that is wonderfully suited to the emotional style of acting that audiences are fond of in Quebec. While the comic virtues of the "maître canadien de l'humour noir," as he is described in the Théâtre de Quat'Sous's program, are appreciated, the tragic quality of his comedies is underscored nonetheless: "En surface, le sarcasme et l'ironie émergent, de sorte que le spectateur est ballotté du rire aux serrements de coeur, écartelé entre le dérisoire et le tragique."[95] There is an admiration for the sincerity in the acting that brings "un maximum de vérité à ces soubresauts loufoques."[96] It must be noted that, in Québécois theatre, generosity and authenticity of emotion are fundamental components of acting. It has to be rousing and it has to rouse. The audience readily laughs and willingly cries.

In the same vein, Aurèle Parisien's comparison of French and English productions of the plays is quite revealing: "the two striking ways in which the Quat'Sous production stands apart from the Toronto production—the use of a highly integrated non-naturalistic visual aesthetic and an intensely emotional style of delivery—are...characteristics of Quebecois theatre that set it apart from British, French and English Canadian theatre."[97] Commenting on the set design at the Théâtre de Quat'Sous, which consisted of a tiny room on a very low platform situated at the front of an already narrow stage, Parisien notes, "the effect is to create a confined, claustrophobic space where everything is pushed up front and in-your-face. In this space, every action is exaggerated and out of proportion."[98] The reduced space on stage results in intensified body movements, which are already accentuated by the emotional acting style favoured in Quebec.

As was the case in Fraser's play, the translator has resorted to a language other than the joual of the earlier plays. We're dealing here with a colloquial language that is very close to the vernacular and bears markers of orality. The translation is a model of efficiency in its faithfulness to the original text, from which it reproduces all the character names and sociocultural references. In a play stripped of onomastic and toponymic markers, the only contextual references that are clearly indicated are the names of well-known hosts of American televison talk shows and reality shows. Far from revealing an Anglo-Canadian specificity, the discourse presented here is anchored in a North American culture dominated by the United States, a culture with which we are familiar whether we are French or English, Canadian or American;

this familiarity renders the play easily exportable in English and in translation.

This completes the descriptive analysis of the French versions of English-Canadian plays included in the corpus.

Norms at Work in the Corpus

More than anything else, what is initially apparent in the statistical study undertaken to determine the corpus is the pronounced asymmetry not only in the number of plays translated for each repertoire, but in the number of translations that gave rise to a publication before 1990. As Annie Brisset pointed out, this is a veritable "forclusion," as up to this point the Canadian repertoire had been ignored, especially during the 1980s when there were only two publications.[99]

With respect to preliminary data, the title of the translation, the names of the playwright and the translator as well as the indication of the genre are considered primary norms inasmuch as they accompany each text. In most instances, the original title is also mentioned. It should be noted that this was not the case with *Charbonneau et le Chef*, a play that originated in Quebec and that underwent significant changes before becoming an enormous success in Quebec in translation. With the exception of Fraser's text, published in 1993, neither the publications nor the manuscript versions furnish any information on the playwright or the English publications. The lack of information on the original English work in the published translations of the plays in 1971 and in 1974 is suprising since plays were most often published in Quebec with an introductory text, as demonstrated by the publications of Tremblay's plays and later those of Marchessault, Chaurette, and Bouchard. More eloquent in this regard is the publication of Paul Zindel's *L'effet des rayons gamma sur les vieux-garçons* that inaugurated Éditions Leméac's collection Traduction et adaptation, which would later include both Herbert's and McDonough's texts. Published in 1970, Tremblay's adaptation of Zindel's play was accompanied by a prologue in which Alain Pontaut sings the praises of a "Tremblay plus créateur qu'adaptateur"; Pontaut's preface replaced Zindel's original preface.[100] The inclusion of an introductory text was therefore a common practice that had, however, been deemed unnnecessary for Herbert's and McDonough's texts, in spite of the great "creativity" displayed by the translators of McDonough's play. This presents us with a primary norm, applicable until the early 1990s, that saw English-Canadian texts in translation published without a preface, introduction, or information on the creation of the original play and the productions it generated. Therefore, the original text was concealed in the introduction and metatexts that accompanied the translation.

As was the case for the translations into English, there is no indication of any strategy applied to the translation. So, here we find a primary norm that requires that the work of the translation and any resulting modifications remain invisible. Even when a metatext accompanies the play, as it does with Fraser's *L'homme laid*, there is no mention of the mediation effected by the translation. Once again, the emphasis is placed on the product, to the detriment of the translation process, to facilitate the acceptance of the borrowed text within the target literary system.

This silence concerning the preliminary data continues at the macrostructural level. Such silence is all the more problematic when it comes to adaptation because it maintains a certain ambiguity concerning the translation devices applied at the microstructural level. In *Aux yeux des hommes*, for example, while an effort has been made to delete information deemed unnecessary, the play is presented without factoring in the modification of the spatial axis in the text. The action is situated in "une maison de redressement, au Canada,"[101] as described in the original play, while all the play's toponymic, onamastic, and sociocultural references have been transposed to Quebec. If one admits that Quebec is also in Canada, it must somehow be a different Canada as the system of references alluded to in the translation had to be changed. Thus reworked, the text becomes increasingly accessible, allowing it to function at various levels within its adoptive context. Not only does it bear the particular linguistic and sociocultural markers of a Québécois product, but it results from an event that gives it great legitimacy since the original play was a success in the United States. It must be remembered that the vast majority of dramatic texts translated in Quebec before 1990 were British or American hits. Indeed, the press kit accompanying the publication of *Aux yeux des hommes* stressed the pertinence of the play and its treatment in translation.

The situation with *Charbonneau et le Chef* is very different because, although it was a relatively unknown play, it was already situated in Quebec. Consequently, it made sense to appropriate the prologue by replacing the Canadian audience targeted by the author with the Quebec audience targeted by the translation. The translating operation introduces a subtle increase in the Québécois value of the play. As for the plays by Freeman and Foster, the action has been transposed into the context of Quebec by eliminating all references to the original context. By reducing the marks of alterity in the text in this manner, the adaptation becomes solipsistic in that it no longer refers to anything but itself.

Given that adaptation calls for the play to be resituated, it requires revisions at the onomastic and toponymic levels. The stage directions are also reworked in all the texts under study, except in the case of Fraser and Walker. As for McDonough's and Freeman's plays, adaptation also affects the works' textual structure and dramatic effects by substantially modifying the composition and distribution of scenes. Here we're in the presence of norms that are aimed at appropriating the play to the receptive context and that are more pronounced in translations described as "adaptations." In each of these four plays, the names of the characters and places have been naturalized, whereas the two that are labelled as adaptations, *Charbonneau et le Chef* and *Le bélier*, have led to a reworking of the dramatic structure.

Even though the indications provided at the preliminary and macrostructural levels can suggest the overall strategy applied to the translation, it is actually the analysis of the microstructures that reveals the strategies at work in the body of the text. This analysis leads us to a primary norm that affects all the language choices, whether matricial or textual in nature, and to which all the texts under study correspond: the target language is distinctly Franco-Québécois. While the subject matter of Herbert's play justifies the recourse to a slang-filled Québécois French, and McDonough's text only occasionally indulges in it, the translation of the texts by Foster and Freeman decidedly lower the level of language through the use of an accentuated *joual*. However, the texts by Fraser and Walker elude this rule, as they are translated in an informal Québécois French. Another primary norm ensures that the spelling of the texts translated into French reproduces the specificities of the oral language in a much more accentuated fashion in the first four texts, in which the grammar, vocabulary, and syntax borrow extensively from the spoken language's local expressions.

Yet, what is surprising in these translations into a vernacular strewn with Anglicims is the systematic rejection of English references, however familiar they are to Canadian francophone audiences, such as those to Bob Hope, Bette Davis, Glenn Ford, or Kirk Douglas, Buckingham Palace, the Brooklyn Bridge, the Royal Winnipeg Ballet, and Disneyland. The fact that these references bear an English name and designate realities outside of Quebec is problematic: within the North American context where Francophones represent a tiny minority, these English designations are rejected to protect and affirm a language and a culture that feels threatened. In the examined translations and adaptations, this attitude ensures that there is a preference for Gallicizing the cultural references and repatriating the referential system of the borrowed play in order to situate it in a francophone space. This was not, however, the case for Walker's play, in which the allusions to American television stars are retained in a play that is not anchored in any specific location.

Another primary norm requires that statements deemed unnecessary, unacceptable, or untranslatable will, in most cases, be deleted or adapted to the target context, thereby creating semantic gaps. The adaptation of McDonough's play is an extremely eloquent example of this. In adjusting to the prevailing doxa, scenes that seemed stereotypical or contrary to the image prevalent in the target context were deleted and adjustments were made to passages deemed overly dogmatic or offensive. It was also an opportune moment to modify the play's dramatic effects, something derived from another norm very active before 1990 that sought to intensify the dramatic or comic effects of a play in translation. In the case of Le bélier, for example, the author rewrote the text by increasing the dramatic effects of the original and endowing the revision with a comic style that was previously nonexistent. In a similar manner, the comic value of Foster's play was intensified through the addition of numerous comments aimed at making the audience laugh. This intrusion into the play's configuration would be handled much more discretely during the 1990s, when one could modify the distribution of scenes, as in *Des restes humains non identifiés*, while conserving the work's dramatic structure.

Lastly, it is only at the microstructural level that it is possible to determine whether adaptation is bound to lead to a transposition of the action into the target context. The plays by Herbert and Freeman, originally situated in Ontario, were both adapted and transposed into a Quebec setting. However, the translation of McDonough's play, which is not transposed as it is already located in Quebec, is also described as an adaptation. Finally, Foster's play, originally situated in New Brunswick, gave rise to a transposition but was not classified as an adaptation.

The end of the 1960s saw the emergence of a Franco-Québécois drama repertoire that developed around the model provided by Tremblay. The recourse to translation would prove a rapid solution to fulfilling the needs of this burgeoning drama repertoire. Once "étouffée par le théâtre étranger," this repertoire "manifeste maintenant assez de force pour l'assimiler" and thus consolidates the established model.[102] To do so, it is prefereable to keep the original at a distance by naturalizing the text through adaptation. Yet, commenting on his adaptation of *L'effet des rayons gamma sur les vieux-garçons*, Tremblay admits to having "à peine ajouté 3 ou 4 répliques" because there were two plays on words impossible to translate, "ça, pis changer les noms de rues" and the names of the characters.[103] Contrary to popular opinion that assumes that adaptation involves more numerous and more important modifications than translation, here the function of the designation is rather to move away from the original work, to keep it at a distance by insisting on the necessary process of naturalization due to a considerable cultural difference that can only be bridged through substantial reworking of the text.

Whether a play had been qualified as translation or adaptation, the transposition of the action in the translation of Anglo-Canadian plays constituted a primary norm between 1970 and 1990, given that all the plays situated in English Canada were relocated to Quebec.[104] Stripped of their inconvenient origins, these plays served to reproduce and to promote the models of writing and translating established by Tremblay in 1968 and 1970 respectively. However, things changed in 1990 as not a single translation listed after 1990 involved a transposition into a Quebec context, as we just saw in the examination of the plays by Fraser and Walker. Though Anglo-Canadian plays were no longer adapted, the recourse to a highly-accentuated vernacular remained an often-employed process of appropriation into the target context that served to naturalize the borrowed text, as is shown by some of the following critical excerpts.

When referring to Peter Madden's *Crime du siècle*, a play translated by Guy Beausoleil and produced in 1992 at the Théâtre d'Aujourd'hui, *Le Devoir*'s Robert Lévesque questioned the choice of translating a text inspired by the trial of the Rosenbergs, an American couple accused of spying and sentenced to death in 1953, in an idiom "pauvre et joual-isante."[105] Following the production of Sally Clark's *La vie sans mode d'emploi*, translated by Maryse Pelletier and presented at La Licorne in 1993, this same critic deplored the recourse to a "purée de sous-français qui n'a plus de qualité" in translating a play that takes place in 1608 and in which the characters speak "à peu près comme les personnages du *Cid Maghané* après édulcoration du genre, naviguant sans élégance entre un demi-joual, des sacres et un français sans finesse."[106] While the action was not transposed to Quebec in Tomson Highway's play, *Les reines de la réserve*, presented that same year at the Théâtre populaire du Québec in a translation by Jocelyne Beaulieu, the *Voir*'s Marie Labrecque underlines the effect of a translation in *joual* that "accentue l'appropriation québécoise du texte."[107] Therefore, the primary norm favouring the use of the vernacular as the target language was still active during the 1990s. Although the model of adaptation had been set aside, there remained a strong attachment to a highly territorialized vernacular language.

Comparison with the Systemic Context

Within a diglossic context, where English enjoys a hierarchical superiority to French and where it is necessary to translate a great many official documents first written in English, the effects of acculturation brought about by translation are viewed with suspicion. For Gaston Miron, this mistrust is all the more justifiable since "la langue est le fondement même de l'existence d'un peuple," a people entitled to a native tongue.[108]

This mistrust is expressed again in the concept of non-translation in which Jacques Brault proposes a "fidélité qui aspire à l'infidélité," an ambivalent text that "n'arrive pas à départager sa dépendance et son indépendance" and inhabits a "tierce réalité, la seule désormais viable."[109] This ambivalence ensures that translation, freed from its duty to imitate, results from a creative autonomy that will benefit the target language "suspendue entre deux certitudes maintenant problématiques, langue qui reconnaît alors sa difficulté d'être. Et sa raison d'être."[110] As Brault emphasizes at the beginning of his work, "Nous n'aimons ni traduire ni être traduits. Et nous n'avons pas toujours et tout à fait tort. Les clefs de la traduction appartiennent aux puissants. S'il n'y a pas de langue mondiale, il y a des langues colonisatrices."[111] Larry Shouldice would go even farther by maintaining that "it is not uncommon...for English Canadians to view translation as a means of fostering national unity; and while this is no doubt true of some French Canadians as well, one senses in the latter a more pronounced impulse to intelligence gathering for strategic defense purposes."[112]

This distrustful attitude is first manifest in the limited number of texts borrowed from English Canada, only a few of which have been published. Before 1990, these included only plays that were internationally successful, as was the case for *Aux yeux des hommes*, or those that took place in Quebec, such as *Charbonneau et le Chef*. This mistrust is next manifest in the systematic transposition to Quebec of plays situated in English Canada. The result is a distancing from the English-Canadian product in the publishing market and a concealment of the play's origins. With Fraser's arrival, this attitude changed in order to welcome a playwright whose innovation extended to both themes and their treatment.

This wariness towards borrowing from English Canada also shows up in the cultural references contained in the original texts. Although they are often familiar to the target audience, these references bear English names. Because this is threatening within a receptive context concerned with affirming its culture and language, these onomastic and toponymic referents are repatriated and bear French names designating French or Quebec realities. This strategy attests to a will to protect a language already beset with Anglicisms and to resist the hegemonic influence of English. However, in the Walker cycle, there remain some references to an American cultural context familiar to North American audiences, be they anglophone or francophone.

Beginning in 1990, when the action in a translated text was no longer transposed into a Quebec setting, there was still a tendency to use a highly-accentuated vernacular as a means of appropriating the borrowed text. With Warda, the language of translation would be slightly deterritorialized and would less insistently display the marks of its affiliation to the target context. Chapter 6 will demonstrate how the results obtained profile the evolution of each system under study and how they relate to each other through translation.

6

COMPARISON OF THE

REPERTOIRES IN TRANSLATION

THE STATISTICAL ANALYSIS CONDUCTED for this study revealed a profound asymmetry in the number of plays borrowed by each linguistic community and in the practices employed to effect the passage from one drama repertoire to the other. This asymmetry can be attributed to several factors.

To begin with, the very nature of the dramatic work imposes restrictions. Theatre is an art of oral, collective, and immediate communication directed towards a given community at a precise moment in its history. In contrast with performing arts that can circulate through recordings (like songs) or other literary genres that are experienced through multiple individual readings over years and sometimes centuries (e.g., novels, short stories, or poems), the play primarily addresses an audience determined by the "here and now" of the performance. The immediacy of theatrical communication requires that it closely adheres to its targeted sociocultural context. It is also important to note that drama developed more slowly in English Canada than in Quebec, where theatre enjoyed special status within the arts and has long been a favoured genre for affirming distinct francophone identity character-ized by the specificity of the Québécois oral language.

Furthermore, within the diglossic context of Canada's official lan-guages, where English enjoys a hierarchical and statistical superiority to French, it is not surprising that literary translation is more widely practised amongst Anglophones, whose language is not threatened and who can borrow without the risk of acculturation. For E.D. Blodgett, this diglossia within the Canadian context must also be taken into account by the literary critic "as any literary framework that assumes equality of status between these two cultural groups mistakes the nature of the relationship."[1] He therefore proposes to apply the theoretical framework of the polysystem developed by the Tel Aviv School to the comparative study of Canadian literatures. According to Itamar Even-Zohar, the lit-erary polysystem is an aggregate of activities related to various systems consisting of different literary genres, different categories of readers, and literature in translation. Within this aggregation, each system functions according to its own particular model, while remaining inter-dependent with the other systems within the polysystem. Each of these systems is shaped according to a hierarchical structure composed of a centre and peripheral layers, which are all in a state of constant mutation as a result of the centrifugal and centripetal forces affecting the system. At the centre, the dominant literary norm, the canon, groups "les formes les plus prestigieuses et les plus conservatrices" that serve as models for the peripheral layers.[2] To avoid petrification, the centre is forced to con-stantly renew itself. This evolutionary necessity demands that it exploit, with the aid of the literary apparatus at its disposal, the resources of the most recently adopted model and, when its novelty fades, replace this model with a new one. "Change is a function of the need felt in the envi-ronment of a literary system for the system to be or remain functional."[3]

Within the polysystem, a textual product that fails to influence any of the major processes and reproduces norms already established by a dominant model is considered secondary. Contrarily, an element that actively contributes to modelling the centre of the polysystem occu-pies a primary position. In this constant quest for innovation, a literary system, whether it focusses on theatre, novels, or poetry, occasionally borrows new models from other systems. Such borrowing will often be carried out through the agency of translation.

This theoretical framework allowed Blodgett to attribute Quebec's indifference towards English-Canadian writing to its secondary nature: "The writing of English Canada has, until recently, only rarely possessed...a 'primary activity' representing 'the principle of innovation,' as opposed to a secondary activity whose role is to maintain 'the established code.'"[4] This is also true for theatre according to the critic Ray Conlogue, who in a 1993 article explains Quebec's indifference to the English-Canadian drama repertoire before 1990: "English Canada's love affair with a plodding American-style naturalism...bored Quebec to tears."[5] However, Robert Wallace contends that this indifference can be attributed to the political relations between Canada and Quebec rather than to aesthetic differences. Many Québécois theatre directors feel they are not required to present English-Canadian drama on Quebec stages: "not considering themselves part of Canadian culture, they feel no obligation to privilege Canadian plays."[6]

In 1990, Annie Brisset broadened the functionalist theoretical framework to include the socio-discursive context of the literary polysystem. As literature is subject to the prevalent discourse of the target society, literary translation is shaped not only by linguistic and literary constraints but also by "l'ensemble des codes qui régissent à des degrés divers le discours de la société-cible."[7] In her study, Brisset highlights the ethnocentric character of Québécois theatre translation carried out between 1968 and 1988. Entrusted with transmitting the values of the Québécois society at a time of nationalist fervour, the objective of the translation was not to reveal the borrowed work, but to "prêter à cette oeuvre étrangère le dessein de mettre en scène le 'fait québécois.'"[8] In this context, English-Canadian plays, just like the other foreign plays borrowed through translation, occupied a secondary position in the target context, where they were entrusted with consolidating the canon of new Québécois theatre.

Far from being exclusive to Quebec, ethnocentrism, suggests Antoine Berman, has been a dominant principle of Occidental literary translation since the time of ancient Rome.[9] However, as we have been able to observe in this study, the strategies adopted to satisfy this principle vary according to the state of the literary system at the moment when the work is borrowed and introduced into its adoptive context.

Too Much Language

From the perspective of the polysystem theory, the anglophone dramatic system's receptiveness towards Michel Tremblay's works can be explained by the circumstances that gave rise to Toronto alternative theatre in the early 1970s. With the establishment of the network of regional theatres funded by the Canada Council for the Arts as of 1957, Canadian professional theatre began to earn its stripes. As it still borrowed extensively from the British and American repertoires, Canadian theatre was slow to develop. In order to enlarge its Canadian content, the most acclaimed Québécois plays were borrowed. Works by Gratien Gélinas, Jacques Languirand, Marcel Dubé, and Robert Gurik were translated and enjoyed a certain success on Canadian stages, more precisely those of Toronto, between 1951 and 1970.

With the end of the Quiet Revolution and the emergence of a new Québécois theatre, things got more complicated, as noted by Jane Koustas: "With the introduction of 'joual,' which posed more complex translation problems, and of the social and political issues associated with the Nouveau Théâtre québécois, which demanded greater understanding of a radically different 'place' as well as of different theatre practices resulting in part from the collective theatre experience (see Wallace 1988 and Leonard), critical response was less sympathetic towards plays' 'québécitude' or Quebeckness; indeed a play's 'québécitude' seemed to work against it as it rendered it too remote for the Toronto audience."[10]

Then, with the founding of Theatre Passe Muraille (1968), the Factory Theatre (1970), Tarragon Theatre (1971), and the Toronto Free Theatre (1972), a new theatre movement began to take shape in English Canada, a movement dedicated to the promotion of Canadian drama. This alternative network developed on the margins of the dominant norm and the funded regional theatres that embodied it. It was therefore a poor theatre that, to survive, had to find ways to compensate for a lack of financial resources. Here translation offered several advantages, including the ability to present plays whose success had already been proven.

In the nationalist enthusiasm that characterized the new English-Canadian theatre movement, it was impossible to ignore the triumph of Tremblay, the playwright who had just revolutionized Québécois theatre by endowing it with not only new aesthetic means but a distinctly Québécois voice as well. The borrowing thus proceeded from an awareness of Tremblay and his work as a successful model of a modern nationalistic theatrical undertaking.

It appears, however, that the thorny question of the language, though crucial for Québécois playwrights of the day, was a major obstacle to cultural transposition. In 1961, it was deemed preferable to ignore Gratien Gélinas's note in *Bousille et les justes* questioning the legitimacy of a theatrical language stripped of "les mots et expressions propres au Canada français."[11] Subsequently, the translation of plays by Jean Barbeau and Jean-Claude Germain, which included dialogue in *joual*, were not well received by the Toronto public. Out of a concern for acceptability, Tremblay was translated in a generic language that accentuated swear words and Gallicisms, which served to vouch for the inherent "Quebecness" of the translated text. The translations of these plays were then published without any introductions. So, critics could hail a new Canadian playwright without taking into account the specificity of his writing and its revolutionary aspect. Instead, they dwelled upon well-known elements and a quaintness that highlighted certain familiar and reassuring characteristics of this "Quebecness," while failing to mention anything that proved problematic for the mediation of the translation. In that sense, it could be said that the Tremblay presented in Toronto really is Canadian; the translation of his work produced a Canadian reading in which the language issue has been eliminated, however crucial it was in the original, and a non-menacing Québécois alterity has been emphasized. Tremblay's plays were celebrated in English Canada more for what the translations of the plays focussed on than for their so-called universality.

The French text could be translated into English in a way that included obvious marks of linguistic alterity because this alterity does not constitute a threat in the Canadian sociocultural context, where English enjoys total supremacy vis-à-vis the language and culture of the francophone minority. Inasmuch as the norm is defined by the majority, and difference is constructed in relation to this norm, in Canada, where Anglophones constitute the majority, it is the Francophones and ethnic minorities that are invested with alterity.

Thus invested with an alterity that the translation has stripped of its ideological and political implications, Tremblay's work was turned to good account by an alternative movement aimed at creating a distinct national theatre. Borrowed at the outset of the 1970s to contribute to the elaboration of a new Canadian norm within a developing drama repertoire, Tremblay's plays occupy a primary position within a target polysystem in need of innovation at a critical moment of its evolution. Tremblay provides English Canada with a model of dramatic writing whose novelty resides primarily in the aesthetic means it displays. Richard Plant describes Tremblay's style as "a multi-layered poetic drama, rich in imagery and centred around volatile issues and powerful emotions...experiments with form, and his use of musical structures, interwoven aria-like monologues, and choruses."[12] Although the translation of Tremblay's works leans towards a maximum adequacy to the innovative textual-structural codes of the original, it resolutely distances itself from the linguistic and discursive codes of the source text, subject as it is to an initial norm that privileges the accessibility to a familiar, non-threatening Québécois culture.

When the alternative movement disappeared at the end of the 1970s, Anglo-Canadian theatre was well-established. With the drafting of the Gaspé Manifesto in 1971, the Canada Council for the Arts increased its support for the production of Canadian works, which from then on had to account for 50 per cent of the repertoire produced at funded theatres. Organizations responsible for promoting Canadian drama had been established, such as the Vancouver New Play Centre in 1970 and the Playwrights Co-op in 1972, which became the Playwrights Union of Canada in 1984. Festivals grew in number, such as the Blyth Festival, established in 1979, and the Fringe, which was launched in Edmonton in 1982 before expanding to Toronto and Vancouver. Calgary's PlayRites Festival was inaugurated by Alberta Theatre Projects in 1985. Lastly, publishing houses, such as Talonbooks, founded in 1972 in Vancouver, NeWest Press, set up in Edmonton in 1977, and the Dramatists' Co-op, which opened its doors in Halifax the same year, dedicated themselves to the publication of Canadian theatre. Toronto's Coach House as well as Simon & Pierre included theatre in their list of publications. In brief, the Canadian norm prevailed, and playwrights such as George F. Walker, David French, Sharon Pollock and, later, Judith Thompson,

Ann-Marie MacDonald, Tomson Highway, and Brad Fraser quickly became known throughout the country.

Far from disappearing with *joual*, the issue of language continued to shape Québécois dramatic writing, and the theatre of the 1980s pursued the exploration of language with untiring enthusiasm. After more than a decade of developing a voice through characters that had to speak *joual*, and thus belonged to an underprivileged social class, there was now a desire to speak of other things in other ways, but without returning to the normative French once prescribed by the right-thinking elite and from which *joual* had acted as a distancing factor. In searching for other ways to express themselves, creators took up the exploration of the image, to the detriment of the word, in what is referred to as visual theatre. Simultaneously, they explored dialogue freed from daily language and the obligation of verisimilitude. The lyricism of Jovette Marchessault, the poetic dialogue of Michel Garneau, the incantatory vertigo of Normand Chaurette's plays, just like the imbroglios of René-Daniel Dubois and the enunciative variations of Théâtre Ubu bear witness to the importance given to the language as material to explore in the elaboration of the Franco-Québécois theatre. Even in visual theatre, with its accentuation of the visual aspect of the performance, distinct new verbal aesthetics were established, such as the plurilingual montages of Robert Lepage. Elsewhere in Canada, other francophone drama developed, voicing a particular linguistic hybridity that in turn presented new challenges for English translation.

So, although *joual* was no longer an obstacle for translation, the language issue was still problematic, as it was now necessary to translate writing that focussed on an aesthetic research that favoured a hyperliterary language that had little to do with daily speech. Although there was an admiration in English Canada for the audacity with which this research questioned the conventional theatrical structures, the supremacy of the text and a certain naturalism in the tone remained essential. This attitude negatively affected the reception of visual theatre, which in some cases, such as Carbone 14's *Hamlet-Machine* presented at the Du Maurier World Stage in 1987, gave rise to scathing criticism.[13] Plays that displayed discursive or narrative novelty were readily borrowed, such as the radical feminist works of Marchessault and the elaborate textual constructions with which Chaurette depicts his homosexual characters. In the case of the latter, care was taken to naturalize what is a highly stylized language while, faithful to her translating position, Marchessault's translator would not reduce the extreme literariness of the language, and *The Edge of Earth is Too Near, Violette Leduc* was met with a certain reserve within the target theatre system.

Thus, despite the obstacle presented by the specific verbal aesthetic of the source texts, plays continued to be borrowed for textual models whose structural and narrative novelty was translated with the greatest adequacy. Discursive models that readily drew from gay and feminist discourses were sought out and subsequently grew in importance. At the same time, Tremblay's work continued to be staged in revised versions in which the question of the language's specificity still remained unaddressed.

The end of the 1980s saw the beginning of an awareness of the inherent difficulty in translating the ceaseless exploration of the language characteristic of the source text. As Koustas observed, the Toronto critics more readily acknowledged translation's role and underlined the existence of "linguistic, rather than cultural barriers" in the sometimes chilly reception of Québécois theatre in translation.[14] What nevertheless remained difficult for an anglophone audience to understand was the francophone theatre's preoccupation with language, a preoccupation expressed through theatrical aesthetics anchored within the linguistic material itself. This difficulty can be attributed to the very success of English, which has managed to impose itself as the common language worldwide. Unburdened with doubt because it speaks a hegemonic language, the anglophone audience cannot conceive that the way of saying something, the very act of speaking, can be the site of such an investment, the object of such insistence. The resulting excess of language conveys a preoccupation with French within the Canadian and North American context, wherein it occupies a minority position. This attitude towards the function of language appears to be one of the fundamental differences between French and English drama in Canada.

English-Canadian critics became aware of the difficulty of translating certain verbal aesthetics at work in the source text because concealing them was no longer the function of translation. In the search for a formal equivalence, the position between adequacy and acceptability shifted accordingly, as some translators felt free to reproduce the literariness of the original language. This new attitude coincided with the elaboration of a Québécois translation marketplace that, beginning in 1987, exported plays to English Canada that were translated in Quebec. Still a widely practised activity, English translation of the French repertoire was from then on concentrated in Quebec, centred around the Centre d'essai des auteurs dramatiques (CEAD), which inaugurated an exchange program for plays in translation. Translation was thus better able to address the specific problems of the language and its primacy within a theatre system where "the presence of that spoken language...is a statement in itself, a statement of cultural survival, aspiration, and communion."[15] In this case, however, borrowing no longer reflects the target system's need for novelty as much as the desire of a source system to present and promote its drama to an anglophone audience through works selected and translated in Quebec.

Although there was a greater awareness of language issues in the source text, translation still had to factor in the reticence expressed by the critics. Having attempted to reproduce the original's literariness and exuberance in the English version, it was now necessary to take into account the incompatibility of certain stylistic codes applied to the theatrical language within each system. So, to translate Bouchard's *Les muses orphelines*, the translator adopted a tone that minimized the extreme language gaps that the author uses to express irony. While it provoked some ultraconservative reviews during its New York production, the text was well received when it was presented in Vancouver. It must be noted that the setting of the play, which covers the years from 1955 to 1965 in Quebec, represents a period in Quebec history to which the anglophone public is much attached. However, in contrast with Tremblay's "belles-sœurs" and transvestites, some of Bouchard's characters manage to escape the family mould and their immediate community to better come to terms with their autonomy.

Now that it had its own institution, the Anglo-Canadian theatre system built itself a national repertoire that borrowed certain theatrical models from its francophone neighbour. Initially prompted by curiosity in the other's culture, the English translations displayed an alterity that often clung to the picturesque. Later on, with the arrival of the new Québécois theatre, this alterity would represent a threat at the same time that it proposed extremely interesting models for a drama seeking to assert itself. For this to occur, the point of equivalence had to slightly shift in order to render the new Québécois model acceptable. Although the aesthetic audacity of the model was retained, its linguistic and discursive aspects would pose problems to its reception. The borrowed text would then occupy a primary position within the target system.

As it gradually constructed a national repertoire, in which the translated text occupied a place of choice, the Canadian theatre system gained its autonomy and the need to borrow became less urgent. Relieved of the obligation to please, translation could shift toward the adequacy pole. A newly-discovered verbal exuberance proved to be incompatible with the linguistic codes in effect within the receptive system and a slight readjustment was required in order to inject a certain naturalism into the dialogue and thereby foster greater acceptance of the translated product in the receptive context. In this way, the search for equivalence in the English translation of the French repertoire was determined by the evolutionary needs of the Anglo-Canadian theatre system.

Quebec Ink

If there was a change in how Québécois and Franco-Canadian theatre were translated into English after 1985, it is because the itinerary followed by translation had been modified. With the inauguration of an exchange program for translated theatre texts at the Centre d'essai des auteurs dramatiques in 1985, there was a progressive centralization of theatre translation in Quebec. Not only were English-language plays translated into French in Quebec, French-language plays selected locally to represent the Quebec drama repertoire were also translated into English. Contrary to the usual mediation that sees a translated work migrating from one cultural context to another to fill a need in the target system, here the borrowing arises from the source system's internal desire to promote its own drama to an anglophone audience in Canada or abroad. It should be noted that, in the officially unilingual province of Quebec, Montreal's sizeable bilingual population readily allows for translation to be done in either of the two languages.

With the centralization of theatre translation in Quebec, the English translation of a Québécois or Franco-Canadian text became an exportable product generated by the source text's literary institution and theatrical system. This inversion of the mediation axis taken by the translation affects the representation of the source text through translation and, consequently, the perception of the francophone culture transmitted to English Canada and abroad. One of the consequences of this shift resulted in these translations being done by Anglophones who lived and worked in Quebec or in a Canadian francophone community, and who were familiar with the linguistic context of the source text. They were therefore more sensitive to the delicate question of language and the issues surrounding it in Québécois and French-Canadian drama.

Thus, in the English translations of plays by Marchessault, Chaurette, Bouchard, and Dalpé, all carried out under the aegis of the CEAD, strategies were used that carefully avoid exoticism while attempting to take into account the linguistic specificity of the source text. In Marchessault's *The Edge of Earth is Too Near, Violette Leduc*, the translator favoured an adequacy to the lyricism and the hyperliterary language of the source text, which has been perceived in English as a manifestation of verbosity. In Bouchard's *The Orphan Muses*, there was a slight reduction in the extreme language gaps that may not have been well received by an anglophone audience unfamiliar with this linguistic exuberance. In Dalpé's *Le Chien*, the concern for authenticity in the dialogue, necessary for a play adopting a naturalistic aesthetic, called for the deletion of the code-switching that reflects the difficulties faced by the French language in a minority situation. It would not be easy to transpose this code-switching into English for an audience that did not share such a reality and for whom this linguistic hybridity would have sounded artificial.

In this vein, the translation insists less than before on the origin of the borrowed text and abandons its ethnographic function. It should be noted that in renouncing *joual*, the Québécois dramatic text ceases to examine its own alienation and opens up to other discursive horizons, thereby exploring a more varied thematic menu from which English Canada readily borrows, but without insisting on the marks of linguistic alterity, as was the case with Tremblay. There are no exotic Gallicisms to be found in the translations of Chaurette's and Marchessault's plays, which employ a rather literary language, nor in the translations of the texts by Bouchard and Dalpé, which call on colloquial and vernacular levels of language. In every instance, the choice has been made to Anglicize or delete a sociocultural reference that could disorient an audience in a discourse that is resolutely modern and has therefore ceased to invite an ethnographic reading. In this respect, the CEAD's reaction to the English translation of Serge Boucher's text *Motel Hélène* is most eloquent.

After having invited Judith Thompson to translate Boucher's text into English, from an initial literal English translation completed by Morwyn Brebner, the CEAD advised Thompson against the use of numerous Gallicisms scattered throughout the English text, where several French expressions and the majority of the swear words had been retained in French. Thompson refused to revise her translation and this version was produced at the Tarragon Theatre in 2000 and published the same year by the Playwrights Union of Canada. What follows is an excerpt in which the Gallicisms have been underlined.

> **MARIO.** Saturday, eh? Calvaire, that makes me think! What's today? Wednesday? Tabernak. Did I tell you my story about the ticket?...Ben Tabernak that pissed me off I start yellin' at him "You lie, cop, it was green it changed after I was already in the middle." I mean like as if I would go right through the light with a cop right there, right? Like I just love gettin' tickets, right? He gives me the ticket anyway the fat pig hosti you know what it cost me? 110 bucks hosti I've got to pay it before Friday, and Ti-Poil owes me money calice and I can't get it off him. I mean where am I going to get it? It's always the same when you lend someone money you have to go running after them I can't take it no more, Johanne, I'm telling you I'm not lending money ever again c'est fini.[16]

Thompson applied strategies borrowed from the English versions of Tremblay's plays to the pronounced vernacular of Boucher's text. This manner of representing *joual* in English has profoundly influenced the anglophone public and had become an unavoidable model for Thompson. Faced with this situation, the CEAD decided to entrust the revision of the English text to Crystal Béliveau and Serge Boucher, and their revised version, in which all the Gallicisms have been removed, is now available at the CEAD. Here is the same excerpt as it appears in this second version:

> **MARIO.** Saturday, eh? Ah shit, that reminds me! What day's today? Wednesday? Shit. Did I tell you my story about the ticket?...Jesus that pissed me off I start yellin' at him "What a crock of shit, it was green, I was already in the middle when it changed." "That's enough" he goes "we were right there. We saw everything." God they are so full of it sometimes, I mean like as if I would go through the light with a cop sitting right there, come on! Like I just love gettin' tickets, right? Fuckin' crook, fuckin' hypocrite, he didn't give a god damn about my side of the story, it was that fat ass, what's his name, everyone knows him, fuckin' pig, d'you know what it cost me? 110 bucks for Christ sake, and I just remembered I gotta pay it by Friday, and Marcel owes me money and I can't get it off him, shit, it's always the same, you lend someone money and then you gotta go running after it, well that's it, no more, enough's enough, I'm not lending money ever again, friend or no friend.[17]

If the preoccupation with language in francophone playwriting has been expressed in various ways over time, the strategies to take this into account in English Canada also display a diversity that corresponds to the needs the translation was asked to fulfill within the Canadian context. With the exportation of francophone texts translated into English in Quebec, the translation's function is determined less by the target context and its needs than by a desire of the source context to export its own repertoire. Plays are thus chosen that are meant to be representative of francophone drama without having been actively sought out by the target system. This means that there may be a discrepancy between the expectations of the recipient and the aspirations governing the choice of plays to be presented to a little-known or, for that matter, unknown audience. The translative strategies employed could then fail to take into account the context in which the play will be produced and the possibilities and constraints peculiar to this context that would influence how the translated work is received. This is a specific aspect of theatre translation related to the immediacy of a performance that is anchored in a given location, period, and community—all factors that profoundly affect the reading of the work presented. This gap between supply and demand could explain the sometimes negative reactions elicited by a translated work when it proposes an aesthetic or a discourse that fails to meet an audience's expectations within the receptive context, even though it has been acclaimed in the source context.

Made in Canada

After French-Canadian theatre gradually came to be known, through, among other ways, the reviews and plays produced by Gélinas as early as 1938, the theatrical renewal of the 1960s gave it a voice meant to be specifically Québécois. In 1968, Tremblay consolidated this new Québécois drama by putting forward a model that enabled a recently inaugurated institution to build a repertoire. As was the case for English-Canadian theatre of the same period, borrowing offered many advantages. However, unlike English-Canadian drama, which was still hesitant and unsure of itself, its nascent Québécois counterpart was flourishing, with each play fashioned after a commonly accepted model. With the overwhelming consensus generated around Tremblay at the end of the 1960s, Québécois drama could affirm an identity that it felt was threatened and examine its relationship to the alterity.

It must be noted that with the emergence of a postcolonial consciousness in Quebec, there was a keen resentment towards what was perceived as domination on the part of France and English Canada. While there was an attempt to rebuff a hegemonic English, there was also a rejection of the standard French from France formerly imposed as the only language capable of expressing a true francophone culture. So, the recourse to joual had the advantage of rebuffing them both by substituting the original English with a dialect completely separate from standard French. In light of this double bind, the Québécois translation imposed the newly prevalent linguistic code on the borrowed text.

To do this, the action of the play had to be relocated, which involved a transposition of all the onomastic, toponymic, and sociocultural references. Concealing the site of the action in the original play in this manner was intended to prevent any representation of English Canada on francophone stages. Along the same lines, even though various realities evoked in the original text were known to a North American francophone audience, they had to be Quebecicized or, if not, Gallicized. These strategies were aimed at resisting an anglophone majority, dominant and threatening, that had to be rebuffed. Thus, beginning in 1970, adaptation, and all its variations, became the favoured mode of translation for a system in which the borrowed text occupied a secondary position, as it was responsible for reproducing the dominant model within the target context. It follows that under such circumstances, the search for equivalence tends towards the greatest acceptability of the translated product.

It is in this spirit that the plays by Herbert, McDonough, and Freeman were borrowed, as they contained discursive and linguistic codes compatible with those favoured by the target system. *Fortune and Men's Eyes* lent itself the most admirably well to a transposition into *joual* and its subject matter conforms to a paradigm favouring the representation of oppression by exterior forces. *Charbonneau and Le Chef* is about a page in Quebec history, but it necessitated some revisions in an effort not to upset an audience that might be offended by some of the play's assertions. While *Battering Ram* has a certain thematic interest, it is not overly pertinent on a discursive level. It was therefore totally rewritten, transformed into a comedy, and proletarianized so that the vernacular could be used. As for the textual codes, the plays by McDonough and Freeman have been completely restructured. Thereby annexed to the target polysystem, the borrowed plays tend towards a specular function, which means they serve as a mirror for a community anxious to affirm its identity.

At the end of the 1980s, Quebec boasted an impressive repertoire, to which translation had contributed, and the necessity to borrow had become less urgent. Adaptation had begun to be frowned upon. In this context, there was less insistence on a compatibility of discursive codes than on the textual novelty that the English-Canadian repertoire had to offer. Foster's comedy, *The Melville Boys*, was borrowed especially for the efficiency of these textual codes, and their comic effects were accentuated by the addition of dialogue and the recourse to a vernacular loaded with dialectical expressions. What is surprising about this insistence on translating into a decidedly vernacular language is that it contrasts sharply with the verbal aesthetics being explored in Quebec at the time. It is as if this research with respect to form is restricted to creation, while translation remains subject to the previous norm favouring the use of *joual*; it is as if a translated text had to bear the marks of a linguistic appropriation to compensate for the decline of adaptation and the transposition it sanctioned.

This compensatory strategy calls into question the unjustified utilization of a vernacular that has lost its emblematic value. If it is evident that Québécois is spoken in plays transposed to Quebec, how does one justify using *joual* in plays solidly anchored within an anglophone context in Canada or abroad? The question could be reformulated: is there another variation of spoken French that would be more appropriate to represent the foreign play? Would it be preferable, for example, to ascribe to it a standard French, which would give the impression that the action was occurring in France, or a Belgian, Swiss, West-Indian, or African French? If not, could one utilize an international French that would give the impression that the play could take place anywhere? What is apparent here is that there is no such thing as a neutral spoken language, one without an identity. The French that is described in Quebec as "international" is in fact a formal level of spoken language that resembles the standard Parisian French. However, this French—described as "international" because it bears a minimal amount of local characteristics—nonetheless exhibits an accent and is no less Québécois, Canadian, or North American. With theatre, short of situating the play within a foreign context or experimenting with new aesthetics based on the linguistic material, the language employed on stage can hardly be anything other than that of the target audience. In this sense it is less the site of the action than the target public that influences the choice of the translation language.

Where things get more complicated is in the choice of the level of language attributed to the characters. In this respect, we noted the insistence placed on the use of a highly-accentuated vernacular, even if it modifies the play's dynamics and proletarianizes the characters. The 1990s, however, saw a break with this strategy, as the translated versions of Brad Fraser's first two plays demonstrate. In these translations, not only does the action take place in the same site as it does in the original, the language moves away from the vernacular towards something more colloquial or informal. Therefore, the point of equivalence had slightly shifted towards adequacy to the original text, which the translation was no longer obliged to conceal.

At the start of the 1990s, the English-Canadian repertoire enjoyed growing popularity on francophone stages not only in terms of numbers, but for the strictly theatrical value of the textual audacity of this new drama. Fraser's arrival on francophone stages combined with that of Thompson to change the way English-Canadian theatre was perceived. As Pat Donnelly reported during the production of *Poor Super Man* in April 1995, "If there is any tenet held sacred in Quebec theatre criticism, it is the assumption that English-Canadian theatre is boring, puritanical, and behind the times. Or at least that's how it was before Edmonton's Brad Fraser came along."[18] This new perception entailed a shift in the position occupied by the translated text within the target polysystem, where the English-Canadian playwright then offers up a model to be reproduced. Donnelly goes on to note in this same article that Fraser "has influenced a school of urban-lifestyle playwriting best exemplified by François Archambault's *Cul sec*."[19] Thus positioned as a model, Fraser's work occupies a primary function within a target system interested in the novelty of the textual codes put forward by the Canadian playwright. It is a novelty, however, that cannot be appreciated unreservedly.

In fact, if the crude language and the violence of *Des restes humains non identifiés et la véritable nature de l'amour* gave off a slight scent of scandal, *L'homme laid*, the second of Fraser's plays to be produced in French, provoked indignation. *Poor Super Man* would then be seen as routine for an author who was by then seen as the most obscene of the contemporary playwrights. Be that as it may, it took this sometimes shocking audacity to draw attention to the spectacular virtues of anglophone drama and reveal that English-Canadian theatre was not necessarily "boringly naturalistic." It was, however, a conditional acknowledgement because it depended on strategies of legitimization that drew upon sensationalism. In other words, the spectacular, shocking, and even scandalous virtues of the borrowed plays had to be praised to justify the sudden interest devoted to them.

The productions of the French versions of the George F. Walker cycle at once break with and conform to the preceding model. From the outset, Walker's plays' referential nonspecificity muddy the waters and dilute the question of origins, which were so problematic from 1969 to the end of the 1980s. While the origin of the texts that comprise Suburban Motel is underlined in the metatexts and in the discourse that accompanies the production, it is not alluded to in the dialogue, which has affinities with a familiar American neighbour often present on Canadian anglophone and francophone stages. The translation is then able to favour an extreme adequacy to the source text and retain all references to sociocultural realities that, when they are not generic, are borrowed from mass American culture.

These translations display a relatively non-accentuated colloquial language that is almost informal, which is a clean break from the strategies previously favoured and the variations observed in the different translations of Fraser's plays. Finally, the scenography, the acting, and the staging of the play have the effect of accentuating its dramatic value, so much so that the author of Le génie du crime was criticized for indulging in "la grosse caricature," which would have completely destroyed the characters' credibility.[20]

Walker's work circumvents the constraints to which Canadian plays were previously exposed, as it no longer presents itself as being Canadian but North American and offers up a hybrid cultural product intended to easily circulate within a global marketplace dominated by the Americans. As the program for the Quebec Walker cycle announces, we can therefore celebrate "le dramaturge canadien-anglais le plus joué dans le monde" in plays that, far from revealing a typically Canadian specificity, reveal the American cultural influence to which Canada is subject.

CONCLUSION

THE INTENTION OF THIS STUDY WAS to compare the strategies applied to plays translated from one official language into the other in Canada. From this comparative perspective, the functionalist methodology advanced a descriptive model that enables certain determinant aspects of each repertoire to be identified and compared. This method also allowed for a synchronic and diachronic analysis of the translation phenomenon. Furthermore, selecting the corpus based on statistical criteria and applying a frame of reference that acted as a third element for the comparison of the texts had the advantage of leaving as little room as possible to value judgements.

According to Antoine Berman, literary translation, as it has been developed and practised in the Occident, is governed by the principle of ethnocentrism. This fundamentally teleological principle ensures that one essentially translates for oneself, contingent on one's own norms and values, in order to enhance the richness of one's culture. In this sense, all translation defends individual, collective, or national inter-ests. As this study demonstrates, the Canadian drama repertoire is no exception to this rule. However, the historic and political dynamics unique to each linguistic and cultural community act on the strategies chosen to satisfy this principle. Within a context where the two official languages occupy asymmetric positions, translation is called upon to perform decidedly divergent functions.

While one side willingly borrows from a minority repertoire that is nonthreatening, the other chooses to hold a hegemonic language and an invasive culture at bay. What is exotic for one represents a danger for the other. Within the texts, dramatic writing itself is shaped by a linguistic dynamic specific to the Canadian context and exhibits quite a different relationship to language depending on whether it is the language of an apprehensive minority or that of a self-assured majority. Called upon to ensure that the threatened language resonates throughout the public sphere on behalf of a community whose linguistic identity lies primarily in the oral specificity of its language, the texts that make up the francophone repertoire display an insistent orality that invests the dialogue with a strong identity coefficient, which has little equivalent in the anglophone context. This gap between the function attributed to language and speech within each repertoire has a determinant effect on the circulation of translated works.

At the end of the 1960s, while Francophones and Anglophones were questioning their attachment to a colonial past, the drama on both sides was influenced by the issue of identity. Translation, then, responded to a desire to create a national repertoire, one that the Anglophones would claim to be specifically Canadian and that Quebec's Francophones would claim to be specifically Québécois. This desire called for difference to be highlighted in order to emphasize what was perceived as essential to a distinct national identity. Common to each linguistic group, this emphasis placed on difference was, however, subject to a power struggle that required specific approaches based on one's respective position.

When the Québécois system rallied around a new model that affirmed a specific identity, it was an extremely compact system that benefitted from a collective consensus. Playwriting flourished while emphasizing the expression of its own "difference." Resorting to adaptation then allowed for the rapid development of a local repertoire imbued with this difference, symbolized above all by the use of a distinct oral language. To better highlight this difference, adaptation required the action to be transposed into the context of Quebec, and, if necessary, changes were made to lower the level of language. However, little was borrowed from English Canada. The only texts selected were those whose discursive codes were highly compatible with the discourse prevalent in the receptive context.

For its part, the English-Canadian system represented a linguistic majority dispersed throughout the country, whose search for identity was articulated in various often indecisive ways. This young and still hesitant drama massively borrowed Québécois plays that provided much sought-after textual novelty. To facilitate its reception, the highly-accentuated vernacular of the source text gave way to a more standard level of language, and a more familiar, nonthreatening alterity was emphasized. This had the effect of eliminating the linguistic and discursive difference to which the initial work laid claim. So, while the translation towards French readily concealed the source text in order to invest it with identity markers of the target audience, the translation towards English did not hesitate to denature the source text in order to canonize it within its own drama repertoire.

As the 1980s came to a close, a rupture occurred within both systems, and they each exhibited new tendencies. English translation was no longer faced with the problem presented by the use of *joual*, as the new Québécois drama opted to explore verbal aesthetics removed from daily language. This resulted in an exuberant language that triggered certain reservations when reproduced in the English translations. A new approach in search of more naturalistic dialogue had to be adopted to facilitate the reception of plays that would henceforth be exported from Quebec in English translation. As for the linguistic hybridity of the text originating in a francophone minority outside of Quebec, the English translation had to erase it in order to preserve the believability of the dialogue.

At the same time, English-Canadian theatre enjoyed a growing popularity on Québécois stages, not only in terms of the number of plays translated, but because it was a drama whose textual audacity was now acknowledged. The trend towards adaptation faded, but the new interest expressed toward the English-Canadian text remained subject to certain conditions. The specular imperative had given way to a spectacular aesthetic, and it was the provocative theatricality of the borrowed English-Canadian play that legitimized borrowing it. Thereafter, the matter of the plays' origins faded as it was eclipsed by a Canadian repertoire that laid claim to a North American identity.

If there is a constant on both sides that transcends time and place, it is the silence, not to say muteness, observed regarding the process of translation devoted to the borrowed text. Such a silence has the effect of denying the work performed on the text by translation, even though the function fulfilled by most of the translated plays within their receptive context is largely a result of the translative strategies applied to them. This makes it a crucial step in the transcultural exchange that remains unacknowledged. Out of a concern for transparency, one would hope that translators, and all those involved at different steps of the production or publication of translated works, acknowledge and draw attention to the role of translation in the text's passage from one linguistic, cultural, and discursive context to the other.

The analysis put forward in this study would surely benefit from the inclusion of other theatre texts translated during the same periods. Yet the dynamic curve that emerges from this study is nonetheless based on a highly representative corpus. From a functionalist perspective, it would be interesting to not only increase the number of plays in the corpus, but to enlarge the study undertaken here to include plays from other repertoires. This expansion would make it possible to compare the strategies employed elsewhere to respond to the necessities determined by each linguistic, literary, theatrical, social, political, and historical context. Finally, it is necessary to broaden the reflection on the "positionality" of the translator and to develop theoretical tools applicable to the study of the translating subject and its effects on the translated work.

Given that translation is the result of a power struggle between languages, we cannot ignore what is at stake in translating. We are a far cry here from the humanistic intentions and static theories that would like to view translation as a disinterested act of communication defined by a unique and ideal operating model. Likewise, the invisibility enjoyed by a practice whose merit consists in passing unnoticed effectively obscures the highly strategic issues at work. As a site of power and resistance, translation informs what it represents as much as it is informed by the circumstances in which it takes place. If translation is shaped by the struggle between the languages and cultures that it brings into contact, it is only to more effectively shape this struggle in return.

APPENDICES

The translation repertoires presented in the appendices are limited to plays written for an adult audience and that have been published or produced professionally. The plays are presented in a chronological order and then arranged alphabetically by author for works produced in the same year.

The translations of the plays by Joseph Quesnel, Antoine Gérin-Lajoie, Louis-Honoré Fréchette, and Elzéar Paquin appeared in the fourth volume of the 1982 anthology *Canada's Lost Plays, Colonial Quebec: French-Canadian Drama, 1606 to 1966* edited by Anton Wagner. Although they were not written in the period under study, they were translated in this period and were thus included in the corpus, as were the works of the Acadian Antonine Maillet, whose plays were translated, published and produced in English in Quebec. The various English translations of the mega-hit *Broue*, which since 1979 has toured world stages in versions most often adapted to the immediate context by the author and actors themselves, were excluded.

The list of plays has been compiled from the following works.

Forsyth, Louise. "Translations, English to French." In *The Oxford Companion to Canadian Theatre*, edited by Eugene Benson and L.W. Conolly, 564–66. Toronto: Oxford University Press, 1989.

Gaboriau, Linda, and Daniel Gauthier, eds. *Québec Plays in Translation: A Catalogue of Québec Playwrights and Plays in English Translation.* Montreal: CEAD, 1998 and 2001 supplement.

Giguère, Richard. "Traduction littéraire et 'image' de la littérature au Canada et au Québec." In *Translation in Canadian Literature: Symposium 1982,* edited by Camille La Bossière, 47–60. Ottawa: University of Ottawa Press, 1983.

Johnston, Denis W. *Up the Mainstream: The Rise of Toronto's Alternative Theatres, 1968–1975.* Toronto: University of Toronto Press, 1991.

Labonté, Maureen, and Linda Gaboriau, eds. *Québec Plays in Translation: A Catalogue of Québec Playwrights and Plays in English Translation.* Montreal: CEAD, 1990 and 1994 supplement.

Nichols, Glen F. *From Around the World & at Home: Translations and Adaptations in Canadian Theatre.* Toronto: Playwrights Union of Canada, 2001.

O'Connor, John J. "Translations, French to English." In *The Oxford Companion to Canadian Theatre,* edited by Eugene Benson and L.W. Conolly, 566–67. Toronto: Oxford University Press, 1989.

The lists, catalogues, and websites of the Centre des auteurs dramatiques, the National Theatre School library, the Playwrights' Workshop Montreal, and the Association québécoise des auteurs dramatiques were also consulted.

APPENDIX 1:

Repertoire of Anglophone Plays for Adults Produced or Published in French Translation, 1966–2000

1960

Ravel, Aviva. *Les épaulettes (Shoulder Pads)*. Translated by Luce Guilbault. Produced by Instant Theatre, Montreal, 1966.

Ryga, George. *Rita Joe (The Ecstasy of Rita Joe)*. Adapted by Gratien Gélinas. Produced by Comédie-Canadienne, Montreal, November 1969.

1970

Herbert, John. *Aux yeux des hommes (Fortune and Men's Eyes)*. Translated and adapted by René Dionne. Produced by Théâtre de Quat'Sous, Montreal, April 1970. Montreal: Leméac, 1971.

McDonough, John. *Charbonneau et le Chef (Charbonneau and Le Chef)*. Translated and adapted by Paul Hébert and Pierre Morency. Produced by Théâtre du Trident, Quebec City, March 1971, May 1972; Compagnie Jean-Duceppe, Montreal, November 1973, February 1986. Montreal: Leméac, 1974.

Richler, Mordecai. *Les cloches d'enfer (The Bells of Hell Ring Ting-a-Ling)*. Translated and adapted by Gilles Rochette. Produced by Radio-Canada, 1974. Montreal: Leméac, 1974.

Fennario, David. *A l'ouvrage (On the Job)*. Translated by Robert Guy Scully. Produced by Centaur Theatre, Montreal, 1975. Saint-Lambert, QC: Heritage, 1976.

Fielden, Charlotte. *Une heure de vie (One Crowded Hour)*. Translated by René Dionne. Produced by Théâtre de Quat'Sous, Montreal, 1977.

Poirier, Léonie. *La nuit blanche (The White Night)*. Translated by Léonie Poirier. Published by Dramatists' Co-op of Nova Scotia, 1977.

Mitchell, William O. *Aux hirondelles (Back to Beulah)*. Adapted by Arlette Francière and translated by Albert Millaire. Produced by Compagnie Jean-Duceppe, Montreal, 1978.

1980

Charlebois, Gaëtan. *Aléola (Aleola)*. Translated by Jean Daigle. Produced by Théâtre du Rideau Vert, Montreal, March 1980.

Slade, Bernard. *Chapeau! (Tribute)*. Translated by Luis de Céspedes. Produced by Théâtre du Rideau Vert, Montreal, 1980–1981. Montreal: Leméac, 1981.

Freeman, David. *Les tout-croches (Creeps)*. Translated by Pierre Collin and Louison Danis. Produced by Salle Fred-Barry, Montreal, April 1981.

Griffiths, Linda. *Margaret et Pierre* (*Maggie and Pierre*). Translated by Elizabeth Bourget. Théâtre d'la Corvée, Vanier, ON, 1983.

Palmer, John. *Hystérie bleu banane* (*Bland Hysteria*). Translated by Christian Bédard. Produced by Théâtre de la Dame de coeur, Upton, QC, 1983.

Slade, Bernard. *Deux à dos* (*Special Occasion*). Translated by Luis de Céspedes. Produced by Théâtre du Rideau Vert, Montreal, 1982–1983.

Freeman, David. *Le bélier* (*Battering Ram*). Adapted by Louison Danis. Produced by Théâtre d'Aujourd'hui, Montreal, January 1984.

Chislett, Ann. *La boîte à surprise* (*The Tomorrow Box*). Translated by Paul Latreille. Produced by Théâtre les femmes Collin, Saint-Esprit, QC, 1984. Théâtre des Filles du Roy, Quebec City, 1985.

Gray, John. *Rock and Roll*. Translated by René Dionne. Produced by Théâtre de Quat'Sous, Montreal, 1985.

Martin, Eric. *Les oubliés* (*Stragglers*). Translated by Guy Pariseau. Produced by Théâtre français d'Edmonton, 1985.

Foster, Christine. *Extases* (*Raptures*). Translated by Michelle Daigle and Claude Vignault. Produced by Théâtre de l'Île, Hull, 1986.

Gross, Paul. *Tension Zéro* (*Sprung Rhythm*). Translated by René Dionne. Produced by Théâtre de la Bordée, Quebec City, 1986.

Lushington, Kate. *Sexe en boîte* (*Sex in a Box*). Translated by Louise Ladouceur. Produced by Théâtre Espace Go, Montreal, 1986.

Pollock, Sharon. *Liens de sang* (*Blood Relations*). Translated by Francine Pominville. Produced by Théâtre de la Commune, Quinzaine internationale de Québec, 1986.

Walker, George. *Le théâtre du film noir* (*Theatre of the Film Noir*). Translated by Louise Ringuet. Produced by Théâtre d'la Corvée, Vanier, ON, 1986.

Rapoport, Janis. *Dreamgirls*. Translated by Francine Pominville. Produced by Théâtre de la Commune, Quebec City, 1987.

Burdman, Ralph. *Tête-à-tête* (*Eye to Eye*). Translated by Jean-Louis Roux. Produced by Café de la Place, 1987. Montreal: Boréal, 1988.

Brown, Ken. *La vie après le hockey* (*Life after Hockey*). Translated by Michel Garneau. Produced by Théâtre français d'Edmonton, 1987.

Murrell, John. *Sarah et le cri de la langouste* (*Memoir*). Adapted by Georges Wilson. Produced by Café de la Place, Montreal, 1987.

Colley, Peter. *J'vais revenir avant minuit* (*I'll Be Back before Midnight*). Translated and adapted by Josée Labossière. Produced by Théâtre de l'Île, Hull, 1988.

Lechay, Jo, and Eugene Lion. *Affamée* (*Affamée / Want*). Translated by Isabelle Cauchy and Michel Garneau. Produced by Création Isis, Montreal, 1988.

Pollock, Sharon. *Doc*. Translated by Francine Pominville. Produced by Théâtre de la Commune, Quebec City, 1988.

Foster, Norm. *Péché mortel* (*Sinners*). Translated by Robert Marinier. Produced by Théâtre de l'Île, Hull, 1989.

Foster, Norm. *Les frères Mainville* (*The Melville Boys*). Translated by Paul Latreille. Produced by Théâtre de l'Île, Hull, 1989.

Stetson, Ken. *Comme un vent chaud de Chine* (*Warm Wind in China*). Translated by Ronald Guèvremont. Produced by Théâtre de l'Île, Hull, 1988. Montreal: NuAge Editions, 1989.

Walker, George F. *Amours passibles d'amendes* (*Criminals in Love*). Translated by Louison Danis. Produced by Théâtre Denise-Pelletier, Montreal, 1989.

1990

Thompson, Judith. *Je suis à toi* (*I Am Yours*). Translated by Robert Vézina. Produced by Théâtre de la Manufacture, Montreal, 1990.

Fraser, Brad. *Des restes humains non identifiés et de la véritable nature de l'amour* (*Unidentified Human Remains and the True Nature of Love*). Translated by André Brassard. Produced by Théâtre de Quat'Sous, Montreal, 1991. Montreal: Boréal, 1993.

Liitoja, Hillar. *Voilà ce qui se passe à Orangeville* (*This Is What Happens in Orangeville*). Translated by Paul Lefebvre. Produced by Salle Fred-Barry, Montreal, 1991. Montreal: Les Herbes Rouges, 1994.

Mother, Frank. *L'homme à tout faire* (*Odd Jobs*). Translated by Simon Verville and Laurier Gareau. Produced by La Troupe du Jour, Saskatoon, 1991.

Moses, Daniel David. *Belle fille de l'aurore* (*The Dreaming Beauty*). Translated by Daniel David Moses. Produced by La Troupe du Jour, Saskatoon, 1991.

Thompson, Judith. *Lion dans les rues* (*Lion in the Streets*). Translated by Robert Vézina. Produced by Théâtre de Quat'Sous, Montreal, 1991.

Foster, Norm. *L'amour compte double* (*The Affections of May*). Translated by Josée Labossière. Produced by Théâtre d'été de Stoneham, Quebec City, 1992.

Lion, Eugene. *Zéro absolu* (*Absolute Zero*). Translated by Michel Garneau and Isabelle Cauchy. Produced by Création Isis, Théâtre d'Aujourd'hui, Montreal, 1992.

Madden, Peter. *Crime du siècle* (*Crime of the Century*). Translated by Guy Beausoleil. Produced by Théâtre d'Aujourd'hui, Montreal, 1992.

Clark, Sally. *La vie sans mode d'emploi* (*Life Without Instruction*). Translated by Maryse Pelletier. Produced by Théâtre populaire du Québec, Montreal, 1993.

Fraser, Brad. *L'homme laid* (*The Ugly Man*). Translated by Maryse Warda. Produced by Théâtre de Quat'Sous, Montreal, 1993. Montreal: Boréal, 1993.

Highway, Tomson. *Les reines de la réserve* (*The Rez Sisters*). Translated by Jocelyne Beaulieu. Produced by Théâtre populaire du Québec, Montreal, 1993.

Lill, Wendy. *Les traverses du coeur* (*Memories of You*). Translated by Guy Beausoleil. Produced by Théâtre populaire du Québec, Montreal, January 1993.

Foster, Norm. *Une chance sur un million* (*Wrong For Each Other*). Translated by Josée Labossière. Produced by Théâtre de l'Île, Hull, 1994.

Hayes, Eliot. *Tout va pour le mieux* (*Homeward Bound*). Translated by Jean Marc Dalpé and Robert Marinier. Produced by Théâtre du Rideau Vert, Montreal, 1994.

Mackenzie, Michael. *Le précepteur* (*Geometry in Venice*). Translated by Jean Asselin. Produced by Theatre Omnibus, Montreal, 1994. Montreal: Les Herbes Rouges, 1995.

Fraser, Brad. *Poor Super Man*. Translated by Robert Vézina. Produced by Théâtre de Quat'Sous, Montreal, 1995.

Hausvater, Alexandre. *La dernière mazurka* (*The Last Mazurka*). Translated by Jean Marchand. Rosemère, QC: Humanitas, 1995.

Foster, Norm. *L'homme accessoire* (*My Darling Judith*). Translated and adapted by Josée Labossière. Produced by Théâtre Quatre/Corps, Chateauguay, QC, 1996.

Nostbaken, Janis. *Le défi de la capitale* (*Capital Quiz*). Translated by Patrick Leroux. Produced by Le Théâtre de la rue York, Ottawa, 1996.

Lion, Eugene. *Chrysanthème* (*Chrysantemum*). Translated by Guy Beausoleil. Produced by Théâtre d'aujourd'hui, Montreal, 1997. Montreal: Dramaturges Éditeurs, 1997.

Mackenzie, Michael. *Le cercle* (*The Circle*). Translated by Jean Asselin. Produced by Théâtre Omnibus, Montreal, 1997.

Roy, Edward. *O.V.N.I.R.E.X.* (*U.F.O.R.E.X.*). Translated by Marc Prescott. Produced by Cercle Molière, Saint-Boniface, MB, 1997.

Sherman, Jason, *Trois dans le dos, deux dans la tête* (*Three in the Back, Two in the Head*). Translated by Pierre Legris. Public reading, Festival de théâtre des Amériques, CEAD, PWM and Difusion Cultural UNAM, Mexico, 1995. Produced by Théâtre de la Manufacture, 1997.

Walker, George F. *L'enfant-problème* (*Problem Child*). Translated by Maryse Warda. Produced by Théâtre de Quat'Sous, Montreal, 1998. Montreal: VLB Éditeur, 2001.

Dykstra, Ted, and Richard Greenblatt. *Deux pianos, quatre mains* (*Two Pianos, Four Hands*). Translated by Danièle Lorrain. Produced by Théâtre du Rideau Vert, Montreal, 1999.

French, David. *Une lune d'eau salée* (*Salt-Water Moon*). Translated by Antonine Maillet. Produced by Théâtre de l'Île, Hull, 1999.

Hunter, Maureen. *L'Atlantide* (*Atlantis*). Translated by Michelle Allen. Public reading, CEAD and Playwrights' Workshop Montreal, 1997. Produced by Théâtre de la Manufacture/La Licorne, Montreal, 1999.

Mackenzie, Michael. *La baronne et la truie* (*The Baroness and the Pig*). Translated by Paul Lefebvre. Produced by Theatre Omnibus, Montreal, 1998. Montreal: Les Herbes Rouges, 1999.

Stickland, Eugene. *Noël de force (Some Assembly Required)*. Translated by René Gingras. Produced by Compagnie Jean-Duceppe, Montreal, 1999.

Varmal, Rahul. *L'affaire Farhadi (Counter Offence)*. Translated by Pierre Legris. Produced by Théâtre la Licorne, Montreal, 1999.

Walker, George F. *Pour adultes seulement (Adult Entertainment)*. Translated by Maryse Warda. Produced by Théâtre de Quat'Sous, Montreal, 1999. Montreal: VLB Éditeur, 2001.

Walker, George F. *Le génie du crime (Criminal Genius)*. Translated by Maryse Warda. Produced by Théâtre de Quat'Sous, Montreal, 1999. Montreal: VLB Éditeur, 2001.

Walker, George F. *La fin de la civilisation (The End of Civilization)*. Translated by Maryse Warda. Produced by Théâtre de Quat'Sous, Montreal, 1999. Montreal: VLB Éditeur, 2001.

Young, David. *Antatirkos (Inexpressible Island)*. Translated by André Ricard. Produced by Théâtre du Trident, Quebec City, 1999. Montreal: Dramaturges Éditeurs, 2000.

APPENDIX 2:

*Repertoire of Francophone Plays for Adults Produced
or Published in English Translation, 1950–2000*

1950

Gélinas, Gratien. *Tit-Coq*. Translated by Kenneth Johnstone and Gratien
Gélinas. Produced by Monument-National, Montreal, 1950; Royal
Alexandra, Toronto, 1951. Toronto: Clarke, Irwin, 1967.

Languirand, Jacques. *The Eccentrics (Les insolites)*. Translated by Albert Bermel.
Produced by Regional Festival of Dramatic Art, Quebec City, 1956.

Dubé, Marcel. *The Time of the Lilacs (Le temps des lilas)*. Translated by Kenneth
Johnstone. Produced by Royal Alexandra, Toronto, 1958.

1960

Gélinas, Gratien. *Bousille and the Just (Bousille et les justes)*. Translated by
Kenneth Johnstone and Joffre Miville-Deschêne. Produced by Comédie-
Canadienne, 1961; Royal Alexandra, Toronto, 1962. Toronto: Clarke, Irwin,
1961.

Languirand, Jacques. *The Partition (Les cloisons)*. Translated by Albert Bermel.
Produced by Instant Theatre, Montreal, 1965; Central Library Theatre,
Toronto, 1966.

Languirand, Jacques. *The Departures (Les grands départs)*. Translated by Albert
Bermel. Produced by Central Library Theatre, Toronto, 1966. London:
Gambit 5, 1966.

Gélinas, Gratien. *Yesterday, the Children Were Dancing (Hier, les enfants
dansaient)*. Translated by Mavor Moore. Produced by Dominion Drama
Festival, Charlottetown, 1967. Toronto: Clarke, Irwin, 1967.

Basile, Jean. *The Drummer Boy (Joli tambour)*. Translated by Jeremy Brooks.
Produced by Theatre Toronto at the Royal Alexandra, Toronto, 1968.

Gurik, Robert. *Hamlet, Prince of Quebec (Hamlet, prince du Québec)*. Translated
by Marc F. Gélinas. Produced by London Little Theatre, ON, 1968. Toronto:
Playwrights Co-op, 1973; Vancouver: Talonbooks, 1974.

Gurik, Robert. *Api 2967*. Translated by Marc F. Gélinas. Produced by Citadel
Theatre, Edmonton, 1969. Toronto: Playwrights Co-op, 1973; Vancouver:
Talonbooks, 1974.

1970

Germain, Jean-Claude. *Notes from Quebec*. Translated by Paul Thompson.
Produced by Theatre Passe Muraille, Toronto, 1970.

Languirand, Jacques. *Man Inc. (L'âge de pierre)*. Translated by Mavor Moore.
Produced by St. Lawrence Centre, Toronto, 1970.

Barbeau, Jean. *The Way of Lacross (Le chemin de Lacroix)*. Translated by Laurence Bédard and Philip W. London. Produced by WW Theatre at the Poor Alex Theatre, Toronto, 1972. Toronto: Playwrights Co-op, 1973.

Barbeau, Jean. *Manon Lastcall*. Translated by Philip W. London and Suzan K. London. Produced by WW Theatre at the Poor Alex Theatre, Toronto, 1972.

Carrier, Roch. *La guerre, yes sir*. Translated by Sheila Fischman. Produced by Stratford Festival, Stratford, ON, 1972.

Dubé, Marcel. *The White Geese (Au retour des oies blanches)*. Translated by Jean Remple. Toronto: New Press, 1972.

Dufresne, Guy. *The Cry of the Whippoorwill (Le cri de l'engoulevent)*. Translated by Laurence Bédard and Philip W. London. Toronto: New Press, 1972.

Hébert, Anne. *Le Temps Sauvage*. Translated by Elizabeth Mascall. Produced by University Alumnae Dramatic Productions at the Firehall Theatre, Toronto, 1972.

Tremblay, Michel. *Forever Yours, Marie-Lou (À toi pour toujours, ta Marie-Lou)*. Translated by Bill Glassco and John Van Burek. Produced by Tarragon Theatre, Toronto, 1972. Vancouver: Talonbooks, 1975.

Gélinas, Marc F. *Mortier*. Translated by Marc F. Gélinas. Produced by Factory Theatre Lab, Toronto, 1973.

Gurik, Robert. *The Hanged Man (Le pendu)*. Translated by Philip W. London and Laurence Bédard. Produced by Domino Theatre, Kingston, 1973. Toronto: New Press, 1972.

Tremblay, Michel. *Les Belles Soeurs (Les belles-sœurs)*. Translated by Bill Glassco and John Van Burek. Produced by St. Lawrence Centre, Toronto, 1973. Vancouver: Talonbooks, 1974.

Tremblay, Michel. *Like Death Warmed Over (En pièces détachées)*. Translated by Allan Van Meer. Produced by Manitoba Theatre Centre, Winnipeg, 1973; *Montreal Smoked Meat*, New Theatre, Toronto, 1974; *Broken Pieces*, Arts Club Theatre, Vancouver, 1974; *Like Death Warmed Over*, Toronto: Playwrights Co-op, 1973; *En pièces détachées*. Vancouver: Talonbooks, 1975.

Garneau, Michel. *Four to Four (Quatre à quatre)*. Translated by Christian Bédard and Keith Turnbull. Produced by Tarragon Theatre, Toronto, 1974. *A Collection of Canadian Plays*, Toronto: Simon & Pierre, 1978.

Gurik, Robert. *The Trial of Jean-Baptiste M. (Le procès de Jean-Baptiste M.)*. Translated by Allan Van Meer. Produced by Vancouver Players, Vancouver, 1974. Vancouver: Talonbooks, 1974.

Tremblay, Michel. *Hosanna*. Translated by John Van Burek and Bill Glassco. Produced by Tarragon Theatre, Toronto, 1974; Toronto Workshop, 1977. Vancouver: Talonbooks, 1974, 1991.

Barbeau, Jean. *The Binge (Une brosse)*. Translated by John Van Burek. Produced by Young People's Theatre, Toronto, 1975.

Tremblay, Michel. *Bonjour, Là, Bonjour (Bonjour, là, bonjour)*. Translated by John Van Burek. Produced by Tarragon Theatre, Toronto, 1975. Vancouver: Talonbooks, 1975.

Tremblay, Michel. *Surprise! Surprise!* Translated by John Van Burek. Produced by Tarragon Theatre, Toronto, 1975. Vancouver: Talonbooks, 1975.

Barbeau, Jean. *Goglu*. Translated by John Van Burek. Produced by Pleiades Theatre, Toronto, 1976. Toronto: *Canadian Theatre Review* 11 (1976).

Barbeau, Jean. *Solange*. Translated by John Van Burek. Produced by Pleiades Theatre, Toronto, 1976. Toronto: *Canadian Theatre Review* 11 (1976).

Blais, Marie-Claire. *The Execution (L'exécution)*. Translated by David Lobdell. Vancouver: Talonbooks, 1976.

Sirois, Serge. *Summer Holidays (Vacances d'été)*. Translated by Charlotte Fielden. Produced by Centaur Theatre, Montreal, 1976.

Tremblay, Michel. *La Duchesse and Other Plays (Trois Petits Tours)*. Translated by John Van Burek. Vancouver: Talonbooks, 1976.

Tremblay, Michel. *La Duchesse de Langeais*. Translated by John Van Burek. Produced by Black Cat Cabaret, Toronto, 1976. Vancouver: Talonbooks, 1976.

Blais, Marie-Claire. *The Ocean. (L'océan)*. Translated by Ray Chamberlain. *Exile* 3-4 (1977).

Carrier, Roch. *Floralie, Where Are You? (Floralie)*. Translated by Sheila Fischman. Produced by National Arts Centre, Ottawa, 1977. Toronto: Anansi, 1971.

Dubé, Marcel. *Zone*. Translated by Aviva Ravel. Produced by Saidye Bronfman Centre, Montreal, 1977. Toronto: Playwrights Canada, 1982.

Tremblay, Michel. *Johnny Mangano and His Astonishing Dogs*. In *Cues and Entrances*. Translated by Arlette Francière. Gage Educational Publishing: Edmonton, 1977.

Lavigne, Louis-Dominique. *Are You Afraid of Thieves? (As-tu peur des voleurs?)*. Translated by Henry Beissel. In *A Collection of Canadian Plays*. Toronto: Simon & Pierre, 1978.

Lepage, Roland. *Le Temps d'une Vie*. Translated by Sheila Fischman. Produced by Tarragon Theatre, Toronto, 1978.

Mercier, Serge. *A Little Bit Left (Encore un peu)*. Translated by Allan Van Meer. In *A Collection of Canadian Plays*. Toronto: Simon & Pierre, 1978.

Pelletier, Pol. (collective including M.-C. Blais, M. Blackburn, N. Brossard, O. Gagnon, L. Guilbeault, P. Pelletier and F. Theoret). *A Clash of Symbols (La nef des sorcières)*. Translated by Linda Gaboriau. Produced by The Alumni Theatre, Toronto, 1978. Toronto: Coach House Press, 1977.

Roussin, Claude. *Looking for a Job (Une job)*. Translated by Allan Van Meer. In *A Collection of Canadian Plays*. Toronto: Simon & Pierre, 1978.

Simard, André. *Waiting for Gaudreault (En attendant Gaudreault)*. Translated by Henry Beissel and Arlette Francière. In *A Collection of Canadian Plays*. Toronto: Simon & Pierre, 1978.

Sirois, Serge. *Dodo*. Translated by John Van Burek. In *A Collection of Canadian Plays*. Toronto: Simon & Pierre, 1978.

Tremblay, Michel. *Sainte-Carmen of the Main* (Sainte-Carmen de la Main). Translated by John Van Burek. Produced by Tarragon Theatre, Toronto, 1978. Vancouver: Talonbooks, 1981.

Tremblay, Reynald. *Greta, the Divine (La celeste Greta)*. Translated by Allan Van Meer. Toronto: Simon & Pierre, 1978.

Maillet, Antonine. *La Sagouine*. Translated by Luis de Céspedes. Produced by Saidye Bronfman Centre, Montreal, 1979. Toronto: Simon & Pierre, 1979.

Marchessault, Jovette. *Night Cows (Les vaches de nuit)*. Translated by Yvonne Klein. Produced by Women's Salon, New York, 1979; Atthis, Toronto, 1980. In *Lesbian Triptych*. Toronto: Women's Press, 1985.

Tremblay, Michel. *Damnée Manon, Sacrée Sandra*. Translated by John Van Burek. Produced by Arts Club Theatre, Vancouver, 1979. Vancouver: Talonbooks, 1981.

Tremblay, Michel. *The Pedestals (Les socles)*. Translated by John Van Burek. Toronto: *Canadian Theatre Review* 24 (1979).

1980

Provencher, Jean and Gilles Lachance. *Quebec, Spring 1918 (Québec, Printemps 1918)*. Translated by Leo Skir and Jean Provencher. Toronto: *Canadian Theatre Review* 28 (1980).

Roy, Louise, and Louis Saia. *A Childhood Friend (Une amie d'enfance)*. Translated by David MacDonald. Produced by Théâtre de la Poudrière, Montreal, 1980.

Tremblay, Michel. *The Impromptu of Outremont (L'impromptu d'Outremont)*. Translated by John Van Burek. Produced by Arts Club Theatre, Vancouver, 1980. Vancouver: Talonbooks, 1981.

Boucher, Denise. *The Fairies Are Thirsty (Les fées ont soif)*. Translated by Alan Brown. Produced by D.B. Clarke Theatre, Concordia University, Montreal, 1981. Vancouver: Talonbooks, 1982.

Garneau, Michel. *The Snows (Les neiges)*. Translated by Ken Brown. Produced by The First Snow and Workshop West, Edmonton, 1981.

Gauvreau, Claude. *Entrails (Entrailles)*. Translated by Ray Ellenwood. Toronto: Coach House Press, 1981.

Carrier, Roch. *The Celestial Bicycle (La bicyclette céleste)*. Translated by Sheila Fischman. Produced by Tarragon Theatre, Toronto, 1982.

Gurik, Robert. *The Champion (Le champion)*. Translated by Allan Van Meer. Toronto: Playwrights Canada, 1982.

Maillet, Antonine. *Pélagie (Pélagie-la-charette)*. Translated by Philip Stratford. Toronto: Doubleday, 1982.

Marchessault, Jovette. *Saga of the Wet Hens* (*La saga des poules mouillées*). Translated by Linda Gaboriau. Produced by Tarragon Theatre, Toronto, 1982. Vancouver: Talonbooks, 1983.

Micone, Marco. *Voiceless People* (*Gens du silence*). Translated by Maurizia Binda. In *Two Plays*. Toronto: Guernica, 1982.

Micone, Marco. *Addolorata*. Translated by Maurizia Binda. Public reading, CEAD and Ubu Repertory Theater, New York, 1984. In *Two Plays*. Toronto: Guernica, 1982.

Saia, Louis et al. *Brew* (*Broue*). Translated by David MacDonald and Michel Côté. Produced by Centaur Theatre, Montreal, 1982.

Roy, Louise, and Louis Saia. *Single* (*Bachelor*). Translated by Michael Sinelnikoff. Produced by Encore Theatre, Montreal, 1983.

Barbeau, Jean. *The Guys* (*Les gars*). Translated by Linda Gaboriau. Produced by Vancouver Playhouse, Vancouver, 1984.

Caron, Catherine, Brigitte Haentjens and Sylvie Trudel. *Strip*. Translated by Robert Dickson. Produced by Théâtre du P'tit Bonheur, Toronto, 1984.

Hébert, Anne. *The Unquiet State*. Translated by Eugene Benson and Renate Benson. *Canadian Drama* 10, no. 2 (1984).

Tremblay, Michel. *Remember Me* (*Les anciennes odeurs*). Translated by John Stowe. Produced by MTC Warehouse Theatre, Winnipeg, 1984. Vancouver: Talonbooks, 1984.

Bouchard, Denis, Rémy Girard, Raymond Legault, and Julie Vincent. *Terminal Blues* (*La déprime*). Translated by Maureen Labonté. Produced by National Arts Centre, Ottawa, 1985.

Dussault, Louisette. *Mommy* (*Moman*). Translated by Michael Sinelnikoff. Produced by Factory Theatre Lab, Toronto, 1985.

Marchessault Jovette. *The Angel Makers* (*Les faiseuses d'anges*). Translated by Yvonne Klein. In *Lesbian Triptych*. Toronto: Women's Press, 1985.

Chaurette, Normand. *Provincetown Playhouse, July 1919* (*Provincetown Playhouse, juillet 1919, j'avais 19 ans*). Translated by William Boulet. Public reading, CEAD and Ubu Repertory Theater, New York, 1984. Produced by Buddies in Bad Times Theatre, Toronto, 1986. In *Quebec Voices: Three Plays*. Toronto: Coach House Press, 1986.

Dubois, René-Daniel. *Don't Blame the Bedouins* (*Ne blâmez jamais les Bédouins*). Translated by Maureen Labonté. Produced by Prairie Theatre Exchange, Winnipeg, 1987. In *Quebec Voices: Three Plays*. Toronto: Coach House Press, 1986.

Ducharme, Réjean. *Ha! Ha!* Translated by David Homel. Toronto: Exile Editions, 1986.

Gélinas, Gratien. *The Passion of Narcisse Mondoux* (*La passion de Narcisse Mondoux*). Translated by Linda Gaboriau. Produced by Theatre du P'tit Bonheur, Toronto, 1986. Toronto: Anansi, 1992.

Marchessault, Jovette. *The Edge of Earth is Too Near, Violette Leduc (La terre est trop courte, Violette Leduc)*. Translated by Susanne de Lotbinière-Harwood. Produced by Nightwood Theatre, Toronto, 1986.

Tremblay, Michel. *Albertine, in Five Times (Albertine en cinq temps)*. Translated by Bill Glassco and John Van Burek. Produced by Tarragon Theatre, Toronto, 1986. Vancouver: Talonbooks, 1986.

Bersianik, Louky. *The Eugélionne (L'Eugélionne)*. Translated by Cynthia Grant. Produced by Groundswell Festival, Toronto, 1987.

Dubois, René-Daniel. *Being at Home with Claude*. Translated by Linda Gaboriau. Produced by Tarragon Theatre, Toronto, 1987. Toronto: Canadian Theatre Review 50 (1987).

Maillet, Antonine. *Evangeline the Second (Evangéline Deusse)*. Translated by Luis de Céspedes. Produced by CBC Television. Toronto: Simon & Pierre, 1987.

Maillet, Antonine. *Gapi and Sullivan (Gapi)*. Translated by Luis de Céspedes. Toronto: Simon & Pierre, 1987.

Rousseau, André. *Mackenzie King*. Translated by Lib Spry. Produced by Théâtre Dérives Urbaines, Hull, 1987.

Dalpé, Jean Marc. *Le Chien (Le chien)*. Translated by Maureen Labonté and Jean Marc Dalpé. Public reading, CEAD and Factory Theatre, Toronto, 1988. Produced by Factory Theatre, 1988.

Gingras, René. *Breaks (Syncope)*. Translated by Linda Gaboriau. Public reading, CEAD and Playwrights' Workshop Montreal. Produced by The Acting Company, Toronto, 1988. In *Quebec Voices: Three Plays*. Toronto: Coach House Press, 1986.

Laberge, Marie. *Night (L'homme gris)*. Translated by Rina Fraticelli. Public reading, CEAD and Ubu Repertory Theater, New York, 1986. Produced by Toronto Free Theatre, 1988. In *Plays by Women, Vol. 7*. London: Methuen, 1988.

Lepage, Robert. *Vinci*. Translated by Linda Gaboriau. Produced by Théâtre de Quat'Sous, Montreal, 1988.

Rousseau, André. *Black Market (Marché noir)*. Translated by Jennifer Boyes. Produced by Théâtre Dérives Urbaines, National Arts Centre, Ottawa, 1988.

Tremblay, Michel. *The Real World? (Le vrai monde?)*. Translated by Bill Glassco and John Van Burek. Produced by Tarragon Theatre, Toronto, 1988. Vancouver: Talonbooks, 1988.

Canac-Marquis, Normand. *The Cezanne Syndrome (Le syndrome de Cézanne)*. Translated by Louison Danis. Produced by Soho Repertory Theatre, New York, 1989. New York: Playwrights Press, 1989; *Theatrum* 13 (1989).

Works from the Seventeenth, Eighteenth, and Nineteenth Centuries

Fréchette, Louis-Honoré. *Papineau*. Play originally produced in Montreal and Quebec, and published in 1880. Translated by Eugene Benson and Renate Benson. In *Canada's Lost Plays*. Vol 4. Toronto: Canadian Theatre Review Publications, 1982.

Gérin-Lajoie, Antoine. *The Young Latour* (*Le jeune Latour*). Originally produced in Montreal and published in 1844. Translated by Louise Forsyth. In *Canada's Lost Plays*. Vol. 4. Toronto: Canadian Theatre Review Publications, 1982.

Paquin, Elzéar. *Riel*. Originally produced and published in 1886. Translated by Eugene Benson and Renate Benson. In *Canada's Lost Plays*. Vol. 4. Toronto: Canadian Theatre Review Publications, 1982.

Quesnel, Joseph. *Colas and Colinette or The Bailiff Confounded* (*Colas et Colinette ou Le bailli dupé*). First produced in Montreal in 1790 and published in 1808. Translated by Michel Lecavalier and Godfrey Ridout. Toronto: *Canada's Lost Plays*. Vol. 4. Toronto: Canadian Theatre Review Publications, 1982.

Quesnel, Joseph. *The French Republicans or An Evening in the Tavern* (*Les Républicains français ou La soirée du cabaret*). 1800–1801. Publication of the original play in 1970. Translated by Louise Forsyth. In *Canada's Lost Plays*. Vol. 4. Toronto: Canadian Theatre Review Publications, 1982.

1990

Dubois, René-Daniel. *But Laura Didn't Answer* (*Et Laura ne répondait plus*). Translated by Linda Gaboriau. Produced by CBC Radio, Vancouver, 1990; Pink Ink Theatre Productions, Vancouver, 1995.

Garneau, Michel. *Warriors* (*Les guerriers*). Translated by Linda Gaboriau. Public reading, Factory Theatre, Toronto, 1990. Produced by Alberta Theatre Projects, Calgary, 1990. Vancouver: Talonbooks, 1990.

Legault, Anne. *O'Neill*. Translated by Daniel Libman. Toronto: Playwrights Canada, 1990.

Lepage, Robert, and Marie Brassard. *Polygraph* (*Le Polygraphe*). Translated by Raby Gyllian. Produced by Harbourfront Quayworks, Toronto, 1990. *Canadian Theatre Review* 64 (1990); In *Modern Canadian Plays*, 3rd ed., vol. 2, 1994.

Pelletier, Maryse. *Duo for Obstinate Voices* (*Duo pour voix obstinées*). Translated by Louise Ringuet. Produced by Terra Nova Theatre, Ontario, 1990. Toronto: Guernica, 1990.

Tremblay, Michel. *La Maison Suspendue*. Translated by Bill Glassco and John Van Burek. Produced by Canadian Stage, Toronto, 1990. Vancouver: Talonbooks, 1990.

Blais, Marie-Claire. *The Island*, (*L'île*). Translated by David Lobdell. Ottawa: Oberon, 1991.

Bouchard, Michel Marc. *Lilies or The Revival of a Romantic Drama* (*Les feluettes ou la répétition d'un drame romantique*). Translated by Linda Gaboriau. Public reading, CEAD and Factory Theatre, 1988. Produced by Theatre Passe Muraille, Toronto, 1991; Touchstone Theatre, Vancouver, 1994. Toronto: Coach House Press, 1990.

Bouyoucas, Pan. *Three Cops on a Roof* (*Trois policiers sur un toit*). Translated by the author. Produced by POV Productions, Montreal, 1991.

Chaurette, Normand. *Fragments of a Farewell Letter Read by Geologists* (*Lettre d'adieu lue par des géologues*). Translated by Linda Gaboriau. Public reading, CEAD and Prairie Theatre Exchange, Winnipeg, 1989. Produced by Cahoots Theatre Projects, Toronto, 1991. Vancouver: Talonbooks, 1998.

Delisle, Jeanne-Mance. *A Live Bird in Its Jaw* (*Un oiseau vivant dans la gueule*). Translated by Yves Saint-Pierre. Produced by Theatre Passe Muraille/ Particle Zoo, Toronto, 1991. Montreal: NuAge Editions, 1992.

Dugas, Bernard, Bertrand Dugas, and Rychard Thériault. *Ernest and Etienne* (*Ernest et Étienne ou les bessons un peu plus loin*). Translated by Marshall Button. Produced by Upper Canada Playhouse, Morrisburg, ON, 1991.

Marinier, Robert, and Daniel Lalande. *Comeback* (*Deuxième souffle*). Translated by Robert Marinier and Daniel Lalande. Produced by Théâtre du Nouvel Ontario, Sudbury, 1991. Sudbury, ON: Prise de parole, 1992.

Bouchard, Michel Marc. *The Tale of Teeka* (*L'histoire de l'oie*). Translated by Linda Gaboriau. Produced by World Stage Festival, Toronto, 1992; Vancouver East Cultural Centre/Les Deux Mondes, Vancouver, 1995. Toronto: Dundurn Press, 1998.

Chaurette, Normand. *The Queens* (*Les reines*). Translated by Linda Gaboriau (commissioned by Banff Playwrights' Colony). Produced by Canadian Stage Company, Toronto, 1992. Toronto: Coach House Press, 1992.

Marchessault, Jovette. *The Magnificent Voyage of Emily Carr* (*Le voyage magnifique d'Emily Carr*). Translated by Linda Gaboriau. Produced by The Belfry Theatre, Victoria, 1992. Vancouver: Talonbooks, 1992.

Tremblay, Michel. *Marcel Pursued by the Hounds* (*Marcel poursuivi par les chiens*). Translated by Bill Glassco and John Van Burek. Vancouver: Talonbooks, 1992.

Bouchard, Michel Marc. *The Orphan Muses* (*Les muses orphelines*). Translated by Linda Gaboriau (for the Banff Playwrights' Colony). Produced by Ubu Repertory Theater, New York, 1993; Touchstone Theatre, Vancouver, 1996. Winnipeg, MB: Scirocco, 1993.

Champagne, Dominic. *Playing Bare* (*La répétition*). Translated by Shelley Tepperman. Produced by Street People Company, Montreal, 1992. Vancouver: Talonbooks, 1993.

Bellefeuille, Robert. *The Beauty Machine (La machine à beauté).* Translated by
Linda Gaboriau. Produced by National Arts Centre/Théâtre de la Vieille 17,
Ottawa, 1994.

Dalpé, Jean Marc. *In the Ring (Eddy).* Translated by Robert Dickson. Produced
by Stratford Theatre Festival, 1994. *Canadian Theatre Review* 84 (1995).

Danis, Daniel. *Stone and Ashes (Cendres de cailloux).* Translated by Linda
Gaboriau. Public reading, CEAD and Ubu Repertory Theater, New York,
1993. Produced by Factory Theatre, Toronto, 1994; Pink Ink Theatre,
Vancouver 1996. Toronto: Coach House Press, 1995.

Fortin, Simon. *The Country in Her Throat (Un pays dans la gorge).* Translated by
Bill Glassco. Produced by Tarragon Theatre, Toronto, 1994. Winnipeg, MB:
Scirocco, 1994.

Marinier, Robert. *Insomnia (Insomnie).* Translated by the author. Produced by
the National Arts Centre, Ottawa, 1994.

Archambault, François. *Fast Lane (Cul sec).* Translated by Shelly Tepperman.
Produced by National Arts Centre, 1995.

Micone, Marco. *Beyond the Ruins (Déjà l'agonie).* Translated by Jill MacDougall.
Toronto: Guernica, 1995.

Pelletier, Pol. *Joy (Joie).* Translated by Linda Gaboriau. Produced by Theatre
Passe Muraille, Toronto, 1995.

Sioui Durand, Yves, and Georges Henri Michel. *The Sun Raiser (Le porteur des
peines du monde).* Translated by Käthe Roth, Tomson Highway, James
Nickolas. Produced by Banff International Festival, 1995.

Bouchard, Michel Marc. *Desire (Le désir).* Translated by Linda Gaboriau.
Produced by Theatre Lac Brome, Quebec City, 1996.

Bouchard, Michel Marc. *Heat Wave (Les grandes chaleurs).* Translated by Bill
Glassco. Winnipeg, MB: Scirocco, 1996.

Mouawad, Wajdi. *Wedding Day at the Cromagnons' (Journée de noces chez les
Cro-Magnons).* Translated by Shelley Tepperman. Public reading, CEAD and
Factory Theatre, Toronto, 1994. Produced by Theatre Passe Muraille and
the National Arts Centre, Ottawa, 1996. In *Playwrights in Exile.* New York:
Ubu Repertory Theater Publications, 1997.

Dalpé, Jean Marc. *Lucky Lady.* Translated by Robert Dickson. Produced by
Great Canadian Theatre Company, Ottawa, 1997.

Fréchette, Carole. *The Four Lives of Marie (Les quatre morts de Marie).* Translated
by John Murrell. Produced by Tarragon Theatre, 1997.

Marinier, Robert. *But for the Grace of God (À la gauche de Dieu).* Translated by
the author. Produced by the National Arts Centre, Ottawa, 1997.

Blais, Marie-Claire. *Wintersleep (Sommeil d'hiver).* Translated by Nigel Spencer.
Ronsdale: Vancouver, 1998.

Bouchard, Michel Marc. *Pierre and Marie...and the Devil with Deep Blue Eyes
(Pierre et Marie...et le démon).* Translated by Linda Gaboriau. Produced by
Théâtre Lac Brome, Quebec City, 1998.

Boucher, Serge. *Motel Hélène*. Translated by Judith Thompson and Morwyn Brebner. Produced by Tarragon Theatre, Toronto, 1998. Toronto: Playwrights Union of Canada, 2000.

Danis, Daniel. *That Woman (Celle-là)*. Translated by Linda Gaboriau. Vancouver: Talonbooks, 1998.

Dubé, Marcel. *On the Other Side of the Wall (De l'autre côté du mur)*. Translated by Aviva Ravel. Toronto: Playwrights Union of Canada, 1998.

Mouawad, Wajdi. *Alphonse*. Translated by Shelly Tepperman. Produced by Pink Ink Theatre Productions, Vancouver, 1998. Toronto: Playwrights Canada Press, 2002.

Savard, Marie. *Mine Sincerely (Bien à moi)*. Translated by Louise Forsyth. Laval: Éditions Trois, 1998.

Archambault, François. *The Winners (Les gagnants)*. Translated by Shelly Tepperman. Produced by Ruby Slippers, Vancouver, 1999.

Archambault, François. *15 Seconds (15 secondes)*. Translated by Bobby Theodore. Produced by Alberta Theatre Projects, Calgary, 1999. Vancouver: Talonbooks, 2000.

Beaudoin, Manon. *The Suitcase (La valise)*. Translated by Manon Beaudoin and Doug Jamha. Produced by PanCanadian PlayRites, Calgary, 1999.

Bouchard, Michel Marc. *The Coronation Voyage (Le voyage du couronnement)*. Translated by Linda Gaboriau. Vancouver: Talonbooks, 1999.

Danis, Daniel. *Thunderstruck, or The Song of the Say-Sayer (Le chant du dire-dire)*. Translated by Linda Gaboriau. Produced by One Yellow Rabbit, Calgary, 1999. Vancouver: Talonbooks, 1999.

Leroux, Patrick. *Embedded (La litière)*. Translated by Shelley Tepperman. Produced by Year 1 Theatre, Ottawa, 1999.

Tremblay, Larry. *Anatomy Lesson (Leçon d'anatomie)*. Translated by Sheila Fischman. Produced by Pink Ink Theatre, Vancouver, 1999. New York: Ubu Repertory Theater Publications, 1995; In *Talking Bodies*. Vancouver: Talonbooks, 2001.

Works from the Nineteenth Century

De Gaspé, Philippe Aubert. *Archibald Cameron of Locheill, or An Episode in the Seven Years' War (Les Anciens Canadiens*, novel, 1759; adapted for the theatre 1894). Translated by Leonard Doucette. In *The Drama of Our Past: Major Plays from Nineteenth-Century Quebec*. Toronto: University of Toronto Press, 1997.

Fréchette, Louis-Honoré. *Félix Poutré* (1862). Translated by Leonard Doucette. In *The Drama of Our Past: Major Plays from Nineteenth-Century Quebec*. Toronto: University of Toronto Press, 1997.

Petitclair, Pierre. *The Donation* (*La donation*, 1842). Translated by Leonard Doucette. In *The Drama of Our Past: Major Plays from Nineteenth-Century Quebec*. Toronto: University of Toronto Press, 1997.

Petitclair, Pierre. *A Country Outing* (*Une partie de campagne*, 1865). Translated by Leonard Doucette. In *The Drama of Our Past: Major Plays from Nineteenth-Century Quebec*. Toronto: University of Toronto Press, 1997.

Quesnel, Joseph. *Anglomania, or Dinner, English Style* (*L'anglomanie ou le dîner à l'anglaise*, 1803). Translated by Leonard Doucette. In *The Drama of Our Past: Major Plays from Nineteenth-Century Quebec*. Toronto: University of Toronto Press, 1997.

NOTES

1 Literary Translation in Canada

1. See Louise Ladouceur, "A Firm Balance: questions d'équilibre et rapport de force dans les représentations des littératures anglophone et francophone du Canada," *Canadian Literature* 175 (2003): 96–114.

2. For an overview of the situation from 1760 to 1860, see Philip Stratford, *Bibliographie de livres canadiens traduits de l'anglais au français et du français à l'anglais*, 2nd ed. (Ottawa: Social Sciences and Humanities Research Council of Canada, 1977). See also Jean Delisle, *La traduction au Canada / Translation in Canada* (Ottawa: University of Ottawa Press, 1987).

3. Stratford, *Bibliographie de livres*, x.

4. Stratford, *Bibliographie de livres*, x.

5. Stratford, *Bibliographie de livres*, xvi.

6. Clément Moisan, *L'âge de la littérature canadienne* (Montreal: HMH, 1969), 30.

7. According to the 2006 census, the Canadian population is composed of 67.6 per cent anglophone, 17.43 per cent bilingual, and 13.25 per cent francophone residents.

8. Stacy Churchill, *Official Languages in Canada: Changing the Language Landscape*, New Canadian Perspectives (Ottawa: Canadian Heritage, 1998), 10.

9. D.G. Jones, "Grounds for Translation," *Ellipse* 21 (1977): 82.

10. D.G. Jones, *Butterfly on a Rock: A Study of Themes and Images in Canadian Literature* (Toronto: University of Toronto Press, 1970), 84.

11. Richard Giguère, "Traduction littéraire et 'image' de la littérature au Canada et au Québec," in *Translation in Canadian Literature: Symposium 1982*, ed. Camille La Bossière (Ottawa: University of Ottawa Press, 1983), 58.

12. Ruth Martin, "Translated Canadian Literature and Canada Council Translation Grants 1972–1992: The Effect on Authors, Translators and Publishers," *Ellipse* 51 (1994): 54.

13. Kathy Mezei, "Translation as Metonomy: Bridges and Bilingualism," *Ellipse* 51 (1994): 88.

14. Louis Dudek and Michael Gnarowski qtd. in Kathy Mezei, "A Bridge of Sorts: The Translation of Quebec Literature in English," *The Yearbook of English Studies: Anglo-American Literary Relations* 15 (1985), 204–05.

15. Mezei, "A Bridge of Sorts," 204.

16. Sherry Simon, "Rites of Passage: Translation and Its Intents," *The Massachusetts Review* 21, no. 1–2 (1990): 96.

17. Larry Shouldice, "On the Politics of Literary Translation in Canada," in *Translation in Canadian Literature: Symposium 1982*, ed. Camille La Bossière (Ottawa: University of Ottawa Press, 1983), 80.

18. Shouldice, "Politics of Literary Translation," 75.

19. Ben-Zion Shek, "Quelques réflexions sur la traduction dans le contexte socio-culturel canado-québécois," *Ellipse* 21 (1977): 111.

20. Shek, "Réflexions sur la traduction," 112.

21. Sherry Simon, *L'inscription sociale de la traduction au Québec* (Quebec City: Office de la langue française, 1989), 31.

22. Jacques Brault, *Poèmes des quatre côtés* (Saint-Lambert, QC: Noroît, 1975), 15.

23. Brault, *Poèmes des quatre côtés*, 16.

24. Brault, *Poèmes des quatre côtés*, 15.

25. E.D. Blodgett, *Configuration: Essays on the Canadian Literatures* (Downsview, ON: ECW Press, 1982), 32.

26. Blodgett, *Configuration*, 34.

27. André Brochu, *L'instance critique* (Montreal: Leméac, 1974), 66.

28. Blodgett, *Configuration*, 34.

29. E.D. Blodgett, "How Do You Say 'Gabrielle Roy'?" in *Translation in Canadian Literature: Symposium 1982*, ed. Camille La Bossière (Ottawa: University of Ottawa Press, 1983), 25.

30. Brault, *Poèmes des quatre côtés*, 16.

31. Barbara Godard, "Language and Sexual Difference: The Case of Translation," *The Atkinson Review of Canadian Studies* 2, no. 1 (1984): 17.

32. Barbara Godard, "Theorizing Feminist Discourse / Translation," *Tessera* 6 (1989): 46.

33. Kathy Mezei, "Translation as Metonomy: Bridges and Bilingualism," *Ellipse* 51 (1994): 94.

34. The *mise en abyme* is a formal technique used in visual art and literature in which an image contains a reproduction of itself that appears to recur infinitely.

35. Sherry Simon, *Le trafic des langues: traduction et culture dans la littérature québécoise* (Montreal: Boréal, 1994), 52.

36. Simon, *Le trafic des langues*, 52, 55.

2   From One Stage to the Other

1. Plays such as Marc Lescarbot's *Le Théâtre de Neptune en la Nouvelle-France*, written in 1609 and translated in 1926, and Louvigny de Montigny's, *Je vous aime*, written in 1902 and translated thirty years later. See *The Oxford Companion to Canadian Theatre* (1989).

2. Jean-Cléo Godin and Laurent Mailhot, *Le théâtre québécois* (Montreal: Hurtubise, 1973), 29.

3. Christopher Innes qtd. in Eugene Benson and L.W. Conolly, eds. *English-Canadian Theatre* (Toronto: Oxford University Press, 1987), 81.

4. The source material that served for the statistical study and a list of the plays it contains are included in the appendices.

5. Henry Deyglun qtd. in Chantal Hébert, *Le burlesque au Québec: un divertissement populaire* (Montreal: Hurtubise, 1981), 34.

6. Hébert, *Le burlesque au Québec*, 44.

7. Lorraine Camerlain and Pierre Lavoie, "Drama in French," in *Canadian Encyclopedia* (Edmonton: Hurtig, 1985), 513.

8. Annie Brisset, *Sociocritique de la traduction: théâtre et altérité au Québec (1968–1988)* (Longueuil: Préambule, 1990), 264.

9. Henri Gobard, *L'aliénation linguistique: analyse tétraglossique* (Paris: Flammarion, 1976), 34.
    i. A *vernacular language*, local, spoken spontaneously, used less as a means of communication than of communion and that alone can be considered as a mother tongue (or native tongue).
    ii. A *vehicular language*, national or regional, learned out of necessity, intended for *communications* on an urban scale.

III. A *referential language*, connected to cultural, oral and written traditions, assuring the continuity of values through a systematic reference to enduring works of the past....

IV. A *mythic language*, which functions as an ultimate resource; verbal magic whose incomprehensibility is understood as an irrefutable proof of the sacred (my translation).

10. Itamar Even-Zohar, "Polysystem Theory," *Poetics Today* 1, no. 1–2 (1979): 295.

11. Jean-Luc Denis, "Traduire le théâtre en contexte québécois: essai de caractérisation d'une pratique," *Jeu* 56 (1990): 12.

12. Jean Delisle, "Dans les coulisses de l'adaptation québécoise," *Circuit* 12 (1986): 4.

13. Louise Ladouceur, "Les paramètres de l'adaptation théâtrale au Québec de 1980 à 1990" (MA thesis, Université de Montréal, 1991), 46.

14. Denis, "Traduire le théâtre en contexte québécois,"16–17.

15. Annie Brisset, "Ceci n'est pas une trahison," *Spirale* 62 (1986): 12.

16. Brisset, *Sociocritique de la traduction*, 312.

17. Brisset, *Sociocritique de la traduction*, 317.

18. Edmond Cary qtd. in Paul Horguelin, *Anthologie de la manière de traduire: domaine français* (Montreal: Linguatech, 1981), 43.

19. Edmond Cary, *La traduction dans le monde modern* (Geneva: Georg, 1956), 70.

20. For further details, refer to Appendix 1: Repertoire of Anglophone Plays for Adults Produced or Published in French Translation, 1966–2000.

21. Pat Donnelly, "English-Canadian Playwrights Finally Get Attention Here," review of *Les traverses du coeur* by Wendy Lill, *Montreal Gazette*, January 18, 1993, C3.

22. Ray Conlogue, "Quebec's Surprising New Wave," *Globe and Mail* (Toronto), January 26, 1993, A12.

23. Robert Wallace, *Producing Marginality: Theatre and Criticism in Canada* (Saskatoon: Fifth House, 1990), 38.

24. Bernard qtd. in Conlogue, "Quebec's Surprising New Wave," A12.

25. Bernard qtd. in Conlogue, "Quebec's Surprising New Wave," A12.

26. Cynthia Zimmerman, "A Conversation with Judith Thompson," *Canadian Drama / L'art dramatique canadien* 16, no. 2 (1990): 190.

27. Luc Boulanger, "Illusion comique," *Voir* (Montreal), November 22–28, 1990, 28.

28. Gilles Lamontagne, "Judith Thompson frappe au Quat'Sous: *Lion dans les rues*," *La Presse* (Montreal), September 18, 1991, C10.

29. Robert Lévesque, "Des restes humains bien identifiés," *Le Devoir* (Montreal), September 20, 1991, B5.

30. Pat Donnelly, "The Shrill of It All. Thompson Play a Passionate Screech," *Montreal Gazette*, September 26, 1991, D13.

31. Benoit Melançon, "*Des restes humains non identifiés et la véritable nature de l'amour*," *Jeu* 60 (1994): 151.

32. Jean Beaunoyer, "Des coups et des douleurs, on ne discute pas," review of *L'homme laid* by Brad Fraser, *La Presse* (Montreal), March 27, 1993, E3.

33. Robert Lévesque, "Une farce bizarre et maléfique pour grands enfants," review of *L'homme laid* by Brad Fraser, *Le Devoir* (Montreal), March 26, 1993, B9.

34. Marie Labrecque, "L'homme laid," review of *L'homme laid* by Brad Fraser, *Voir* (Montreal), April 1–7, 1993, 36.

35. Robert Lévesque, "Un bon moment avec Brad. L'auteur albertain et sulfureux donne dans le melodrama gay," review of *Poor Super Man* by Brad Fraser, *Le Devoir* (Montreal), April 14, 1995, B11.

36. For a detailed analysis, see Louise Ladouceur, "Du spéculaire au spectaculaire: le théâtre anglo-canadien traduit au Québec au début des années 90," in *Nouveaux regards sur le théâtre québécois*, eds. Betty Bednarski and Irene Oore, 185–94. Halifax: XYZ/Dalhousie French Studies, 1997.

37. For a more detailed account, see Eugene Benson and L.W. Conolly, eds. *English-Canadian Theatre*, Toronto: Oxford University Press, 1987. 85–89.

38. Jerry Wasserman, ed., introduction to *Modern Canadian Plays*, 3rd ed., 2 vols. (Vancouver: Talonbooks, 1994), 15.

39. Benson and Conolly, eds., *English-Canadian Theatre*, 85.

40. Herbert Whittaker qtd. in Jane Koustas, "From Gélinas to Carrier: Critical Response to Translated Quebec Theatre in Toronto," *Studies in Canadian Literature* 17, no. 2 (1992): 114.

41. Koustas, "From Gélinas to Carrier," 114.

42. Koustas, "From Gélinas to Carrier," 115.

43. Urjo Kareda qtd. in Koustas, "From Gélinas to Carrier," 115.

44. Herbert Whittaker qtd. in Denis Johnston, *Up the Mainstream: The Rise of Toronto's Alternative Theatres, 1968–1975* (Toronto: University of Toronto Press, 1991), 155.

45. Jane Koustas, "From 'Homespun' to 'Awesome': Translated Quebec Theatre in Toronto," in *Essays on Modern Quebec Theatre*, eds. Joseph I. Donohue Jr. and Jonathan M. Weiss (East Lansing: Michigan State University Press, 1995), 93.

46. Carl Honoré, "The Best Playwright Scotland Never Had," *Globe and Mail* (Toronto), October 31, 1992, C5.

47. Honoré, "Best Playwright," C5.

48. Pierre Hébert qtd. in Koustas, "From Gélinas to Carrier," 85.

49. Jill Humphries, *Who's Who in the Playwrights Union of Canada* (Toronto: Playwrights Union of Canada, 1995), 42.

3 Translating for the Stage

1. Susan Bassnett-McGuire, "Ways through the Labyrinth, Strategies and Methods for Translating Theatre Texts," in *The Manipulation of Literature, Studies in Literary Translation*, ed. Theo Hermans (London: Croom Helm, 1985), 87.
2. Georges Mounin, *Linguistique et traduction* (Bruxelles: Dessart et Mardaga, 1976), 163.
3. Paul Lefebvre and Pierre Ostiguy, "L'adaptation théâtrale au Québec," *Jeu* 9 (1984): 34.
4. Robert Spickler, preface to *La culture contre l'art: essai d'économie politique du théâtre* by Josette Féral. (Montreal: Les Presses de l'Université du Québec, 1990), xi.
5. Tadeusz Kowzan, *Littérature et spectacle* (The Hague and Paris: Mouton, 1976), 52–80.
6. Anne Ubersfeld, *Lire le theatre* (Paris: Messidor, 1982), 140.
7. Jan Ferencik, "De la spécification de la traduction de l'oeuvre dramatique," in *The Nature of Translation*, ed. James Holmes (Bratislava: Slovak Academy of Sciences, 1970), 144.
8. Ferencik, "De la spécification de la traduction," 147.
9. Ferencik, "De la spécification de la traduction," 147.
10. See Louise Ladouceur, "Les paramètres de l'adaptation théâtrale au Québec de 1980 à 1990" (MA thesis, Université de Montréal, 1991).
11. Georges Mounin, *Linguistique et traduction* (Bruxelles: Dessart et Mardaga, 1976), 133.
12. Robert Larose, *Théories contemporaines de la traduction* (Quebec City: Les Presses de l'Université du Québec, 1987), 227.
13. Larose, *Théories contemporaines de la traduction*, 228.
14. Lefebvre and Ostiguy, "L'adaptation théâtrale au Québec," 44, 45.
15. Jean Delisle, "Dans les coulisses de l'adaptation québécoise," *Circuit* 12 (1986): 3, 5.
16. See Eugène Nida and Charles Taber, *The Theory and Practice of Translation* (Leiden: E.J. Brill, 1969).
17. Delisle, "Les coulisses de l'adaptation," 3.
18. The methodological framework was developed in several stages. See Louise Ladouceur, "Normes, fonctions et traduction théâtrale," *Meta. Journal des traducteurs* 40, no. 1 (1995): 31–38; and Ladouceur, "Separate Stages: la traduction du théâtre dans le contexte Canada/Québec" (PHD diss., University of British Columbia, 1997).
19. Gideon Toury, *Descriptive Translation Studies and Beyond* (Amsterdam: Benjamins, 1995), 12.
20. Roman Jakobson, *Essais de linguistique générale* (Paris: Les Éditions de Minuit, 1963), 214.

21. Itamar Even-Zohar, "The 'Literary' System," *Poetics Today* 11, no. 1 (1990): 30, 31.

22. Even-Zohar, "The 'Literary' System," 31.

23. Even-Zohar, "The 'Literary' System," 42.

24. Even-Zohar, "Polysystem Theory," 290.

25. Gideon Toury, *In Search of a Theory of Translation* (Tel Aviv: The Porter Institute for Poetics and Semiotics, 1980), 37.

26. Iouri Lotman, *La structure du texte artistique* (Paris: Gallimard, 1973), 36.

27. Lotman, *La structure du texte artistique*, 37.

28. Annie Brisset, *Sociocritique de la traduction: théâtre et altérité au Québec (1968–1988)* (Longueuil: Préambule, 1990), 30.

29. Marc Angenot qtd. in Brisset, *Sociocritique de la traduction*, 30.

30. Antoine Berman, *Toward a Translation Criticism: John Donne*, trans. Françoise Massardier-Kenney (Kent, OH: Kent State University Press, 2009), 45.

31. Paul Horguelin, *Pratique de la révision* (Montreal: Linguatech, 1985), 111.

32. Toury, *In Search of a Theory of Translation*, 55.

33. Itamar Even-Zohar, "Translated Literature within the Literary System," *Poetics Today* 11, no. 1 (1990): 51.

34. E.D. Blodgett, "How Do You Say 'Gabrielle Roy'?" in *Translation in Canadian Literature: Symposium 1982*, ed. Camille La Bossière (Ottawa: University of Ottawa Press, 1982), 30.

35. Blodgett, "How Do You Say 'Gabrielle Roy'?" 33.

36. E.D. Blodgett, "Translation as a Key to Canadian Literature," *New Comparison* 1 (1986): 96.

37. E.D. Blodgett, "Towards a Model of Literary Translation in Canada," *TTR. Études sur le texte et ses transformations* 4, no. 2 (1991): 191.

38. Toury, *Descriptive Translation Studies*, 58, 59.

39. Toury, *Descriptive Translation Studies*, 59.

40. Toury, *In Search of a Theory of Translation*, 60.

41. See Louise Ladouceur, "Le sujet en question: *I Am Yours* de Judith Thompson, version québécoise," *TTR. Études sur le texte et ses transformations* 11, no.1 (1998): 89–112.

42. Pierre Bourdieu, *Questions de sociologie* (Paris: Les Éditions de Minuit, 1980), 119.

43. Jean-Marc Gouanvic, "Pour une sociologie de la traduction: le cas de la littérature américaine traduite en France après la Seconde Guerre mondiale (1945–1960)," in *Translations as Intercultural Communication*, eds. Mary Snell-Hornby, Zuzana Jettmarova, and Klaus Kaindl (Amsterdam: Benjamins, 1997), 37.

44. Luise von Flotow, "Translating the Women of the Eighties: Erotocism, Anger, Ethnicity," in *Culture in Transit: Translating the Literature of Quebec*, ed. Sherry Simon (Montreal: Véhicule Press, 1995), 32.

45. Berman, *Toward a Translation Criticism*, 3.
46. Berman, *Toward a Translation Criticism*, 75.
47. Berman, *Toward a Translation Criticism*, 74.
48. Hans Robert Jauss, *Pour une esthétique de la reception* (Paris: Gallimard, 1978), 49.
49. Berman, *Toward a Translation Criticism*, 63.
50. Berman, *Toward a Translation Criticism*, 64.
51. Berman, *Toward a Translation Criticism*, 58.
52. Berman, *Toward a Translation Criticism*, 58.
53. Berman, *Toward a Translation Criticism*, 58.
54. Berman, *Toward a Translation Criticism*, 59.
55. Berman, *Toward a Translation Criticism*, 59.
56. Berman, *Toward a Translation Criticism*, 59.
57. Berman, *Toward a Translation Criticism*, 60.
58. Berman, *Toward a Translation Criticism*, 61.
59. Berman, *Toward a Translation Criticism*, 61.
60. Berman, *Toward a Translation Criticism*, 69.
61. Berman, *Toward a Translation Criticism*, 69.
62. Berman, *Toward a Translation Criticism*, 70.
63. José Lambert and Hendrik van Gorp, "On Describing Translations," in *The Manipulation of Literature*, ed. Theo Hermans (London: Croom Helm, 1985), 52.
64. The development of the various versions of this table can be traced in Louise Ladouceur, "Normes, fonctions et traduction théâtrale," *Meta. Journal des traducteurs* 40, no. 1 (1995): 31–38; and Ladouceur, "Separate Stages: la traduction du théâtre dans le contexte Canada/Québec" (PHD diss., University of British Columbia, 1997).

4 Descriptive Analysis: The French Repertoire Translated into English

1. Jean-Cléo Godin and Laurent Mailhot, *Le théâtre québécois* (Montreal: Hurtubise, 1973), 29.
2. Gratien Gélinas and Victor-Lévy Beaulieu, *Gratien, Tit-Coq, Fridolin, Bousille et les autres* (Montreal: SRC/Stanké, 1993), 181.
3. Gratien Gélinas, *Bousille et les justes* (Montreal: Institut littéraire du Québec, 1960), 10.
4. Renate Usmiani, *Gratien Gélinas*, Profiles in Canadian Drama (Agincourt, ON: Gage Educational, 1977), 62.
5. Gratien Gélinas, *Bousille and the Just*, trans. Kenneth Johnstone and Joffre Miville-Deschêne (Toronto: Clarke, Irwin and Company, 1961), 61.

6.   Gélinas, *Bousille et les justes*, 10.

7.   Gélinas, *Bousille et les justes*, 121.

8.   Gélinas, *Bousille and the Just*, trans. Johnstone and Miville-Deschêne, 60.

9.   Gélinas, *Bousille and the Just*, trans. Johnstone and Miville-Deschêne, 78.

10. Gélinas, *Bousille et les justes*, 122.

11. Gélinas, *Bousille and the Just*, trans. Gélinas and Johnstone and Miville-Deschêne, 60.

12. Gélinas, *Bousille et les justes*, 65.

13. Gélinas, *Bousille and the Just*, trans. Johnstone and Miville-Deschêne, 29.

14. Gélinas, *Bousille et les justes*, 75.

15. Gélinas, *Bousille and the Just*, trans. Johnstone and Miville-Deschêne, 34.

16. Gélinas, *Bousille et les justes*, 34; Gélinas, *Bousille and the Just*, trans. Johnstone and Miville-Deschêne, 14.

17. Marc Angenot defines an "idéologème" this way: every maxim, underlying an utterance, the subject of which circumscribes a field of particular relevance. These subjects are determined and defined by the collection of maxims where the ideological system allows them to appear. The "idéologèmes" act as regulating principles underlying social discourses to which they bestow authority and coherence (my translation). *Glossaire pratique de la critique littéraire contemporaine* (Montreal: Hurtubise, 1979), 99–100.

18. Johnson qtd. in Conolly, ed. *Canadian Drama and the Critics* (Vancouver: Talonbooks, 1995), 37.

19. Herbert Whittaker qtd. in Jane Koustas, "From Gélinas to Carrier: Critical Response to Translated Quebec Theatre in Toronto," *Studies in Canadian Literature* 17, no. 2 (1992): 112.

20. Nathan Cohen qtd. in Koustas, "Gélinas to Carrier," 112.

21. Cohen qtd. in Koustas, "Gélinas to Carrier," 112.

22. Whittaker qtd. in Koustas, "Gélinas to Carrier," 112.

23. Cohen qtd. in Koustas, "Gélinas to Carrier," 112.

24. Paul Leonard, "Critical Questioning," *Canadian Theatre Review* 57 (1988): 6.

25. Excerpts from this section have appeared in the following articles: Louise Ladouceur, "A Version of Quebec: le théâtre québécois au Canada anglais," *L'Annuaire théâtral* 27 (2000): 108–19; and Ladouceur, "From Other Tongue to Mother Tongue in the Drama of Quebec and Canada," in *Changing the Terms: Translating in the Postcolonial Era*, eds. Sherry Simon and Paul St-Pierre (Ottawa: University of Ottawa Press, 2000), 207–26.

26. To avoid the confusion created by the calque of the original in the translated versions, it is necessary to note the different spellings attributed to the original title, *Les belles-sœurs*, and to its translations, *Les Belles Soeurs* (1974), and *Les Belles-Soeurs* (1992).

27. Saving stamps are given to customers and can be exchanged for goods such as toys, personal items, housewares, furniture, and appliances.

28. Herbert Whittaker, "Les Belles Soeurs Milestone Play," *Globe and Mail* (Toronto), April 4, 1973, 13.

29. Herbert Whittaker, "Belles Soeurs Bright Light for St. Lawrence," *Globe and Mail* (Toronto), May 7, 1973, 14.

30. Urjo Kareda qtd. in Conolly, ed. *Canadian Drama*, 311.

31. Kareda qtd. in Renée Hulan, "Surviving Translation: *Forever Yours Marie-Lou* at Tarragon Theatre," *Theatre Research in Canada* 15, no. 1 (1994): 49.

32. Stephen Mezei, "Tremblay's Toronto Success," *Performing Arts in Canada* 10 (1973): 26.

33. Whittaker, "Les Belles Soeurs Milestone Play," 13.

34. Myron Galloway qtd. in Conolly, ed. *Canadian Drama*, 310.

35. Whittaker, "Les Belles Soeurs Milestone Play," 13.

36. Herbert Whittaker, "*Forever Yours* Offers Some Familiar Novelty," *Globe and Mail* (Toronto), June 5, 1972, 12.

37. Marianne Ackerman, "Sweet Jesus! Who's That, Ma?" *Saturday Night* (Toronto), June 1988, 47.

38. Kareda and David McCaughna qtd. in Koustas, "From Gélinas to Carrier," 118.

39. Kareda and Galloway qtd. in Koustas, "From Gélinas to Carrier," 118.

40. Vivien Bosley, "Diluting the Mixture: Translating Michel Tremblay's *Les Belles-Soeurs*," TTR 1, no. 1 (1988): 139.

41. Jane Koustas, "Hosanna in Toronto: 'Tour de force' or 'Détour de traduction,'" TTR 2, no. 2 (1989): 135.

42. Michel Tremblay, *Hosanna*, trans. John Van Burek and Bill Glassco (Vancouver: Talonbooks, 1974), 29.

43. According to Paul Horguelin, the term Gallicism signifies "construction[s] peculiar to the French language." *Pratique de la révision* (Montreal: Linguatech, 1985), 112.

44. Tremblay, *Hosanna*, trans. Van Burek and Glassco, 26.

45. Sherry Simon, *Le trafic des langues: traduction et culture dans la littérature québécoise* (Montreal: Boréal, 1994), 52.

46. Sir Charles G.D. Roberts qtd. in Simon, *Le trafic des langues*, 53.

47. Linda Gaboriau and Daniel Gauthier, eds., *Québec Plays in Translation: A Catalogue of Québec Playwrights and Plays in English Translation* (Montreal: Centre des auteurs dramatiques, 1998).

48. Jean-Claude Germain, "J'ai eu le coup de foudre," in *Les belles-sœurs*, by Michel Tremblay (Montreal: Holt, Rinehart and Winston, 1968), 5.

49. Alain Pontaut, preface to *Les belles-sœurs* by Michel Tremblay, revised edition (Montreal: Leméac, 1972), i.

50. Michel Tremblay, *Les Belles Soeurs*, trans. Van Burek and Glassco (1974), 13; Michel Tremblay, *Les Belles-Soeurs*, trans. John Van Burek and Bill Glassco, in *Modern Canadian Plays*, 3rd ed., vol. 1, ed. Jerry Wasserman (Vancouver: Talonbooks, 1993), 105.

51. Michel Tremblay, *Les belles-sœurs* (Montreal: Holt, Rinehart and Winston, 1968), 9; Michel Tremblay, *Les belles-sœurs* (Montreal: Leméac, 1972), 18.

52. Tremblay, *Les Belles Soeurs*, trans. Van Burek and Glassco (1974), 10; Tremblay, *Les Belles-Soeurs*, trans. John Van Burek and Bill Glassco, rev. ed. (Vancouver: Talonbooks, 1992), 8.

53. Tremblay, *Les belles-sœurs* (1968), 61; Tremblay, *Les belles-sœurs* (1972), 96.

54. Tremblay, *Les Belles Soeurs*, trans. Van Burek and Glassco (1974), 97; Tremblay, *Les Belles-Soeurs*, trans. Van Burek and Glassco, rev. ed. (1992), 94.

55. Tremblay, *Hosanna*, trans. Van Burek and Glassco (1974), 12, 27.

56. For an outline of the variations between curses, swear words, and blasphemies, see the work by Renate Usmiani, *Michel Tremblay* (Vancouver: Douglas & McIntyre, 1982), 48.

57. Tremblay, *Les belles-sœurs* (1968), 9; Tremblay, *Les belles-sœurs* (1972), 17.

58. Tremblay, *Les Belles Soeurs*, trans. Van Burek and Glassco (1974), 9.

59. Tremblay, *Les Belles-Soeurs*, trans. Van Burek and Glassco, rev. ed. (1992), 7.

60. Tremblay, *Les belles-sœurs* (1968), 33; Tremblay, *Les belles-sœurs* (1972), 54.

61. A.J. Greimas, *Du sens* (Paris: Seuil, 1966), 10.

62. Tremblay, *Les belles-sœurs* (1968), 10 and (1972), 18; (1968), 14 and (1972), 25; (1968), 14 and (1972), 26.

63. Tremblay, *Les Belles Soeurs*, trans. Van Burek and Glassco (1974), 7, 9, 10, 11, 14, 15, 18, 20.

64. Tremblay, *Les Belles-Soeurs*, trans. Van Burek and Glassco, rev. ed. (1992), 5, 7, 8, 12, 13, 16, 18, 19, 20, 21.

65. Tremblay, *Les belles-sœurs* (1968), 66; Tremblay, *Les belles-sœurs* (1972), 102.

66. Tremblay, *Les Belles Soeurs*, trans. Van Burek and Glassco (1974), 105; Tremblay, *Les Belles-Soeurs*, trans. Van Burek and Glassco, rev. ed. (1992), 102.

67. Tremblay, *Les belles-sœurs* (1968), 12–13.

68. Tremblay, *Les Belles Soeurs*, trans. Van Burek and Glassco (1974), 14–16.

69. Tremblay, *Les belles-sœurs* (1968), 25; Tremblay, *Les belles-sœurs* (1972), 40.

70. Tremblay, *Les Belles Soeurs*, trans. Van Burek and Glassco (1974), 34.

71. Tremblay, *Les belles-sœurs* (1968), 29; Tremblay, *Les belles-sœurs* (1972), 48.

72. Tremblay, *Les Belles Soeurs*, trans. Van Burek and Glassco (1974), 44.

73. Tremblay, *Les Belles-Soeurs*, trans. Van Burek and Glassco, rev. ed. (1992), 32, 41.

74. Tremblay, *Les belles-sœurs* (1972), 46; Tremblay, *Les Belles Soeurs*, trans. Van Burek and Glassco (1974), 41.

75. Van Burek qtd. in Don Rubin, "John Van Burek: Tremblay in Translation," *Canadian Theatre Review* 24 (1979): 45.

76. Michel Tremblay, *Hosanna / La Duchesse de Langeais* (Montreal: Leméac, 1973), 29.

77. Tremblay, *Hosanna / La Duchesse de Langeais* (1973), 75.

78. Tremblay, *Hosanna*, trans. Van Burek and Glassco (1974), 101–02; Tremblay, *Hosanna*, trans. John Van Burek and Bill Glassco, rev. ed. (Vancouver: Talonbooks, 1991), 87.

79. *Backyard Theatre*, National Film Board of Canada, 1972. This film contains excerpts from the plays *Les belles-sœurs* and *Demain matin, Montréal m'attend* as well as interviews with Michel Tremblay and André Brassard.

80. This is also what Tremblay maintains when talking about Hosanna: "This Québécois always wanted to be an English actress in an American movie about an Egyptian myth in a movie shot in Spain. In a way, this is a typically Québécois problem. For the past 300 years we were not taught that we were a people, so we were dreaming about somebody else instead of ourselves." Qtd. in Koustas, "Hosanna in Toronto," 134.

81. Michel Tremblay, *Bonjour, Là, Bonjour*, trans. John Van Burek and Bill Glassco (Vancouver: Talonbooks, 1975), 29; Tremblay, *Bonjour, Là, Bonjour*, trans. John Van Burek and Bill Glassco, rev. ed. (Vancouver: Talonbooks, 1988), 22.

82. Tremblay, *Bonjour, Là, Bonjour*, trans. Van Burek and Glassco (1975), 20; Tremblay, *Bonjour, Là, Bonjour*, trans. Van Burek and Glassco, rev. ed. (1988), 14.

83. Tremblay, *Bonjour, là, bonjour* (Montreal: Leméac, 1974), 40; Tremblay, *Bonjour, Là, Bonjour*, trans. Van Burek and Glassco (1975), 28; Tremblay, *Bonjour, Là, Bonjour*, trans. Van Burek and Glassco, rev. ed. (1988), 19.

84. Michel Tremblay, *La Maison Suspendue*, trans. John Van Burek and Bill Glassco (Vancouver: Talonbooks, 1991), 34–35.

85. John Van Burek qtd. in Rubin, "John Van Burek," 45.

86. Bosley, "Diluting the Mixture," 141.

87. Jacques Saint-Pierre, "Michel Tremblay, dramaturge québécois et canadien: bilan de la réception d'une pièce et sa traduction," in *Littérature québécoise: la recherche en émergence. Actes du deuxième colloque interuniversitaire des jeunes chercheur(e)s en littérature québécoise* (Quebec: Centre de recherche en littérature québécoise/Nuit blanche éditeur, 1991), 65.

88. Barbara Godard, "Letters in Canada. Translations," *University of Toronto Quarterly* 58, no. 1 (1988): 85.

89. Simon, *Le trafic des langues*, 55.

90. Richard Plant, "Drama in English," in *The Oxford Companion to Canadian Theatre*, eds. Eugene Benson and L.W. Conolly (Toronto: Oxford University Press, 1989), 164.

91. Eugene Benson and L.W. Conolly, *The Oxford Companion to Canadian Theatre* (Toronto: Oxford University Press, 1989), x.

92. This phrase, "in the tone," is an excerpt from the prologue in which Jovette Marchessault cites Violette Leduc, who wrote in *L'affamée* that she would like to be "dans le ton comme le violon." *La terre est trop courte, Violette Leduc* (Montreal: Pleine Lune, 1982), 13.

93. I was the assistant director on this production.

94. Martial Dassylva, "Les tourbillons Leduc, Guilbault et Marchessault," *La Presse* (Montreal), November 24, 1981, B3.

95. Jacques Larue-Langlois, "Un pas de géant pour le théâtre d'ici," *Le Devoir* (Montreal), November 13, 1981, 14.

96. Maureen Peterson, "Play a Marathon of Dubious Taste," *Montreal Gazette*, November 16, 1981, 52.

97. Peterson, "Play a Marathon," 52.

98. Francine Pelletier, "Violette-Jovette, Jovette-Violette," preface to *La terre est trop courte, Violette Leduc* by Jovette Marchessault (Montreal: Les Éditions de la pleine lune, 1982), 7.

99. Pelletier, "Violette-Jovette, Jovette-Violette," 7.

100. Pelletier, "Violette-Jovette, Jovette-Violette," 7.

101. Violette Leduc, *La bâtarde* (Paris: Gallimard, 1964), 117.

102. Jovette Marchessault, *La terre est trop courte, Violette Leduc*, 1982, 48.

103. Jovette Marchessault, *The Edge of Earth is Too Near, Violette Leduc*, trans. Susanne de Lotbinière-Harwood (unpublished manuscript, Montreal: National Theatre School of Canada, 1985), III: 1.

104. Susanne de Lotbinière-Harwood, *Re-belle et infidèle: La traduction comme pratique de réécriture au féminin / The Body Bilingual: Translation as a Rewriting in the Feminine* (Montreal: Les Éditions du remue-ménage; Toronto: Women's Press, 1991), 108.

105. Violette Leduc, *La bâtarde* (Paris: Le Livre de poche n° 2566), 435.

106. Violette Leduc, *La Bâtarde*, translation by Derek Coltman (Frogmore: Panther Books, 1967), 361.

107. de Lotbinière-Harwood, *Re-belle et infidèle*, 107.

108. de Lotbinière-Harwood, *Re-belle et infidèle*, 108, 109.

109. Marchessault, *The Edge of Earth is Too Near, Violette Leduc*, trans. de Lotbinière-Harwood, III:11.

110. de Lotbinière-Harwood, *Re-belle et infidèle*, 109.

111. Marchessault, *La terre est trop courte, Violette Leduc*, 1982, 23, 24.

112. Marchessault, *La terre est trop courte, Violette Leduc*, 1982, 27, 41, 139.

113. Marchessault, *La terre est trop courte, Violette Leduc*, 1982, 114.

114. de Lotbinière-Harwood, *Re-belle et infidèle*, 107.

115. Robert Wallace, *Producing Marginality: Theatre and Criticism in Canada* (Saskatoon: Fifth House, 1990), 222–23.

116. Wallace, *Producing Marginality*, 223.

117. Mietkiewicz qtd. in Robert Wallace, "D'où cela vient-il? Réflexions sur la réception critique du théâtre francophone récent à Toronto," trans. Michel Vaïs, *Jeu* 49 (1988): 16.

118. Conlogue qtd. in Wallace, "D'où cela vient-il?" 16.

119. Norma Harris qtd. in Koustas, "From Gélinas to Carrier," 123.

120. Linda Gaboriau, "The Cultures of Theatre," in *Culture in Transit: Translating the Literature of Quebec*, ed. Sherry Simon (Montreal: Véhicule Press, 1995), 84.

121. Gaboriau, "The Cultures of Theatre," 85.

122. Gaboriau, "The Cultures of Theatre," 85.

123. With regards to the English version of Garneau's play, Conlogue writes, "Gilles' exuberant language and his passion for ideas are distinctly Gallic. An anglophone adman might well have Gilles' talent and encounter his moral dilemma, but there is no way he would *talk about it* in this fashion" ("Warriors Succumbs to Faulty Adaptation," *Globe and Mail* [Toronto], February 28, 1990, C9). An article by Conlogue commenting on the production of Chaurette's *Le passage de l'Indiana* is entitled "Fuelled by Long Monologues, Play's Verbosity Is Its Engine" (*Globe and Mail* [Toronto], November 9, 1996, C15.)

124. Louise Forsyth, "Feminist Theatre," in *The Oxford Companion to Canadian Theatre*, eds. Eugene Benson and L.W. Conolly (Toronto: Oxford University Press, 1989), 204.

125. Forsyth, "Feminist Theatre," 205.

126. After *La terre est trop courte, Violette Leduc*, Jovette Marchessault published the play *Alice et Gertrude, Nathalie et Renée et ce cher Ernest*, which brought Alice Toklas, Gertrude Stein, Renée Vivien, Nathalie Barney, and Ernest Hemingway to the stage. This play was not translated. Next came *Anaïs dans la queue de la comète*, a play focussing on Anaïs Nin, translated by Susanne de Lotbinière-Harwood under the title *Anaïs in the Comet's Wake*, a short excerpt of which appeared in the collection *Plays/Playwrights from Quebec* published in Canada by the CEAD in 1987.

127. Rodrigue Villeneuve, "*Provincetown Playhouse, juillet 1919, j'avais 19 ans, à la lettre*," *Jeu* 64 (1992): 123.

128. Paul Lefebvre, introduction to *Quebec Voices: Three Plays*, ed. Robert Wallace (Toronto: Coach House, 1986), 9.

129. Lefebvre, introduction, 10.

130. Jean-Cléo Godin, "Quebec Voices: Three Plays," *Canadian Theatre Review* 56 (1988): 86.

131. Normand Chaurette, *Provincetown Playhouse, juillet 1919, j'avais 19 ans* (Montreal: Leméac, 1981), 25–26.
132. Normand Chaurette, *Provincetown Playhouse, July 1919*, trans. William Boulet, in *Quebec Voices: Three Plays*, ed. Robert Wallace (Toronto: Coach House, 1986), 23–24.
133. Chaurette, *Provincetown Playhouse, juillet 1919, j'avais 19 ans*, 31.
134. Chaurette, *Provincetown Playhouse, July 1919*, trans. Boulet, 25.
135. Toury, *In Search of a Theory of Translation*, 60.
136. Chaurette, *Provincetown Playhouse, juillet 1919, j'avais 19 ans*, 96.
137. Chaurette, *Provincetown Playhouse, July 1919*, trans. Boulet, 45.
138. Chaurette, *Provincetown Playhouse, juillet 1919, j'avais 19 ans*, 102; Chaurette, *Provincetown Playhouse, July 1919*, trans. Boulet, 48.
139. Chaurette, *Provincetown Playhouse, juillet 1919, j'avais 19 ans*, 102; Chaurette, *Provincetown Playhouse, July 1919*, trans. Boulet, 48.
140. Chaurette, *Provincetown Playhouse, July 1919*, trans. Boulet, 39; Chaurette, *Provincetown Playhouse, juillet 1919, j'avais 19 ans*, 77.
141. Chaurette, *Provincetown Playhouse, juillet 1919, j'avais 19 ans*, 95; Chaurette, *Provincetown Playhouse, July 1919*, trans. Boulet, 45.
142. Chaurette, *Provincetown Playhouse, juillet 1919, j'avais 19 ans*, 83; Chaurette, *Provincetown Playhouse, July 1919*, trans. Boulet, 41.
143. Chaurette, *Provincetown Playhouse, July 1919*, trans. Boulet, 24.
144. Robert Crew, "Mystery Explores Madness," *Toronto Star*, December 7, 1986, C2.
145. Eleanor Crowder, "*Provincetown Playhouse, juillet 1919, j'avais 19 ans*," *Theatrum* 40 (1994): 37.
146. Wallace, "D'où cela vient-il?," 10.
147. Jean Barbe, "Les Feluettes. Le retour de l'âme," *Voir* (Montreal), September 3–9, 1987, 6.
148. Michel Marc Bouchard, *The Orphan Muses*, trans. Linda Gaboriau (Victoria: Scirocco Drama, 1995), 62.
149. Dominique Lafon, "La relecture d'une pièce: mouture textuelle et meule scénique," *Jeu* 74 (1995): 83.
150. Bouchard, *The Orphan Muses*, trans. Gaboriau, 11.
151. Bouchard, *The Orphan Muses*, trans. Gaboriau, 12.
152. Linda Gaboriau, "The Cultures of Theatre," in *Culture in Transit: Translating the Literature of Quebec*, ed. Sherry Simon (Montreal: Véhicule Press, 1995), 83.
153. Gaboriau, "The Cultures of Theatre," 87.
154. Gaboriau, "The Cultures of Theatre," 87.
155. Michel Marc Bouchard, *Les muses orphelines*, rev. 2nd ed. (Montreal: Leméac, 1995), 20.
156. Bouchard, *The Orphan Muses*, trans. Gaboriau, 15.
157. Gaboriau, "The Cultures of Theatre," 88.

158. Gaboriau, "The Cultures of Theatre," 88.
159. Wallace, *Producing Marginality*, 220.
160. Bouchard, *Les muses orphelines*, rev. 2nd ed., 63–64.
161. Bouchard, *The Orphan Muses*, trans. Gaboriau, 49.
162. Bouchard, *The Orphan Muses*, trans. Gaboriau, 42.
163. Michel Bouchard, *Les muses orphelines* (Montreal: Leméac, 1989), 116; Bouchard, *Les muses orphelines*, rev. 2nd ed., 82.
164. Bouchard, *The Orphan Muses*, trans. Gaboriau, 62.
165. Bouchard, *Les muses orphelines*, rev. 2nd ed., 79.
166. Bouchard, *Les muses orphelines*, rev. 2nd ed., 20.
167. Bouchard, *The Orphan Muses*, trans. Gaboriau, 16.
168. Bouchard, *Les muses orphelines*, rev. 2nd ed., 26, 32.
169. Bouchard, *The Orphan Muses*, trans. Gaboriau, 19, 46, 46.
170. Bouchard, *The Orphan Muses*, trans. Gaboriau, 46.
171. Bouchard, *Les muses orphelines*, rev. 2nd ed., 51.
172. Bouchard, *The Orphan Muses*, trans. Gaboriau, 38.
173. Barbara Crook, "Vancouver Production of a Quebec Play Shows a Universal Symbol for Survival," *Vancouver Sun*, March 11, 1996, B6.
174. Colin Thomas, "*The Orphan Muses* Strikes a Universal Chord," *Georgia Straight* (Vancouver), March 11–18, 1996, 51.
175. Wallace, *Producing Marginality*, 10.
176. Linda Hutcheon qtd. in Wallace, *Producing Marginality*, 10–11.
177. Ann Wilson qtd. in Wallace, *Producing Marginality*, 11.
178. Koustas, "From 'Homespun' to 'Awesome,'" 93.
179. Michel Bélair, *Le nouveau théâtre québécois* (Montreal: Leméac, 1973), 36.
180. Bélair, *Le nouveau théâtre québécois*, 36.
181. Association des théâtres francophones du Canada, accessed June 21, 2011, http://atfc.ca.
182. To avoid confusion between the original play and the translation, it should be noted that "chien" is not capitalized in the French title.
183. Dalpé, *Le Chien*, 2; Dalpé, *Lucky Lady*, 2.
184. Jean Marc Dalpé, *Le Chien*, trans. Maureen Labonté and Jean Marc Dalpé (unpublished manuscript, Montreal: Centre d'essai des auteurs dramatiques, 1988), 23.
185. Dalpé, *Le chien* (Ottawa: Éditions Prise de parole, 1987), 45.
186. Dalpé, *Le chien*, 59.
187. Dalpé, *Le Chien*, trans. Labonté and Dalpé, 56.
188. Dalpé, *Le Chien*, trans. Labonté and Dalpé, 74–75.
189. Kathy Mezei, "Speaking White: Translation as a Vehicle of Assimilation in Quebec," in *Culture in Transit: Translating the Literature of Quebec*, ed. Sherry Simon (Montreal: Véhicule Press, 1995), 136.
190. Jean Marc Dalpé, *Lucky Lady*, trans. Robert Dickson (unpublished manuscript, Montreal: Centre des auteurs dramatiques, 1995), 100.

191. Rémy Charest, "À bride abattue," *Le Devoir* (Montreal), January 13, 1995, B8.

192. Robert Crew, "*Le Chien's* English Debut an Underwhelming Event," *Toronto Star*, November 18, 1988, B18, accessed November 20, 2002, http://www.iduna.demon.co.uk/roy_dupuis/rdtheatre/lechien.htm.

193. Janice Kennedy, "*Lucky Lady* Is an Also-ran," *Ottawa Citizen*, May 2, 1997, final edition, E4.

194. Wallace, "D'où cela vient-il?" 15.

195. Louis Dudek and Michael Gnarowski qtd. in Mezei, "A Bridge of Sorts," 205; John Glassco, *The Poetry of French Canada in Translation* (Toronto: Oxford University Press, 1970), xii; Mezei, "A Bridge of Sorts," 201; Philip Stratford, "Literary Translation: A Bridge between Two Solitudes," *Language and Society* 11 (1983): 8.

196. Ray Conlogue, "Fuelled by Long Monologues, Play's Verbosity is Its Engine," *Globe and Mail* (Toronto), November 9, 1996, C15.

5 Descriptive Analysis: The English Repertoire Translated into French

1. Jean-Paul Brousseau qtd. in John Herbert, *Aux yeux des hommes (Fortune and Men's Eyes)*, trans. and adapted by René Dionne (Montreal: Leméac, 1971), 99.

2. Paul Lefebvre and Pierre Ostiguy, "L'adaptation théâtrale au Québec," *Jeu* 9 (1978): 38.

3. Lefebvre and Ostiguy, "L'adaptation théâtrale," 42.

4. Lefebvre and Ostiguy, "L'adaptation théâtrale," 45.

5. Herbert, *Aux yeux des hommes*, trans. and adapted Dionne, 9; John Herbert, *Fortune and Men's Eyes* (New York: Grove, 1967), 9.

6. Herbert, *Fortune and Men's Eyes*, 15.

7. Herbert, *Aux yeux des hommes*, trans. and adapted Dionne, 16.

8. Herbert, *Fortune and Men's Eyes*, 60.

9. Herbert, *Aux yeux des hommes*, trans. and adapted Dionne, 17.

10. Herbert, *Fortune and Men's Eyes*, 70.

11. Lawrence Sabbath, "Duplessis vs. an Archbishop," *Montreal Star*, November 10, 1973, D15.

12. John Thomas McDonough, *Charbonneau and Le Chef* (Toronto: McClelland & Stewart, 1968), 103.

13. McDonough, *Charbonneau and Le Chef*, 7; John Thomas McDonough, *Charbonneau et le chef*, trans. and adapted Paul Hébert and Pierre Morency (Montreal: Leméac, 1974), 11; McDonough, *Charbonneau and Le Chef*, 8; McDonough, *Charbonneau et le chef*, trans. and adapted Hébert and Morency, 12.

14. McDonough, *Charbonneau and Le Chef*, 65; McDonough, *Charbonneau et le chef*, trans. and adapted Hébert and Morency, 72.

15. McDonough, *Charbonneau and Le Chef*, 67; McDonough, *Charbonneau et le chef*, trans. and adapted Hébert and Morency, 73.

16. McDonough, *Charbonneau and Le Chef*, 78.

17. McDonough qtd. in Sabbath, "Duplessis vs. an Archbishop," D15.

18. McDonough qtd. in Sabbath, "Duplessis vs. an Archbishop," D15.

19. McDonough, *Charbonneau and Le Chef*, 22–23.

20. McDonough, *Charbonneau et le chef*, trans. and adapted Hébert and Morency, 20–21.

21. Jean-Pierre Bonhomme, "De bons comédiens débusquent le syndrome de la dame patronnesse," *La Presse* (Montreal), January 24, 1984, A12.

22. Marie Laurier, "Une pièce qui mérite des bravos," *Le Devoir* (Montreal), January 25, 1984, 14.

23. Laurier, "Une pièce qui mérite des bravos," 14.

24. David Freeman, *Le bélier*, trans. and adapted Louison Danis (unpublished manuscript, Montreal: National Theatre School of Canada, 1984), 11.

25. Freeman, *Le bélier*, trans. and adapted Danis, 35.

26. David Freeman, *Battering Ram* (Vancouver: Talonbooks, 1974), 40.

27. Freeman, *Le bélier*, trans. and adapted Danis, 32.

28. Freeman, *Le bélier*, trans. and adapted Danis, 35.

29. Laurier, "Une pièce qui mérite des bravos," 14.

30. Annie Brisset, *Sociocritique de la traduction: théâtre et altérité au Québec (1968–1988)* (Longueuil: Préambule, 1990), 292.

31. Louison Danis qtd. in Jean-Luc Denis et al., "Le statut du québécois comme langue de traduction," *Jeu* 56 (1990): 25.

32. Marie-Ève Pelletier, "Gamme d'émotions aérées d'humour," *Le Droit* (Ottawa), November 4, 1989, 13.

33. John Hare, "Bitter-sweet Comedy Gets Magical Touch," *Ottawa Citizen*, November 2, 1989, E3.

34. Colette Godin, "*Les frères Mainville*: deux frères drôles et attachants," *ARTicles*, November/December, 1989, 10.

35. Gilles Provost qtd. in Godin, "*Les frères Mainville*," 10.

36. Norm Foster, *Les frères Mainville*, trans. Paul Latreille (unpublished manuscript, Montreal: National Theatre School of Canada, 1989), 19, 6.

37. Norm Foster, *The Melville Boys* (Toronto: Playwrights Canada, 1984), 30; Foster, *Les frères Mainville*, trans. Latreille, 30.

38. Foster, *Les frères Mainville*, trans. Latreille, 31, 36.

39.   Foster, *The Melville Boys*, 37.

40.   Foster, *Les frères Mainville*, trans. Latreille, 33.

41.   Foster, *The Melville Boys*, 34.

42.   Foster, *The Melville Boys*, 3; Foster, *Les frères Mainville*, trans. Latreille, 5.

43.   Foster, *Les frères Mainville*, trans. Latreille, 23. The title of the French version of the television series *Father Knows Best*.

44.   Foster, *The Melville Boys*, 22.

45.   Foster, *Les frères Mainville*, trans. Latreille, 39; Foster, *The Melville Boys*, 41.

46.   Foster, *The Melville Boys*, 68; Foster, *Les frères Mainville*, trans. Latreille, 63, 64.

47.   Foster, *Les frères Mainville*, trans. Latreille, 5, 5, 6, 12, 16, 19, 25, 32, 39, 48, 54, 55, 55, 56, 61, 61, 66, 66, 67, 67, 68, 69, 76, 82, 85, 90, 90, 92, 94, 97.

48.   Foster, *Les frères Mainville*, trans. Latreille, 8, 8, 8, 14, 15, 16, 13, 17.

49.   Foster, *Les frères Mainville*, trans. Latreille, 16.

50.   Foster, *Les frères Mainville*, trans. Latreille, 25; Foster, *The Melville Boys*, 25.

51.   Foster, *The Melville Boys*, 10; Foster, *Les frères Mainville*, trans. Latreille, 10; Foster, *The Melville Boys*, 20; Foster, *Les frères Mainville*, trans. Latreille, 21.

52.   Foster, *The Melville Boys*, 14.

53.   Foster, *The Melville Boys*, 111.

54.   Jean-Luc Denis, "Traduire le théâtre en contexte québécois: essai de caractérisation d'une pratique," *Jeu* 56 (1990): 16–17.

55.   For a detailed study of the translation of this play, see Louise Ladouceur, "Le sujet en question: *I Am Yours* de Judith Thompson, version québécoise," TTR. *Études sur le texte et ses transformations* 11, no. 1 (1998): 89–112.

56.   Claude Poissant qtd. in Robert Nunn, "Canada Incognita: Has Quebec Theatre Discovered English Canadian Plays?" *Theatrum* 24 (1991): 17.

57.   Micheline Letourneur, "*Je suis à toi* de Judith Thompson," *Jeu* 58 (1990): 172.

58.   Denis, "Traduire le théâtre en contexte québécois," 12.

59.   Liam Lacey, "Humour amid Horror," *Globe and Mail* (Toronto), March 2, 1992, C1.

60.   Liz Nicholls, "Fraser Play Hot Draw at Calgary Fest," *Edmonton Journal*, March 3, 1992, C6.

61.   Benoit Melançon, "*Des restes humains non identifiés et la véritable nature de l'amour*," *Jeu* 60 (1994): 152.

62.   Brad Fraser, *The Ugly Man* (Edmonton: NeWest, 1993), 12, 20, 26, 24, 45, 82.

63.   Brassard qtd. in Diane Pavlovic, "Ce reste, l'humain," in *Des restes humains non identifiés et la véritable nature de l'amour* by Brad Fraser (Montreal: Boréal, 1993), 200.

64. Brad Fraser, *Des restes humains non identifiés et la véritable nature de l'amour*, trans. André Brassard (Montreal: Boréal, 1993), 21.

65. Jean Beaunoyer, "Des coups et des douleurs, on ne discute pas," review of *L'homme laid* by Brad Fraser, *La Presse* (Montreal), March 27, 1993, E3.

66. Robert Lévesque, "Une farce bizarre et maléfique pour grands enfants," review of *L'homme laid* by Brad Fraser, *Le Devoir* (Montreal), March 26, 1993, B9.

67. Gaëtan Charlebois, "Blood 'n' Guts in Polite Company. Two Theatres Take Us to the Nut-house Door," *Mirror* (Montreal), April 1–8, 1993, 25.

68. Marie Labrecque, "L'homme laid," review of *L'homme laid* by Brad Fraser, *Voir* (Montreal), April 1–7, 1993, 36.

69. The original version upon which the translation is based was generously provided by Maryse Warda.

70. For a detailed analysis of "camp," see Shawn Huffman, "Draguer l'identité: le *camp* dans *26bis, impasse du Colonel Foisy* et *Ne blâmez jamais les Bédouins* de René-Daniel Dubois," *Voix et images* 72 (1999): 558–72.

71. Brad Fraser, *The Ugly Man* (Edmonton: NeWest, 1993), 9.

72. Robert Claing, "Rencontre avec Derek Goldby, metteur en scène de *L'Homme laid* de Brad Fraser," in *L'homme laid* by Brad Fraser, trans. Maryse Warda (Montreal: Boréal, 1993), 259.

73. Fraser, *L'homme laid*, trans. Warda, 26.

74. Fraser, *The Ugly Man*, 22.

75. Fraser, *L'homme laid*, trans. Warda, 56.

76. Fraser, *The Ugly Man*, 35; Fraser, *L'homme laid*, trans. Warda, 84.

77. Fraser, *The Ugly Man*, 22; Fraser, *L'homme laid*, trans. Warda, 18; Fraser, *The Ugly Man*, 24; Fraser, *L'homme laid*, trans. Warda, 22.

78. Fraser, *The Ugly Man*, 25; Fraser, *L'homme laid*, trans. Warda, 62.

79. Fraser, *L'homme laid*, trans. Warda, 34.

80. Fraser, *The Ugly Man*, 42; Fraser, *L'homme laid*, trans. Warda, 99.

81. Fraser, *The Ugly Man*, 89; Fraser, *L'homme laid*, trans. Warda, 207.

82. Fraser, *L'homme laid*, trans. Warda, 239, 242.

83. Fraser, *The Ugly Man*, 29; Fraser, *L'homme laid*, trans. Warda, 10.

84. Sylvain Campeau, "*Amours passibles d'amendes*," *Voir* (Montreal), May 4–10, 1989, 22.

85. Campeau, "*Amours passibles d'amendes*," 22.

86. Jean Beaunoyer, "À voir un soir de pleine lune," *La Presse* (Montreal), February 3, 1989, B4.

87. George F. Walker, *Criminals in Love* (Toronto: Playwrights Canada, 1985), 100; George F. Walker, *Amours passibles d'amendes*, trans. Louison Danis (Montreal: National Theatre School Library, 1988), 83.

88. Daniel de Raey qtd. in George F. Walker, *Suburban Motel* (Vancouver: Talonbooks, 1997), 4.

89. Walker qtd. in Raymond Bernatchez, "L'enfant-problème," *La Presse* (Montreal), October 10, 1998, D4.

90. George F. Walker, *Problem Child*, in *Suburban Motel* (Vancouver: Talonbooks, 1997), 42.

91. Walker, *Problem Child*, 8, 8, 8, 9, 10.

92. Hervé Guay, "L'art de s'effacer pour faire sentir sa presence," *Le Devoir* (Montreal) April 3–4, 1999, B5.

93. George F. Walker, *L'enfant-problème*, in *Motel de passage*, tome 1, trans. Maryse Warda (Montreal: VLB Éditeur, 2001), 54–55.

94. Solange Lévesque, "Le prix de la vie," *Le Devoir* (Montreal), April 13, 1999, B7.

95. S. Lévesque, "Le prix de la vie," B7.

96. Robert Lévesque, "Motel Caprice," *Ici* (Montreal), May 6–13, 1999, 40.

97. Aurèle Parisien, "Taking a Walker on the French Side," *Canadian Theatre Review* 102 (2000): 29.

98. Parisien, "Taking a Walker on the French Side," 29.

99. Brisset, *Sociocritique de la traduction*, 76.

100. Alain Pontaut, preface to *L'effet des rayons gamma sur les vieux-garçons* by Paul Zindel, trans. Michel Tremblay (Montreal: Leméac, 1970), 7.

101. Herbert, *Aux yeux des hommes*, trans. and adapted Dionne, 9.

102. Paul Lefebvre and Pierre Ostiguy, "L'adaptation théâtrale au Québec," *Jeu* 9 (1984): 47.

103. Tremblay qtd. in Annie Brisset, *Sociocritique de la traduction*, 61.

104. See Louise Ladouceur, "Du spéculaire au spectaculaire: le théâtre anglo-canadien traduit au Québec au début des années 90," in *Nouveaux regards sur le théâtre québécois*, eds. Betty Bednarski and Irene Oore (Halifax: XYZ/Dalhousie French Studies, 1997), 185–94.

105. Robert Lévesque, "La figure imprécise d'Ethel Rosenberg," *Le Devoir* (Montreal), April 18, 1992, C5.

106. Robert Lévesque, "Une renaissance 'maghanée,'" *Le Devoir* (Montreal), April 29, 1993, B8.

107. Marie Labrecque, "Les reines de la réserve," *Voir* (Montreal), September 30, 1993, 37.

108. Gaston Miron, *L'homme rapaillé* (Montreal: Les Presses de l'Université de Montréal, 1970), 124.

109. Jacques Brault, *Poèmes des quatre côtés* (Saint-Lambert, QC: Noroît, 1975), 34.

110. Brault, *Poèmes des quatre côtés*, 15.

111. Brault, *Poèmes des quatre côtés*, 16.

112. Larry Shouldice, "On the Politics of Literary Translation in Canada," in *Translation in Canadian Literature: Symposium 1982*, ed. Camille La Bossière (Ottawa: University of Ottawa Press, 1983), 75.

6 Comparison of the Repertoires in Translation

1. E.D. Blodgett, *Configuration: Essays on the Canadian Literatures* (Downsview, ON: ECW Press, 1982), 32.
2. Barbara Folkart, *Le conflit des énonciations: traduction et discours rapporté* (Candiac: Préambule, 1991), 449.
3. André Lefevere, *Translation, Rewriting and the Manipulation of Literary Fame* (London: Routledge, 1992), 23.
4. Blodgett, *Configuration*, 30.
5. Ray Conlogue, "Quebec's Surprising New Wave," *Globe and Mail* (Toronto), January 26, 1993, A12.
6. Robert Wallace, *Producing Marginality: Theatre and Criticism in Canada* (Saskatoon: Fifth House, 1990), 38.
7. Annie Brisset, *Sociocritique de la traduction: théâtre et altérité au Québec (1968–1988)* (Longueuil: Préambule, 1990), 26.
8. Brisset, *Sociocritique de la traduction*, 312.
9. Antoine Berman, "La traduction et la lettre, ou l'auberge du lointain," in *Les Tours de Babel: essais sur la traduction* (Mauvezin, FR: Trans-Europ-Repress, 1985), 50.
10. Jane Koustas, "From Gélinas to Carrier: Critical Response to Translated Quebec Theatre in Toronto," *Studies in Canadian Literature* 17, no. 2 (1992): 110.
11. Gratien Gélinas, *Bousille et les justes* (Montreal: Institut littéraire du Québec, 1960), 10.
12. Richard Plant, "Drama in English," in *The Oxford Companion to Canadian Theatre*, eds. Eugene Benson and L.W. Conolly (Toronto: Oxford University Press, 1989), 164.
13. See Robert Wallace, "D'où cela vient-il? Réflexions sur la réception critique du théâtre francophone récent à Toronto," trans. Michel Vaïs, *Jeu* 49 (1988): 9–23.
14. Jane Koustas, "From 'Homespun' to 'Awesome': Translated Quebec Theatre in Toronto," in *Essays on Modern Quebec Theatre*, eds. Joseph I. Donohue Jr. and Jonathan M. Weiss (East Lansing: Michigan State University Press, 1995), 100.
15. Linda Gaboriau, "The Cultures of Theatre," in *Culture in Transit: Translating the Literature of Quebec*, ed. Sherry Simon (Montreal: Véhicule Press, 1995), 87.
16. Serge Boucher, *Motel Hélène*, trans. Judith Thompson and Morwyn Brebner (Toronto: Playwrights Union of Canada, 2000), 12.
17. Serge Boucher, *Motel Hélène* (English version revised by Crystal Béliveau and Serge Boucher, from an adaptation by Judith Thompson based on a literal translation by Morwyn Brebner, unpublished manuscript, Montreal: CEAD, 2001), 9–10.

18. Pat Donnelly, "Edmonton's Fraser a Quebec Favorite," *Montreal Gazette,* April 19, 1995, G6.
19. Donnelly, "Edmonton's Fraser a Quebec Favorite," G6.
20. Patricia Belzil, "Par le trou de la serrure," *Jeu* 94 (2000): 104.

BIBLIOGRAPHY

Primary References—Dramatic works composing the corpus

Bouchard, Michel Marc. *Les feluettes ou la répétition d'un drame romantique.*
    Montreal: Leméac, 1987.

———. *Lilies or The Revival of a Romantic Drama.* Translated by Linda Gaboriau.
    Toronto: Coach House Press, 1990.

———. *Les muses orphelines.* Montreal: Leméac, 1989.

———. *Les muses orphelines.* Revised 2nd edition. Montreal: Leméac, 1995.

———. *The Orphan Muses.* Translated by Linda Gaboriau. Victoria: Scirocco
    Drama, 1995.

Chaurette, Normand. *Provincetown Playhouse, juillet 1919, j'avais 19 ans.*
    Montreal: Leméac, 1981.

———. *Provincetown Playhouse, July 1919.* Translated by William Boulet. In
    Quebec Voices: Three Plays, edited by Robert Wallace, 23–125. Toronto:
    Coach House, 1986.

Dalpé, Jean Marc. *Le chien.* Ottawa: Éditions Prise de parole, 1987.

———. *Le Chien.* Translated by Maureen Labonté and Jean Marc Dalpé.
    Unpublished manuscript, Montreal: Centre d'essai des auteurs
    dramatiques, 1988.

———. *Lucky Lady.* Montreal: Boréal, 1995.

———. *Lucky Lady*. Translated by Robert Dickson. Unpublished manuscript, Montreal: Centre des auteurs dramatiques, 1995.

Foster, Norm. *The Melville Boys*. Toronto: Playwrights Canada, 1984.

———. *Les frères Mainville*. Translated by Paul Latreille. Unpublished manuscript, Montreal: National Theatre School of Canada, 1989.

Fraser, Brad. *The Ugly Man*. Edmonton: NeWest, 1993.

———. *L'homme laid*. Translated by Maryse Warda. Montreal: Boréal, 1993.

Freeman, David. *Battering Ram*. Vancouver: Talonbooks, 1974.

———. *Le bélier*. Translated and adapted by Louison Danis. Unpublished manuscript, Montreal: National Theatre School of Canada, 1984.

Gélinas, Gratien. *Bousille et les justes*. Montreal: Institut littéraire du Québec, 1960.

———. *Bousille and the Just*. Translated by Kenneth Johnstone and Joffre Miville-Deschêne. Toronto: Clarke, Irwin and Company, 1961.

Herbert, John. *Fortune and Men's Eyes*. New York: Grove Press, 1967.

———. *Aux yeux des hommes*. Translated and adapted by René Dionne. Montreal: Leméac, 1971.

Lepage, Robert, and Marie Brassard. *Le Polygraphe*. Unpublished manuscript, Quebec City: La Caserne, 1992.

———. "Polygraph." Translated by Gyllian Raby. In *Modern Canadian Plays*, 3rd edition, vol. 2, edited by Jerry Wasserman, 297–316, Vancouver: Talonbooks, 1994.

Marchessault, Jovette. *La terre est trop courte, Violette Leduc*. Montreal: Les Éditions de la pleine lune, 1982.

———. *The Edge of Earth is Too Near, Violette Leduc*. Translated by Susanne de Lotbinière-Harwood. Unpublished manuscript, Montreal: National Theatre School of Canada, 1985.

McDonough, John Thomas. *Charbonneau and Le Chef*. Toronto: McClelland & Stewart, 1968.

———. *Charbonneau et le chef*. Translated and adapted by Paul Hébert and Pierre Morency. Montreal: Leméac, 1974.

Tremblay, Michel. *Les belles-sœurs*. Montreal: Holt, Rinehart and Winston, 1968.

———. *Les belles-sœurs*. Montreal: Leméac, 1972.

———. *Les Belles Soeurs*. Translated by John Van Burek and Bill Glassco, Vancouver: Talonbooks, 1974.

———. *Les Belles-Soeurs*. Translated by John Van Burek and Bill Glassco, revised edition. Vancouver: Talonbooks, 1992.

———. *Les Belles-Soeurs*. Translated by John Van Burek and Bill Glassco. In *Modern Canadian Plays*, 3rd ed., vol. 1, edited by Jerry Wasserman, 97–133. Vancouver: Talonbooks, 1993.

———. *Bonjour, là, bonjour*. Montreal: Leméac, 1974.

———. *Bonjour, Là, Bonjour*. Translated by John Van Burek and Bill Glassco. Vancouver: Talonbooks, 1975.

——. *Bonjour, Là, Bonjour.* Translated by John Van Burek and Bill Glassco, revised edition. Vancouver: Talonbooks, 1988.

——. *Hosanna / La Duchesse de Langeais.* Montreal: Leméac, 1973.

——. *Hosanna.* Translated by John Van Burek and Bill Glassco. Vancouver: Talonbooks, 1974.

——. *Hosanna.* Translated by John Van Burek and Bill Glassco, revised edition. Vancouver: Talonbooks, 1991.

——. *La maison suspendue.* Montreal: Leméac, 1990.

——. *La Maison Suspendue.* Translated by John Van Burek and Bill Glassco. Vancouver: Talonbooks, 1991.

Walker, George F. *Problem Child.* In *Suburban Motel*, 7–48. Vancouver: Talonbooks, 1997.

——. *L'enfant-problème.* In *Motel de passage.* Tome 1, 7–86. Translated by Maryse Warda. Montreal: VLB Éditeur, 2001.

——. *Amours passibles d'amendes.* Translated by Louison Danis. Unpublished manuscript, Montreal: National Theatre School, 1988.

Secondary References—Reference works, critical and theoretical texts, newspaper articles, and theatre reviews

Ackerman, Marianne. "Sweet Jesus! Who's That, Ma?" *Saturday Night* (Toronto), June 1988, 40–47.

Angenot, Marc. *Glossaire pratique de la critique littéraire contemporaine.* Montreal: Hurtubise, 1979.

Barbe, Jean. "Les Feluettes. Le retour de l'âme." *Voir* (Montreal), September 3–9 1987, 6.

Bassnett-McGuire, Susan. *Translation Studies.* London: New Accents, 1980.

——. "Ways through the Labyrinth, Strategies and Methods for Translating Theatre Texts." In *The Manipulation of Literature, Studies in Literary Translation*, edited by Theo Hermans, 87–102. London: Croom Helm, 1985.

Beaunoyer, Jean. "À voir un soir de pleine lune." *La Presse* (Montreal), February 3, 1989, B4.

——. "Des coups et des douleurs, on ne discute pas." Review of *L'homme laid* by Brad Fraser. *La Presse* (Montreal), March 27, 1993, E3.

Bélair, Michel. *Le nouveau théâtre québécois.* Montreal: Leméac, 1973.

Belzil, Patricia. "Par le trou de la serrure." *Jeu* 94 (2000): 100–07.

Benson, Eugene, and L.W. Conolly, eds. *English-Canadian Theatre.* Toronto: Oxford University Press, 1987.

——. *The Oxford Companion to Canadian Theatre.* Toronto: Oxford University Press, 1989.

Berman, Antoine. *Pour une critique des traductions: John Donne*. Paris: Gallimard, 1995.

——. *Toward a Translation Criticism: John Donne*. Translated by Françoise Massardier-Kenney. Kent, OH: Kent State University Press, 2009.

——. "La traduction et la lettre, ou l'auberge du lointain." In *Les tours de Babel: essais sur la traduction* 31–151. Mauvezin, FR: Trans-Europ-Repress, 1985.

Bernatchez, Raymond. "L'enfant-problème." *La Presse* (Montreal), October 10, 1998, D4.

Blodgett, E.D. *Configuration: Essays on the Canadian Literatures*. Downsview, ON: ECW Press, 1982.

——. "How Do You Say 'Gabrielle Roy'?" In *Translation in Canadian Literature: Symposium 1982*, edited by Camille La Bossière, 13–34. Ottawa: University of Ottawa Press, 1983.

——. "Towards a Model of Literary Translation in Canada." TTR. *Études sur le texte et ses transformations* 4, no. 2 (1991): 189–203.

——. "Translation as a Key to Canadian Literature." *New Comparison* 1 (1986): 93–103.

Bonhomme, Jean-Pierre. "De bons comédiens débusquent le syndrome de la dame patronnesse." *La Presse* (Montreal), January 24, 1984, A12.

Bosley, Vivien. "Diluting the Mixture: Translating Michel Tremblay's *Les Belles-Soeurs*." TTR 1, no. 1 (1988): 139–45.

Boucher, Serge. *Motel Hélène*. English version by Judith Thompson based on a literal translation by Morwyn Brebner. Toronto: Playwrights Union of Canada, 2000.

——. *Motel Hélène*. English version revised by Crystal Béliveau and Serge Boucher, from an adaptation by Judith Thompson based on a literal translation by Morwyn Brebner. Unpublished manuscript, Montreal: CEAD, 2001.

Boulanger, Luc. "Illusion comique." *Voir* (Montreal), November 22–28, 1990, 28.

Bourdieu, Pierre. *Questions de sociologie*. Paris: Les Éditions de Minuit, 1980.

Brault, Jacques. *Poèmes des quatre côtés*. Saint-Lambert, QC: Noroît, 1975.

Brisset, Annie. "Ceci n'est pas une trahison." *Spirale* 62 (1986): 12–13.

——. *Sociocritique de la traduction: théâtre et altérité au Québec (1968–1988)*. Longueuil: Préambule, 1990.

Brochu, André. *L'instance critique*. Montreal: Leméac, 1974.

Camerlain, Lorraine, and Pierre Lavoie. "Drama in French." In *Canadian Encyclopedia*. Edmonton: Hurtig, 1985.

Campeau, Sylvain. "Amours passibles d'amendes." *Voir* (Montreal), May 4–10, 1989, 22–23.

Cary, Edmond. *La traduction dans le monde modern*. Geneva: Georg, 1956.

Charest, Rémy. "À bride abattue." *Le Devoir* (Montreal), January 13, 1995, B8.

Charlebois, Gaëtan. "Blood 'n' Guts in Polite Company. Two Theatres Take Us to the Nut-house Door," *Mirror* (Montreal), April 1–8, 1993, 25.

———. "Breaking Boundaries," *Mirror* (Montreal), September 26–October 3, 1991, 20–21.

Churchill, Stacy. *Official languages in Canada: Changing the Language Landscape.* New Canadian Perspectives. Ottawa: Canadian Heritage, 1998.

Claing, Robert. "Rencontre avec Derek Goldby, metteur en scène de *L'Homme laid* de Brad Fraser." In *L'homme laid* by Brad Fraser, 253–63. Montreal: Boréal, 1993.

Conlogue, Ray. "Fuelled by Long Monologues, Play's Verbosity is Its Engine." *Globe and Mail* (Toronto), November 9, 1996, C15.

———. "Quebec's Surprising New Wave." *Globe and Mail* (Toronto), January 26, 1993, A12.

———. "Warriors Succumbs to Faulty Adaptation." *Globe and Mail* (Toronto), February 28, 1990, C9.

Conolly, L.W., ed. *Canadian Drama and the Critics.* Vancouver: Talonbooks, 1995.

Crew, Robert. "Mystery Explores Madness." *Toronto Star*, December 7, 1986, C2.

———. "Le Chien's English Debut an Underwhelming Event." *Toronto Star*, November 18, 1988, B18. Accessed November 20, 2002. http://www.iduna. demon.co.uk/roy_dupuis/rdtheatre/lechien.htm.

Crook, Barbara. "Vancouver Production of a Quebec Play Shows a Universal Symbol for Survival." *Vancouver Sun* (BC), March 11, 1996, B6.

Crowder, Eleanor. "*Provincetown Playhouse, juillet 1919, j'avais 19 ans.*" *Theatrum* 40 (1994): 37.

Dassylva, Martial. "Les tourbillons Leduc, Guilbault et Marchessault." *La Presse* (Montreal), November 24, 1981, B3.

David, Gilbert, and Pierre Lavoie, eds. *Le monde de Michel Tremblay.* Montreal: Jeu/Lansman, 1993.

Delisle, Jean. *Au coeur du trialogue canadien: Bureau des traductions 1934–1984 / Bridging the Language Solitudes: Translation Bureau 1934–1984.* Ottawa: Minister of Supply and Services Canada, 1984.

———. "Dans les coulisses de l'adaptation québécoise," *Circuit* 12 (1986), 3–8.

———. *La traduction au Canada / Translation in Canada.* Ottawa: University of Ottawa Press, 1987.

Denis, Jean-Luc, Louison Danis, René Gingras, Louise Ladouceur, Paul Lefebvre, and Gilbert Turp. "Le statut du québécois comme langue de traduction." *Jeu* 56 (1990): 25–37.

Denis, Jean-Luc. "Pourquoi traduire *L'éveil du printemps* en québécois." Program from *L'éveil du printemps* by Frank Wedekind. Montreal: Théâtre de Quat'Sous, 1989.

———. "Traduire le théâtre en contexte québécois: essai de caractérisation d'une pratique." *Jeu* 56 (1990): 9–17.

Donnelly, Pat. "Edmonton's Fraser a Quebec Favorite." *Montreal Gazette*, April 19, 1995, G6.

———. "English-Canadian Playwrights Finally Get Attention Here." Review of *Les traverses du coeur* by Wendy Lill. *Montreal Gazette*, January 18, 1993, C3.

———. "The Shrill of It All. Thompson Play a Passionate Screech." *Montreal Gazette*, September 26, 1991, D13.

Even-Zohar, Itamar. "Laws of Literay Interference." *Poetics Today* 11, no. 1 (1990): 53–72.

———. "The 'Literary' System." *Poetics Today* 11, no. 1 (1990): 27–44.

———. "Polysystem Theory." *Poetics Today* 1, no. 1–2 (1979): 287–310.

———. "Translated Literature within the Literary System." *Poetics Today* 11, no. 1 (1990): 45–51.

Ferencik, Jan. "De la spécification de la traduction de l'oeuvre dramatique." In *The Nature of Translation*, edited by James Holmes, 145–50. Bratislava: Slovak Academy of Sciences, 1970.

Folkart, Barbara. *Le conflit des énonciations: traduction et discours rapporté.* Candiac: Préambule, 1991.

Forsyth, Louise. "Feminist Theatre." In *The Oxford Companion to Canadian Theatre*, edited by Eugene Benson and L.W. Conolly, 203–06. Toronto: Oxford University Press, 1989.

Fraser, Brad. *Des restes humains non identifiés et la véritable nature de l'amour.* Translated by André Brassard. Montreal: Boréal, 1993.

———. *L'homme laid.* Translated by Maryse Warda. Montreal: Boréal, 1993.

———. *The Ugly Man.* Edmonton: NeWest, 1993.

———. *Unidentified Human Remains and the True Nature of Love.* Winnipeg, MB: Blizzard Publishing, 1990.

Gaboriau, Linda. "The Cultures of Theatre." In *Culture in Transit: Translating the Literature of Quebec*, edited by Sherry Simon, 83–90. Montreal: Véhicule Press, 1995.

Gaboriau, Linda, and Daniel Gauthier, eds. *Québec Plays in Translation: A Catalogue of Québec Playwrights and Plays in English Translation.* Montreal: Centre des auteurs dramatiques, 1998.

Gélinas, Gratien, and Victor-Lévy Beaulieu. *Gratien, Tit-Coq, Fridolin, Bousille et les autres.* Montreal: SRC/Stanké, 1993.

Germain, Jean-Claude. "J'ai eu le coup de foudre." In *Les belles-sœurs* by Michel Tremblay, 3–5. Montreal: Holt, Rinehart and Wintson, 1968.

Giguère, Richard. "Traduction littéraire et 'image' de la littérature au Canada et au Québec." In *Translation in Canadian Literature: Symposium 1982*, edited by Camille La Bossière, 47–60. Ottawa: University of Ottawa Press, 1983.

Glassco, John. *The Poetry of French Canada in Translation.* Toronto: Oxford University Press, 1970.

Gobard, Henri. *L'aliénation linguistique: analyse tétraglossique.* Paris: Flammarion, 1976.

Godard, Barbara. "Language and Sexual Difference: The Case of Translation."*Atkinson Review of Canadian Studies* 2, no. 1 (1984): 13–20.

———. "Letters in Canada. Translations." *University of Toronto Quarterly* 58, no. 1 (1988): 76–99.

———. "Theorizing Feminist Discourse / Translation." *Tessera* 6 (1989): 42–53.

Godin, Collette. "*Les frères Mainville*: deux frères drôles et attachants." ARTicles, November/December, 1989, 10.

Godin, Jean-Cléo. "Quebec Voices: Three Plays." *Canadian Theatre Review* 56 (1988): 86–87.

Godin, Jean-Cléo, and Laurent Mailhot. *Le théâtre québécois.* Montreal: Hurtubise, 1973.

Gouanvic, Jean-Marc. "Pour une sociologie de la traduction: le cas de la littérature américaine traduite en France après la Seconde Guerre mondiale (1945-1960)." In *Translation as Intercultural Communication,* edited by Mary Snell-Hornby, Zuzana Jettmarova, and Klaus Kaindl, 33–44. Amsterdam: Benjamins, 1997.

Greimas, A.J. *Du sens.* Paris: Seuil, 1966.

Guay, Hervé. "L'art de s'effacer pour faire sentir sa presence." *Le Devoir* (Montreal), April 3–4, 1999, B5.

Hare, John. "Bitter-sweet Comedy Gets Magical Touch." *Ottawa Citizen,* November 2, 1989, E3.

Hébert, Chantal. *Le burlesque au Québec: un divertissement populaire.* Montreal: Hurtubise, 1981.

Honoré, Carl. "The Best Playwright Scotland Never Had." *Globe and Mail* (Toronto), October 31, 1992, C5.

Horguelin, Paul A. *Anthologie de la manière de traduire: domaine français.* Montreal: Linguatech, 1981.

———. *Pratique de la révision.* Montreal: Linguatech, 1985.

Huffman, Shawn. "Draguer l'identité: le *camp* dans *26bis, impasse du Colonel Foisy* et *Ne blâmez jamais les Bédouins* de René-Daniel Dubois." *Voix et Images* 72 (1999): 558–72.

Hulan, Renée. "Surviving Translation: *Forever Yours Marie-Lou* at Tarragon Theatre." *Theatre Research in Canada* 15, no. 1 (1994): 48–57.

Humphries, Jill. *Who's Who in the Playwrights Union of Canada.* Toronto: Playwrights Union of Canada, 1995.

Jakobson, Roman. *Essais de linguistique générale.* Paris: Les Éditions de Minuit, 1963.

Jauss, Hans Robert. *Pour une esthétique de la reception.* Paris: Gallimard, 1978.

Johnston, Denis W. *Up the Mainstream: The Rise of Toronto's Alternative Theatres, 1968-1975.* Toronto: University of Toronto Press, 1991.

Jones, D.G. *Butterfly on Rock: A Study of Themes and Images in Canadian Literature.* Toronto: University of Toronto Press, 1970.

———. "Grounds for Translation." *Ellipse* 21 (1977): 58–91.

Kennedy, Janice. "*Lucky Lady* Is an Also-ran." *Ottawa Citizen*, May 2, 1997, final edition, E4.

Koustas, Jane. "From Gélinas to Carrier: Critical Response to Translated Quebec Theatre in Toronto." *Studies in Canadian Literature* 17, no. 2 (1992): 109–28.

———. "From 'Homespun' to 'Awesome': Translated Quebec Theatre in Toronto." In *Essays on Modern Quebec Theatre*, edited by Joseph I. Donohue Jr. and Jonathan M. Weiss, 81–107. East Lansing: Michigan State University Press, 1995.

———. "Hosanna in Toronto: 'Tour de force' or 'Détour de traduction.'" TTR 2, no. 2 (1989): 129–39.

Kowzan, Tadeusz. *Littérature et spectacle*. The Hague and Paris: Mouton, 1976.

Labrecque, Marie. "L'homme laid." Review of *L'homme laid* by Brad Fraser. *Voir* (Montreal), April 1–7, 1993, 36.

———. "Les reines de la réserve." *Voir* (Montreal), September 30, 1993, 37.

Lacey, Liam. "Humour amid Horror." *Globe and Mail* (Toronto), March 2, 1992, C1.

Ladouceur, Louise. "A Firm Balance: questions d'équilibre et rapport de force dans les représentations des littératures anglophone et francophone du Canada." *Canadian Literature* 175 (2003): 96–114.

———. "From Other Tongue to Mother Tongue in the Drama of Quebec and Canada." In *Changing the Terms: Translating in the Postcolonial Era*," edited by Sherry Simon and Paul St-Pierre, 207–26. Ottawa: University of Ottawa Press, 2000.

———. "Normes, fonctions et traduction théâtrale." *Meta. Journal des traducteurs* 40, no. 1 (1995): 31–38.

———. "Les paramètres de l'adaptation théâtrale au Québec de 1980 à 1990." MA thesis, Université de Montréal, 1991.

———. "Separate Stages: la traduction du théâtre dans le contexte Canada/ Québec." PHD diss., University of British Columbia, 1997.

———. "Du spéculaire au spectaculaire: le théâtre anglo-canadien traduit au Québec au début des années 90." In *Nouveaux regards sur le théâtre québécois*, edited by Betty Bednarski and Irene Oore, 185–94. Halifax: XYZ/Dalhousie French Studies, 1997.

———. "Le sujet en question: *I Am Yours* de Judith Thompson, version québécoise." TTR. *Études sur le texte et ses transformations* 11, no.1 (1998): 89–112.

———. "A Version of Quebec: le théâtre québécois au Canada anglais." *L'Annuaire théâtral* 27 (2000): 108–19.

Lafon, Dominique. "La relecture d'une pièce: mouture textuelle et meule scénique." *Jeu* 74 (1995): 80–88.

Lambert, José, and Hendrik van Gorp. "On Describing Translations." In *The Manipulation of Literature*, edited by Theo Hermans, 42–53. London: Croom Helm, 1985.

Lamontagne, Gilles. "Judith Thompson frappe au Quat'Sous: *Lion dans les rues*." *La Presse* (Montreal), September 18, 1991, C10.

Larose, Robert. *Théories contemporaines de la traduction*. Quebec City: Les Presses de l'Université du Québec, 1987.

Larue-Langlois, Jacques. "Un pas de géant pour le théâtre d'ici." *Le Devoir* (Montreal), November 13, 1981, 14.

Laurier, Marie. "Une pièce qui mérite des bravos." *Le Devoir* (Montreal), January 25, 1984, 14.

Leduc, Violette. *La bâtarde*. Paris: Gallimard, 1964.

———. *La Bâtarde*. Translated by Derek Coltman. London: Panther Books, 1967.

Lefebvre, Paul. Introduction to *Quebec Voices: Three Plays*. Edited by Robert Wallace, 9–16. Toronto: Coach House, 1986.

Lefebvre, Paul, and Pierre Ostiguy. "L'adaptation théâtrale au Québec." *Jeu* 9 (1978): 32–47.

Lefevere, André. *Translation, Rewriting and the Manipulation of Literary Fame*. London: Routledge, 1992.

Leonard, Paul. "Critical Questioning." *Canadian Theatre Review* 57 (1988): 4–10.

Lepage, Robert, and Ex Machina. *The Seven Streams of the River Ota*. London: Methuen Drama, 1996.

Letourneur, Micheline. "*Je suis à toi* de Judith Thompson." *Jeu* 58 (1990): 170–72.

Lévesque, Robert. "Des restes humains bien identifiés." *Le Devoir* (Montreal), September 20, 1991, B5.

———. "En attendant le bingo." *Le Devoir* (Montreal), September 24, 1993, B7.

———. "Une farce bizarre et maléfique pour grands enfants." Review of *L'homme laid* by Brad Fraser. *Le Devoir* (Montreal), March 26, 1993, B9.

———. "La figure imprécise d'Ethel Rosenberg." *Le Devoir* (Montreal), April 18, 1992, C5.

———. "Motel Caprice." *Ici* (Montreal), May 6–13, 1999, 40.

———. "Une renaissance 'maghanée.'" *Le Devoir* (Montreal), April 29, 1993, B8.

Lévesque, Solange. "Le prix de la vie." *Le Devoir* (Montreal), April 13, 1999, B7.

Lotbinière-Harwood, Susanne de. *Re-belle et infidèle: La traduction comme pratique de réécriture au féminin / The Body Bilingual: Translation as a Rewriting in the Feminine*. Montreal: Les Éditions du remue-ménage; Toronto: Women's Press, 1991.

Lotman, Iouri. *La structure du texte artisque*. Paris: Gallimard, 1973.

Martin, Ruth. "Translated Canadian Literature and Canada Council Translation Grants 1972–1992: The Effect on Authors, Translators and Publishers." *Ellipse* 51 (1994): 54–84.

Melançon, Benoit. "*Des restes humains non identifiés et la véritable nature de l'amour*." *Jeu* 60 (1991): 149–52.

Mezei, Kathy. "A Bridge of Sorts: The Translation of Quebec Literature into English." *The Yearbook of English Studies: Anglo-American Literary Relations Special Number 15* (1985): 202–26.

———. "Speaking White: Translation as a Vehicle of Assimilation in Quebec." In *Culture in Transit: Translating the Literature of Quebec*, edited by Sherry Simon, 133–48. Montreal: Véhicule Press, 1995.

———. "Translation as Metonomy: Bridges and Bilingualism." *Ellipse* 51 (1994): 85–102.

Mezei, Stephen. "Tremblay's Toronto Success." *Performing Arts in Canada* 10 (1973): 26.

Miron, Gaston. *L'homme rapaillé*. Montreal: Les Presses de l'Université de Montréal, 1970.

Moisan, Clément. *L'âge de la littérature canadienne*. Montreal: HMH, 1969.

Mounin, Georges. *Linguistique et traduction*. Bruxelles: Dessart et Mardaga, 1976.

Nichols, Glen F. *From Around the World and at Home: Translations and Adaptations in Canadian Theatre*. Toronto: Playwrights Union of Canada, 2000.

Nicholls, Liz. "Fraser Play Hot Draw at Calgary Fest." *Edmonton Journal*, March 3, 1992, C6.

Nida, Eugène, and Charles Taber. *The Theory and Practice of Translation*. Leiden: E.J. Brill, 1969.

Nunn, Robert. "Canada Incognita: Has Quebec Theatre Discovered English Canadian Plays?" *Theatrum* 24 (1991): 14–19.

Parisien, Aurèle. "Taking a Walker on the French Side." *Canadian Theatre Review* 102 (2000): 28–32.

Pavlovic, Diane. "Ce reste, l'humain." In *Des restes humains non identifiés et la véritable nature de l'amour* by Brad Fraser, 199–212. Montreal: Boréal, 1993.

Pelletier, Francine. "Violette-Jovette, Jovette-Violette." Preface to *La terre est trop courte, Violette Leduc* by Jovette Marchessault. Montreal: Les Éditions de la pleine lune, 1982.

Pelletier, Marie-Ève. "Gamme d'émotions aérées d'humour." *Le Droit* (Ottawa), November 4, 1989, 13.

Peterson, Maureen. "Play a Marathon of Dubious Taste." *Montreal Gazette*, November 16, 1981, 52.

Plant, Richard. "Drama in English." In *The Oxford Companion to Canadian Theatre*, edited by Eugene Benson and L.W. Conolly, 148–69. Toronto: Oxford University Press, 1989.

Pontaut, Alain. Preface to *Les belles-sœurs* by Michel Tremblay, revised edition, i–vi. Montreal: Leméac, 1972.

———. Preface to *L'effet des rayons gamma sur les vieux-garçons* by Paul Zindel. Translated by Michel Tremblay, i–vii. Montreal: Leméac, 1970.

Rubin, Don. "John Van Burek: Tremblay in Translation." *Canadian Theatre Review* 24 (1979): 42–46.

Sabbath, Lawrence. "Duplessis vs. an Archbishop." *Montreal Star*, November 10, 1973, D15.

Saint-Pierre, Jacques. "Michel Tremblay, dramaturge québécois et canadien: bilan de la réception d'une pièce et sa traduction." In *Littérature québécoise: la recherche en émergence. Actes du deuxième colloque interuniversitaire des jeunes chercheur(e)s en littérature québécoise*, 57–69. Quebec: Centre de recherche en littérature québécoise/Nuit blanche éditeur, 1991.

Shek, Ben-Zion. "Quelques réflexions sur la traduction dans le contexte socio-culturel canado-québécois." *Ellipse* 21 (1977): 111–16.

Shouldice, Larry. "On The Politics of Literary Translation in Canada." In *Translation in Canadian Literature: Symposium 1982*, edited by Camille La Bossière, 73–82. Ottawa: University of Ottawa Press, 1983.

Simon, Sherry. *L'inscription sociale de la traduction au Québec*. Quebec City: Office de la langue française, 1989.

———. "Rites of Passage: Translation and Its Intents." *The Massachusetts Review* 31, no. 1–2 (1990): 96–110.

———. *Le trafic des langues: traduction et culture dans la littérature québécoise*. Montreal: Boréal, 1994.

Spickler, Robert. Preface to *La culture contre l'art: essai d'économie politique du théâtre* by Josette Féral, xi–xiii. Montreal: Les Presses de l'Université du Québec, 1990.

Stratford, Philip. *Bibliographie de livres canadiens traduits de l'anglais au français et du français à l'anglais / Bibliography of Canadian Books in Translation: French to English and English to French*, 2nd ed. Ottawa: Social Sciences and Humanities Research Council of Canada, 1977.

———. "Canada's Two Literatures: A Search for Emblems." *Canadian Review of Comparative Literature* 6, no. 2 (1979): 131–38.

———. "Literary Translation: A Bridge between Two Solitudes." *Language and Society* 11 (1983): 8–13.

Thomas, Colin. "*The Orphan Muses* Strikes a Universal Chord." *Georgia Straight* (Vancouver), March 11–18, 1996, 51.

Toury, Gideon. *Descriptive Translation Studies and Beyond*. Amsterdam: Benjamins, 1995.

———. *In Search of a Theory of Translation*. Tel Aviv: The Porter Institute for Poetics and Semiotics, 1980.

Ubersfeld, Anne. *Lire le theatre*. Paris: Messidor, 1982.

Usmiani, Renate. *Gratien Gélinas*. Profiles in Canadian Drama. 1977. Agincourt, ON: Gage Educational, 1982.

———. *Michel Tremblay*. Vancouver: Douglas & McIntyre, 1982.

Villeneuve, Rodrigue. "*Provincetown Playhouse, juillet 1919, j'avais 19 ans, à la lettre.*" *Jeu* 64 (1992): 123–25.

von Flotow, Luise. "Translating the Women of the Eighties: Erotocism, Anger, Ethnicity." In *Culture in Transit: Translating the Literature of Quebec*, edited by Sherry Simon, 31–46. Montreal: Véhicule Press, 1995.

Wallace, Robert. "D'où cela vient-il? Réflexions sur la réception critique du théâtre francophone récent à Toronto." Translated by Michel Vaïs. *Jeu* 49 (1988): 9–23.

———. *Producing Marginality: Theatre and Criticism in Canada.* Saskatoon: Fifth House, 1990.

Wasserman, Jerry, ed. *Modern Canadian Plays*, 3rd ed., 2 vols. Vancouver: Talonbooks, 1994.

Whittaker, Herbert. "Belles Soeurs Bright Light for St. Lawrence." *Globe and Mail* (Toronto), May 7, 1973, 14.

———. "*Forever Yours* Offers Some Familiar Novelty." *Globe and Mail* (Toronto), June 5, 1972, 12.

———. "Les Belles Soeurs Milestone Play." *Globe and Mail* (Toronto), April 4, 1973, 13.

Zimmerman, Cynthia. "A Conversation with Judith Thompson." *Canadian Drama / L'art dramatique canadien* 16, no. 2 (1990): 184–292.

BIOGRAPHICAL NOTE

Born in Montreal at the beginning of the 1950s to a working-class family, Louise Ladouceur graduated from Montreal's Conservatoire d'art drama-tique and went on to participate in numerous stage and screen productions in Quebec and abroad. Primarily interested in experimental and feminist theatre, she joined the Théâtre expérimental de Montréal and subsequently the Théâtre expérimental des femmes, where she initiated the idea of an interdisciplinary festival that would bring together female artists and creators, francophone and anglophone alike. She founded and co-directed the first *Festival de créations de femme* at the Théâtre expérimental des femmes in 1980 and co-ordinated the third edition of this festival at Espace Go in 1983.

She has crossed Canada numerous times and lived on Galiano Island, a Gulf Island located near Vancouver, where she established lasting bonds. After completing a bachelor's and a master's degree in translation at the Université de Montréal, she obtained a PHD in interdisciplinary studies at the University of British Columbia in Vancouver. She then returned to Quebec to undertake postdoctoral research at the Centre de recherche en littérature québécoise at Université Laval in Quebec City. A professor at the University of Alberta's Campus Saint-Jean, she has lived in Edmonton, Alberta since 2000.

INDEX

naturalism:
    departure from, 21, 162–63
    in English works, 20, 21, 137, 143,
        162, 187, 191, 201
    in French works, 65, 125, 157
    and oral language, 186
    translation to *joual*, xi
naturalization, 181
neo-realism, 71
new Quebec theatre, 99–100, 188, 198
New York Drama Desk Award, 150
New York Times, 114
NeWest Press, 166, 190
Nida, Eugène, 43
Night Cows, 33
"Night Cows" (monologue), 101
Nightwood Theatre, 94
1980s:
    adaptations, 18, 150
    comedy, 156
    dramatic structure, 101–02
    explorations, 109
    feminism, 92
    intercultural dialogue, 9–10, 29–30
    joual use, 17–18, 163
    nationalism, 26, 92, 103, 108
    numbers of translations, 5, 29, 33,
        34
    post-nationalism, 156
    publications, 20
    style, 103
    translation studies, 10
    transpositions in, 162
1990s:
    intercultural dialogue, 29–30
    interest in English works, 162
    language variety, 163, 176, 182, 184
    number of translations, 20–21,
        22–23, 31, 162, 184
1970s:
    adaptations, 150
    alterity, 129
    alternative theatres, 5

bridging cultures, 131
joual, 16
number of translations, 91
poetry, 8
publishing, 26, 27
regional theatres, 26
translated works in Quebec, 19
1960s:
    English theatre, 5, 24
    joual's canonization, 4–5, 29
    literary translation, 3–4
    new Quebec theatre, 198
    publishing, 27
    regional theatres, 24
non-translation, 183
nonrealism, 162–63
nonspecificity, 173–75, 176, 184
norm of norms, 50
norms:
    central, 52
    definition, 49–50
    of dialect, 45–46
    discursive, 50–51
    dominant, 186
    and equivalence, 50
    establishment and maintenance
        of, 45–46
    extratextual, 52, 56, 57, 60, 131–32
    in functionalist translation, xviii
    identifying, 51, 62
    ideosyncratic, 51
    initial, 51
    intensity of, 51
    internalized by the translating
        subject, 56
    linguistic, 50–51
    matricial, 50–51
    measuring, 60
    nature of, 51
    operational, 50–51
    peripheral, 52
    preliminary, 50, 60
    primary, 51, 126, 177–78, 179–80

reception of, 198
studies of, 43, 46–47, 53–54, 187
of televison shows, 159–60
as tertiary agent, 6
transposition in, 135–36
visibility of original, 168
vs. adaptation, 18, 41–43, 163–64
See also literary translation;
theatre translation
translation drive, 56
"translation effect," 89–90
translation horizon, 55
translation projects, 57–59, 165
translation strategies:
acceptance, 70, 174–75, 179
in adaptation, 139
avoiding exoticism, 195–96
in Canadian context, 197–98
choice of, 50
for comedy, 159
expressing, 112
importance of, 206
measuring, 60
microstructural analysis, 179–80
post-1985, 194
resisting dominance, 199
sources of information on, 60
study of, 43–44, 60
transpositions, 161–62
for vernacular language, 196–97
translators:
aesthetic judgements, 120
anonymity of, 56–57, 118, 127–28,
178
awards for, 111
effects on translation, 52–54
English in Quebec, 194–95
ethics, 55
individuality of, 2, 40, 47, 51,
52–54, 120
recognition of, 111, 172
sharing text with other players, 40
unconscious influences, 55

visible, 10
See also translating subject

Transmissions, 29–30
transpositions, 135–36, 150–51, 161–
62, 181–82
transvestites, 86
See also homosexuality
Tremblay, Larry, 102
Tremblay, Michel:
acceptability in translation, 88
adaptations by, 16, 134, 177, 181
anthologies, 127
awards, 73
as bridge between cultures, 131
in Canadian repertoire, 72, 91
characters, 76–77, 87, 107
cultural issues, 88
dramatic intensification, 130
forms of address, 132
influence of, 16, 181, 198
and *joual*, 88–89
motivation for translation of, 91
as nationalistic model, 188–89
number of works translated, 29,
31, 91
place names, 130
pre-modern settings, 76, 89
published works, 27
Québécois vs. Canadian, 72
reputation, 27–28, 177, 188
settings, 76–77
style, 91, 129, 190
titles, 75–76, 129
and tradition, 89
translation challenges, 127
translation strategies, 196–97
translations by, 135
universality, 119
works changed through
translation, 189
trialogue, 6
Ubersfeld, Anne, 39n6